LIBERTY SHIP

LIBERTY SHIP

The Voyages of the *John W. Brown,*

1942–1946

Sherod Cooper

Naval Institute Press

ANNAPOLIS, MARYLAND

LIBRARY OF CONGRESS CATALOGING-IN-PUBLICATION DATA
Cooper, Sherod.
   Liberty ship : the voyages of the John W. Brown, 1942–1946 /
Sherod Cooper.
      p.   cm.
   Includes bibliographical references and index.
   ISBN 1-55750-135-1 (alk. paper)
   1. John W. Brown (Ship)   2. Liberty ships—United States.
3. World War, 1939–1945—Naval operations, American.
4. Merchant marine—United States—History.   I. Title.
D774.J64C66   1997
940.54' 5973—dc21   97-1519

Printed in the United States of America on acid-free paper ∞

04 03 02 01 00 99 98 97   9 8 7 6 5 4 3 2
First printing

To Janet

Contents

Maps and Illustrations

Foreword

ON A BALMY spring morning a few years ago an unusual vessel stood up Ambrose Channel bound into the port of New York. Standing tall out of the water, painted in her stark wartime gray, and with the snouts of her cannon protruding in menacing fashion from their old-fashioned gun tubs, she looked like a revenant from an earlier age— the era of World War II, half a century earlier, when ships of her kind had been sunk on the doorsteps of our port cities by an implacable foe bent on world domination.

This may sound like science fiction, but it is historic fact. The Liberty ship *John W. Brown* is a survivor of that terrible time in world history. And not just a survivor, but an absolutely essential instrument of the tremendous effort put forward by Americans in all walks of life, which turned the tides of war in all oceans and enabled America, at the head of a worldwide coalition, to dictate the terms of peace in the conquered enemy capitals of Berlin and Tokyo.

What a cargo of history this great looming hulk of a ship carries, I thought, as the pilot boat delivered our party alongside and we climbed the ladder up her side. Once aboard, I walked fore and aft about the decks of the great steel structure, longer than a city block, and said hello to the crew of volunteers who had gotten this great ship steaming. She rolled ponderously to the swell as I stood chatting with Project Liberty Ship Chairman Captain Brian Hope, who had led the fight to save this vessel from the scrapper's torch and bring her up to New York from her home port in Baltimore for this special visit.

Captain Hope had done this with the help of many people—some grizzled veterans of the great war now half a century behind us, and some as young as the hope that drives mankind to rediscover its past and thereby improve its future. The cheerfulness and energy of this crew brought life to the bare industrial structure as they went about their mundane tasks, from peeling potatoes for the noontime meal to touching up spots where rust had spoiled the fresh gray paint that covered everything in sight.

As the great ship gathered way, I excused myself from the bridge and went below to see the source of the rhythmic thump of her great engine—a sound the author of this utterly authentic book describes as "chunk-um-bum," but others describe more floridly as "roundy-go-thump." There, in the bowels of the ship, grinning oilers did their corybantic act, catching revolving wheels and spindles and flying arms of steel with their oil squirt cans and bits of cotton waste, while seasoned engineers kept a sharp eye on things standing by the gauges that measured the heartbeat and pressure of the great engine that drove the ship.

After my ears grew accustomed to the din of weighty metal parts whirling and thumping around, and my nose to the swampy smell of oil and steam—a smell our author rightly calls "not unpleasant"—I looked around to take stock of my surroundings. The engine room was closed in by steel walls—and outside those plates of steel was the ocean. If a torpedo hit those thin plates, or a bomb fell too near, a torrent of salt water would rush in and drown everyone who couldn't get away. The only way out lay upward—to a skylight far overhead.

The *Brown* came through the war unhit by bomb or torpedo, but her crew saw ships next in line in the convoys hit and sunk. Over one thousand Allied ships were sunk with appalling loss of life in 1942, the year the *Brown* first sailed forth on the dangerous sea lanes of World War II. She sailed from New York Port to carry tanks, aircraft, and supplies to the Persian Gulf, for delivery to the Russian Army locked in battle with the German panzers at Stalingrad on the Volga, the high-water mark of the German invasion of Russia launched a year before.

In this book you can join that first voyage of the *John W. Brown* in a war-torn world. You can learn to know the ship as if you were aboard her. The author, Sherod Cooper, has served in the merchant marine and went on to a shore career as professor of English. He also is a member of Brian Hope's volunteer crew.

It is these volunteers who have given the Liberty ship *John W. Brown* her third career, following her service as cargo ship in war and peace, and then as a floating school in New York City. I first came to know her as a schoolship, guns removed, painted in peaceful black, white, and buff, a stationary relic on the Greenwich Village waterfront of Manhattan's West Side. The young merchant seaman Michael Gillen and Moran Towing's Francis Duffy kept people's interest in the ship alive through the 1960s and '70s, encouraged and abetted by the quintessential ship lover Frank O. Braynard. Our National Maritime Historical Society, under the chairmanship of that grand tugboat man James P. McAllister and his very able associate James Ean (who made possible the preservation of the aircraft carrier *Intrepid* farther upstream on Manhattan's Hudson shore), had a watching brief for the ship backed by the dedicated commitment of former crew members like James P. Farley, honorary trustee of the National Society. The late Harold McCormick, in command of the Armed Guard aboard the Liberty ship *William Gaston* when she was sunk during the war, was another enthusiast in the project. He hunted down Jurgen Oesten, skipper of the U-boat that sank the *Gaston,* and held a wonderful reception for the former U-boat skipper in his home in Connecticut.

These old warriors do not meet to refight the old battles, as people who don't know them might suppose. They meet to find out what it was like on the other side, the U-boat men inquiring about survivors of their sinkings, and the merchant seamen and U.S. Navy Armed Guard crews learning what it was like to be in the narrow steel coffin of a submarine, particularly toward the end of the war when losses began to run over 80 percent.

So it is not to celebrate the supposed glories of war that we need to encourage each generation of Americans to learn about the experience of World War II—it is rather to learn the realities of war in defense of freedom, and to understand how hard-won and infinitely valuable is the peace built on the sacrifices of the Americans who fight our wars for us. Among those people, the unarmed and virtually unprotected civilians of the U.S. Merchant Marine bore one of the heaviest burdens. Their casualty rate was even higher than the casualties among the uniformed servicemen of the U.S. Navy.

Inspired by the example of merchant seamen in San Francisco who had saved and restored to steaming condition the Liberty ship *Jeremiah O'Brien*, the Project Liberty Ship forces in New York joined with supporters in Maryland to bring the *Brown* to Baltimore where she had been hurriedly built forty-six years earlier to meet the emergency shortage of shipping in 1942. There they restored the ship to her wartime condition and trained a crew to steam the giant vessel and tell her story to the public as Sherod Cooper does so well in these pages.

Climb up the boarding ladder then, and sign on for the voyage as Sherod Cooper gets steam up in the boilers. In this authentic account of the extraordinary service of a quite ordinary ship traveling the perilous sea lanes of World War II, you will see why people cheerfully give months and years of hard work to keep the *John W. Brown* steaming today, to deliver her vital message to coming generations of Americans.

Peter Stanford, President
National Maritime Historical Society

Preface

THIS BOOK began on a day in late fall 1988 when as a volunteer crew member I was stripping old varnish off the starboard door of the *John W. Brown*'s wheelhouse. Brian Hope, chairman of Project Liberty Ship, found me there and suggested that because of my academic background I could better serve the cause by delving into the ship's history, about which little was known. With encouragement to do what I had already thought of doing, I stopped stripping and a few days later made the first of many trips to the National Archives. On retirement from the University of Maryland the following year, I was able to give full attention to unearthing information about the *Brown* in the vast research resources of the Washington, D.C., area.

During the course of research, I broadened the scope of the book to include information about the convoys the *Brown* sailed in and to relate her movements and accomplishments to the total war effort. As a result, the following story, although focusing on the *Brown*, is representative of the adventures of most other merchant ships during the war years.

As the notes and bibliography demonstrate, the basic information comes from documents in the National Archives, the Operational Archives of the Naval Historical Center, the Navy Department Library, the Maritime Administration's files, and the Archives and Manuscripts Department of the University of Maryland College Park

Libraries. The knowledgeable and unfailingly helpful staffs of these institutions assisted me greatly in finding the material I needed. Also, logs, letters, reminiscences, and other documents that have accumulated in the Project Liberty Ship Archives were rich sources of anecdotal as well as basic information. With the help of many Project members I located about sixty Navy and Merchant Marine—and two Army—men who had associations with the *Brown*. Many of them shared their memories with me; their names figure in the text, notes, and bibliography.

Others have made important contributions to this book. Brian Hope not only got me started but through the years has answered innumerable technical questions and has read the manuscript. Michael Lawton was able to get valuable American Bureau of Shipping records about the *Brown*. Ray Brubacher, photo archivist of Project Liberty Ship, helped immeasurably by processing snapshots to make them suitable for publication. Marine artist Oswald Brett donated the painting reproduced on the book jacket. My son-in-law, Douglas L. Judy, contributed the map illustrations. Over the years my sons Sherod III, Stephen, and David have helped in various ways large and small. The staff at the Naval Institute Press was always helpful and supportive as the book took shape, and Jonathan Lawrence, the copyeditor assigned by the Press, was expert in detecting problems and smoothing out rough spots.

My greatest help has always come from my wife, Janet. Not only has she supported, encouraged, and advised me in my work, but she has also been actively involved by reading and commenting on the manuscript as it developed over a number of versions—she read them all!—and by proofreading and doing other unpleasant but necessary chores.

LIBERTY SHIP

1

The Beginnings

O N 1 September 1939, Hitler's army invaded Poland. Living up to their pledge to support Poland, Great Britain and France declared war on Germany two days later. Only twenty-one years after the armistice had stopped "the war to end all wars," the countries of Europe were again fighting. By the end of the first year, the German army had overrun most of western Europe and the *Luftwaffe* was hammering Britain with punishing bombing raids. In the United States, President Franklin D. Roosevelt's pro-British impulses were curbed by the political muscles of powerful isolationist groups and a small but nonetheless influential band of German sympathizers. The best he could do to aid Britain was to interpret restrictive neutrality laws freely. Thus in September 1940 he agreed to transfer fifty U.S. destroyers to the British in exchange for some military bases in British possessions, and in December 1940, shortly after his election to a third term, he proposed the Lend-Lease Act to make the United States the "arsenal of democracy," as he phrased it in a 29 December "Fireside Chat."[1] The proposal engendered heated debate in Congress, but by early March 1941 it had passed both the House of Representatives and the Senate by comfortable although not overwhelming margins. This vital legislation in effect reversed the neutrality laws by allowing the government and private firms to send or lease military equipment, supplies, and other goods to Britain and other Allies without demanding immediate payment.

Among the many problems in implementing the Lend-Lease Act, the most crucial was getting arms and supplies across the Atlantic. There were far too few merchant ships to begin with, and the Germans were having great success in further reducing the number. Between the beginning of the war in September 1939 and the entry of the United States in December 1941, 892 merchant ships of the nations at war with the Axis powers were sunk in the North Atlantic, and in 1942, the United States' first full year at war, 1,006 went down, most of them the victims of U-boats.[2]

At about the same time he proposed Lend-Lease, President Roosevelt ordered the Maritime Commission to organize a new shipbuilding program—one that would supply ships faster than the Germans could sink them. The commission responded with an emergency shipbuilding program emphasizing the construction of relatively uncomplicated ships that could be mass-produced quickly. For a design the commission chose a modified version of one that American shipyards were using at the time to build sixty ships for the British. Although the president may or may not have called the ship an "ugly duckling" when he first saw the plans, he called it a Liberty ship in his Liberty Fleet Day address on 27 September 1941 when the first one, the SS *Patrick Henry*, was launched at the Bethlehem-Fairfield Shipyard in Baltimore.

Although beauty may indeed be "in the eye of the beholder"—and certainly Liberty ships did not have the stylish lines of the cargo ships designed for the Maritime Commission in the mid-1930s—calling them "ugly" was not accurate either. They more appropriately could have been called "plain," for that was what they were—unadorned and unsophisticated ships that could be built quickly by inexperienced workers and operated by equally inexperienced crews. They were precisely the ships to meet the needs of the time.

With a length overall of 441 feet, 6 inches, and a beam of 57 feet, Liberty ships when fully loaded drew about 28 feet, leaving not quite 10 feet of freeboard. The approximately ten thousand tons of cargo that a Liberty could carry—equivalent to the capacity of three hundred railway boxcars—was stowed in five holds, three forward of the deckhouse and two aft, serviced by booms on three masts.

In the beginning Liberty ships had fewer navigational aids than the average thirty-five-foot pleasure boat of the 1990s. Actually, Libertys had only three fixed pieces of navigating equipment: three magnetic compasses, one each in the wheelhouse, on the "monkey

bridge" on top of the wheelhouse, and at the emergency steering station in the stern.[3] SS *John W. Brown,* the subject of this book, had in
addition a radio direction finder and a fathometer.[4] As time went on,
some ships, including the *Brown,* got gyrocompasses, and some even
got radar, but not the *Brown* until after the war.

Like the overall design, the triple-expansion steam engine used to
power Liberty ships was outdated, but it had the advantage of being
relatively easy to manufacture and maintain. Although the jumble of
pipes, valves, pumps, and machinery in the engine room looks complicated and difficult to understand, the concept is straightforward.
Water is heated in boilers to make steam, which is piped to the
engine to move the pistons up and down to turn the crankshaft,
which is bolted to the propeller shaft.

Watertube boilers were used in Liberty ships to make steam,
meaning that the water to be heated passed through tubes in a com-
bustion chamber fired by four oil burners. Two such boilers were required. The boilers vaporized the water into steam at 220 pounds per
square inch and 450 degrees Fahrenheit, and the steam was then
piped to the triple-expansion main engine. The term "triple expansion" simply means that the steam, which cools and thus expands in
volume as it journeys through the engine, passes through three
stages of expansion. From the boiler, the steam at its hottest and
densest goes first through an eight-inch pipe to the high-pressure cylinder, which has a diameter of twenty-four and one-half inches; then,
having lost some pressure but gained in volume, it moves on to the
thirty-seven-inch intermediate cylinder; and finally, having lost
more pressure and gained more volume, it enters the seventy-inch
low-pressure cylinder. In the cylinders the steam forces the pistons
up and down through four-foot strokes. From the engine the steam
exhausts through a twenty-six-inch pipe to the main condenser,
where it passes through tubes cooled by seawater, which turns it
back into water that is then pumped back to the boilers to repeat the
process.

On first sight, the engine room of a Liberty ship is both impressive
and intimidating. As one enters from either the main or second deck,
one is immediately aware of a maze of pipes and valves, of narrow
grated walkways, and of steep ladders descending into an area from
which rises a wave of moist heat and the not unpleasant smell of
mixed oil and steam. On arriving at the engine room floor some
twenty-five feet below the second deck, one finds the combination of

sounds overwhelming and so loud that normal conversation is impossible. Dominating all others is the rhythmic deep bass chunk-um-bum, chunk-um-bum, chunk-um-bum of the main engine as the piston rods turn the crankshaft at full speed, about 72 to 76 rpm. Near the generators one also hears a sound like that of a noisy high-speed sewing machine; near the auxiliary condenser one hears a constant loud roar.

There is also heat. On a recent balmy June afternoon when it was a pleasure for the deck crew to be above decks, the temperature by the throttle in the engine room was a steamy 104 degrees and in the aisle between the boilers about 6 degrees hotter. On the hot day in August 1991 when the reactivated *Brown* was put through her trials, the temperature between the boilers reached 130 degrees. In the cold winter months, however, when fierce icy winds whip the deck crew, the engine room is comfortably cozy.

The Liberty ship engine is stately in its dimensions: about 20 feet tall, 21.5 feet long, 12 feet wide, and 135 tons in weight. With the throttle wide open, that is, admitting the maximum amount of steam to the engine, the engine generates 2,500 horsepower to turn the propeller 76 rpm. With four blades, a diameter of 18.5 feet, and a pitch (distance advanced in one revolution) of 16 feet,[5] the propeller at 76 rpm moves the ship at 10 to 11 knots (about 11.5 to slightly over 12.5 miles per hour).

Liberty ships had a fuel capacity of about 13,000 barrels of Bunker C oil. Burning fuel at a rate ranging from as few as 120 to more than 200 barrels a day depending on such variables as speed, condition of hull, weight of cargo, winds, seas, and currents, Liberty ships could steam between sixty and a hundred days without refueling. On her maiden voyage, for example, the *John W. Brown* burned 5,461 barrels, about 165 a day, during the thirty-three-day trip from Panama to Cape Town, South Africa, via the Panama Canal, the west coast of South America, and Cape Horn. On arrival in Cape Town she still had 5,820 barrels left, enough for another thirty-five steaming days.[6]

Although the living quarters for both the officers and crew have been described as "comfortably and conveniently arranged,"[7] even by the standards of the early 1940s they were no more than adequate and fell far short of the accommodations provided for the crews on the ships built for the Maritime Commission's long-range program. Compared with the quarters in Navy ships, however, even Liberty ships were luxurious. The basic Liberty ship design provided accommodations for forty-four officers and crew in the deckhouse amidships. The captain's stateroom and adjoining office were on the bridge deck on the starboard side immediately aft of the chart room and just a few steps from the wheelhouse. The captain had the distinction of being the only person on the ship to have a private head and shower and the additional luxury of an overhead cowl ventilator to direct fresh air into his rooms. His built-in berth, settee, desk, chair, and other furniture were made of golden oak finished with high-gloss varnish. The radio room and the staterooms for the radio operators were on the port side of the bridge deck. The furnishings, like the captain's and those of the other officers, were oak. There was a head on the bridge deck that the radio operators could use, but they had to go below to the boat deck to shower.

The deck, engine, and Armed Guard officers were quartered in ten single rooms on the boat deck directly beneath the bridge deck. Although compact to the point of being small, each officer's room was fitted with a built-in berth, settee, desk and chair, locker, and sink with running water. Like the captain, the chief engineer had an office adjoining his stateroom, but not having a private bath, he had to share the three toilets and three shower stalls on the boat deck with the other officers.

The chief steward's room on the main (or upper) deck was like the officers' rooms topside, but the rooms on the main deck for the unlicensed crew and part of the Navy enlisted men were completely different. First of all, three and sometimes four men shared an eight- by eleven-foot room containing two double-pipe berths. Since the berths, including the railing to keep the men from rolling off in heavy weather, were almost three feet wide and seven feet long, the floor space was reduced to a narrow aisle in the center of the room and only about four feet at the end, some of which was taken up by lockers. The impression of confinement in cramped quarters was enhanced by the overhead (ceiling) being less than seven feet high. Such impressions, of course, are relative: compared with the sleeping quarters on a submarine, or on any Navy ship for that matter, Liberty ship crews enjoyed spacious accommodations. The sanitary facilities for the minimum of thirty-five men housed on the main deck amidships consisted of two rooms each equipped with two toilets, two sinks, and two showers; two rooms each with a toilet and sink; and two shower rooms—a total of six toilets, six showers, and six sinks. The passageways in the deckhouse were so narrow that people had to turn sideways to squeeze past each other, and they couldn't pass on the even narrower ladders.

The Merchant Marine unlicensed crew's mess on the port side of the deckhouse on the main deck was also small for the number of men who ate there. In a room sixteen by a little over eleven feet were two long tables, one for eight men seated on school desk–type swivel chairs on fixed pedestals and the other for six men. There was also a small table with two school desk–type armchairs for the boatswain (bos'n) and carpenter. Thus sixteen men could be served at a time. Separated from the Merchant Marine crew's mess by a pantry was the somewhat smaller Armed Guard mess, which could seat only twelve at a time.

As with their living quarters, the distinction between officers and crew was emphasized by their dining facilities, although not by their meals, which were the same for everyone. The twenty- by fourteen-foot officers' saloon was on the main deck at the forward end of the deckhouse. A settee extended the twenty feet along the forward bulkhead, with three fixed tables placed opposite it. On the other side of each table were two golden oak office desk–type swivel chairs on fixed pedestals. On the aft side of the room there was a built-in oak server and a table with four chairs. Thus, as in the Merchant crew's mess, sixteen people could be seated, but since there were fewer officers, under normal conditions fewer than sixteen would eat at the same time.

Food for the crew was prepared in the galley located in the center of the deckhouse, where the effects of rolling and pitching would be least felt. Cooking was done on a massive coal-burning range about six and a half feet long and forty inches deep with two wrought-iron ovens twenty-two inches wide and sixteen inches high.[8] Wrought-iron railings on the stovetop prevented pots from sliding off, and there was a grab rail along the front of the range for the cooks to hang onto when the ship was rolling and pitching in heavy weather. Among other necessities for food preparation, a twenty-five-gallon stockpot was prominent because of its size.[9]

Although the Liberty ships turned out to be exceptionally seawor-thy, the design caused some problems for the men serving in them. A Navy Armed Guard officer commented that the ships were "ideally built for everything but the comfort of the men. The merchant-crew quarters . . . were all constructed around the stack and directly over the engine, which meant that in warm weather it was almost impossible to enter them at all. In my own cabin the deck was always so hot I couldn't step on it with bare feet. The quarters for the gun crew were on the stern, just over the steering engine, and they likewise were insufferable in hot weather."[10] Besides the heat, the men housed in the stern had to put up with the steering engine's constant rumbling like the sound of a slow freight train, punctuated with loud bangs and clanks as the engine moved the rudder. And when the ship was pitching in heavy seas, they had to hold onto their bunk railings to stay in bed because of the frequently violent and always exaggerated up-and-down motion of the stern. They also "learned to remove the light bulbs in the stern quarters during rough seas. When the propeller came out of the water the vibration broke the bulbs."[11] The heat was especially oppressive at night for everyone aboard because portholes in lighted rooms had to be closed at night to preserve blackout conditions, thus eliminating any possibility for ventilation. There was, of course, no air-conditioning, nor were there ventilators of any kind in the rooms—except the captain's and some others on the bridge deck—but each room was equipped with an electric fan that, if nothing else, kept the hot air moving. Many men slept out on deck, but there was always the risk, especially in the tropics, of being abruptly awakened by a sudden shower.

Another complaint was that Libertys rolled excessively, even when fully loaded, leading one veteran seaman to complain with considerable exaggeration that "the 'Liberty' was the poorest plan for sea transportation that ever came down the ways. . . . Even a passing motorboat can start one rolling."[12] An Armed Guard officer who crossed the Pacific in a Liberty commented that "all Liberty ships I have seen . . . tend to be top heavy, particularly when they are carrying deck cargo, as we did, and I have never rolled more in my life than on that trip across the South Pacific. On the first leg of our journey . . . all of our dishes were broken and we ended up using condensed milk cans for utensils. It was not uncommon for a man to eat with an arm locked about a stanchion. But, roll though they do, those Liberty ships can go places."[13] And that was the point. Their ability to "go places" justified everything else about them.

Between the launching of the *Patrick Henry* and the delivery of the last Liberty ship four years later—the *Albert H. Boe* in October 1945—more than 2,700 were built in shipyards from coast to coast. Bethlehem-Fairfield in Baltimore, incidentally, built the greatest number, 384. More than two hundred were lost during the war to torpedoes, bombs, mines, and the hazards of the sea—about fifty on their maiden voyages[14]—but 2,500 survived to transport the arms, supplies, and personnel needed to win the war.

On 1 May 1941, the day after the *Patrick Henry's* keel was laid,[15] the Maritime Commission awarded contract MCc 7798 to the Bethlehem-Fairfield Shipyard for the construction of twelve Liberty ships, MCE numbers 301–312. Under the terms of the contract, Hull 312, which became the *John W. Brown*, was to be delivered on 5 April 1943.[16] A number of circumstances led to the *Brown's* being delivered about seven and a half months early, but the most obvious was an expansion of the shipbuilding program beyond what the Maritime Commission could have anticipated when the contract was drawn.[17] Another was the success of Bethlehem's innovative adaptation of mass-production methods to shipbuilding. The *Patrick Henry*, the first Liberty ship, required a total of 244 days between keel laying and delivery, while the *William Tilghman*, the fiftieth ship, was delivered in fifty-nine days. Bethlehem-Fairfield had good reason to boast in October 1942 that "the record for the shortest outfitting time has been made at Fairfield; namely, five days from launching to delivery. Twelve ships were delivered complete from this yard in the month of July, 1942, and twelve ships were launched during August. Up to September 1, the delivery figure is an East Coast record; the launching figure, a world's record."[18]

The keel for MCE Hull 312, Builder's Hull 2062, was laid on 28 July 1942[19] in Shipway 12,[20] vacant since the 25 July launching of the *John P. Poe.* When everything was running smoothly at full speed at Bethlehem-Fairfield it took only a matter of hours between launching one ship and laying the keel of the next, but for some reason three days passed before the keel for Hull 312 was laid. During part of this time shipyard workers prepared the shipway for the keel laying. Each of the sixteen shipways at Bethlehem-Fairfield occupied an area some 450 feet long and somewhat wider than the 57-foot beam of a Liberty ship, with the ground along the longer dimension gently inclining toward the Patapsco River. Permanent scaffolding extended along both lengths to the river's edge. To start the process of building a Liberty ship, carpenters laid out a line midway between the two rows of scaffolding, on which at four-foot intervals they stacked four wooden blocks, the "keel blocks" on which the keel would rest. After placing the keel on the blocks, workmen attached frames and bottom plates to it to begin the assembly of the hull. These plates were

This aerial view of the Bethlehem-Fairfield Shipyard in Baltimore shows the sixteen shipways and the two outfitting piers. The *Brown* was built in Shipway 12. *National Archives*

held in position by "shorings," logs wedged between the ground and the bottom plates, about 420 in all by the time the bottom was fully assembled. Next, as the side plates were attached, "cribbings," heavy timber laid end-to-end the length of the ship, were piled against them as support, followed by wooden scaffolding as the hull took shape. Thus during this stage of construction the keel blocks, the shorings, and the cribbings carried the weight of the hull.[21]

On 28 July, the day the *Brown*'s keel was laid, surveyors from the American Bureau of Shipping made the first of their forty visits to the ship during her forty-one days of construction.[22] Because the plates for Hull 312 had been cut to size and shaped in one of the fabricating shops before being delivered to Shipway 12, assembling them took relatively little time. After only three days, the ship was 37.3 percent complete; by the end of August, thirty-four days after the keel laying, she was 73.7 percent complete.[23] Factories in various parts of the country manufactured the machinery and parts: the main engine by the Worthington Pump and Machinery Corporation in Harrison, New Jersey; the boilers by the Edge Moor Iron Works in Edge Moor, Delaware; the main condenser by M. W. Kellogg Company in Jersey City, New Jersey; the auxiliary condenser by Heat Transfer Products, Inc., in Newburgh, New York; the rudder by Bethlehem Steel Company at its Leetsdale, Pennsylvania, plant; and the propeller by the Koppers Company's Bartlett Hayward Division in Baltimore.[24] As early as the 31 July progress report, the ship was expected to be ready for launching on 7 September, and so she was.[25]

Earlier in 1942, Baltimore members of the Industrial Union of Marine and Shipbuilding Workers of America had suggested that naming some Liberty ships for labor leaders would be a good way to highlight organized labor's contribution to the war effort. As part of the plan, they promised to build a Liberty ship in record time, and not knowing that ships could not be named for living persons, they wanted to name it "Philip Murray" in honor of the president of the CIO. Although Murray was not eligible, the idea of naming ships for union leaders was not dropped, and early in July, John Green, president of the Industrial Union, announced that the union, in cooperation with shipyard managements and the Maritime Commission, would name and launch several Liberty ships in special ceremonies at yards across the country on Labor Day, 7 September.[26]

Local 43 at the Bethlehem-Fairfield Shipyard in Baltimore proposed that one of the two Liberty ships scheduled for launching on Labor Day be named for John W. Brown, a member of the General Executive Board of the Industrial Union until his death in 1941, and the other for John Mitchell, who joined the United Mine Workers at its founding in 1890 and was its president between 1899 and 1908. Local 43 also proposed that Mrs. John Green sponsor the *John W. Brown*,[27] but the details about sponsorship were still not settled as late as 4 September, when the *Shipyard Worker*, the Industrial Union's newspaper, reported that Mrs. Green would sponsor the *John Mitchell* and Miss Mercedes Daugherty, Philip Murray's niece and secretary, the *John W. Brown*. It was settled, however, that John Green would give the main address and that the Mutual network would carry it on a coast-to-coast hookup. "The ceremonies," asserted the *Shipyard*

Worker, "will be the high point of a production drive that this week saw the combined efforts of the Industrial Union Local 43 members and management successfully turn out 12 Liberty Ships during August, the largest number of bottoms ever launched by one yard in this country."[28]

Just as it was not clear who would sponsor which ship, so it was also not clear which hull would get which name. Fortunately each hull had both a Maritime Commission Emergency (MCE) hull number and a builder's hull number; otherwise mix-ups could easily occur. A letter from Wade Skinner of the War Shipping Administration to the Commissioner of Customs on 3 September, just four days before the launching date, reveals the potential for confusion: "Under date of August 29, 1942, I wrote you giving new names for the hulls being built for the United States Maritime Commission by the Bethlehem-Fairfield Shipyard Company, Inc., known as Builder's Hull Nos. 2061 and 2062. We are now advised that in the proposed Labor Day celebration to be held at the yard of the Builder, the ceremonial ship, Builder's Hull No. 2062, which we had first named RALPH IZARD and in my letter dated August 29, 1942, I stated we desired to name it JOHN MITCHELL, the parties have now decided that the vessel be named instead JOHN W. BROWN, who was, we are advised, a labor representative local to Baltimore and who I understand lost his life in some daring exploit; that hull No. 2062 was chosen as the ceremonial ship because it is being completed in 40 days."[29] Actually, Hull 2062 was completed in forty days only if the day the keel was laid and the day of launching are not counted. Skinner's use of "we are advised" and "who I understand" in referring to Brown suggests doubt that Brown in fact had roots in Baltimore and died in "some daring exploit." He was right to be skeptical, because both statements are false. Brown's work with the Industrial Union was primarily in Bath, Maine, and he died at his home in Woolwich, Maine. One wonders who said what behind the scenes, and why. At all events, there were no more changes, and Builder's Hull 2062, MCE Hull 312, would be named for Brown.

John W. Brown was born in 1867 in Prince Edward Island, Canada, and became a U.S. citizen in 1896.[30] He first became involved in the labor movement when he took a job as a joiner at the Bath Iron Works in Maine. His experiences there convinced him that only through banding together in unions could workers force employers to improve wages and working conditions. Before the nineteenth century ended, his commitment to the union movement had led him to become an organizer for the United Brotherhood of Carpenters. Sometime later he went over to the United Mine Workers and played a part in the bloody labor conflicts in Colorado in 1913 and 1914, including the Ludlow Massacre in April 1914 when actions by militiamen employed by the Colorado Fuel and Iron Company led to the deaths of twenty-five people, among them two women and fourteen children. In the 1920s he was in the middle of the fight in West Virginia when owners used force against coal miners attempting to organize.[31] John Brown believed deeply in the union movement and accepted the inevitability of bitter and often violent conflict; as he put it, "If I have to live under this system I must fight, and one can't fight alone and accomplish anything."[32]

By the early 1930s he had left the United Mine Workers and was living on his farm in Woolwich, Maine. He continued to be active in union affairs, however, and in 1934 he helped establish Local 4 of the Industrial Union of Marine and Shipbuilding Workers of America at the Bath Iron Works where many years earlier he had first become involved in the union movement. Besides working to organize workers at the Bath Iron Works, Brown served as an adviser to the General Executive Board of the Industrial Union. Perhaps his most significant contribution was his column "Workers Should Know" in the *Shipyard Worker*. Starting on 30 October 1936, the column appeared regularly through 20 June 1941, the day after Brown died. Through his comments in "Workers Should Know," Brown became a combination of teacher, guide, and motivator. The point that underlay virtually every column was that it was essential that workers band together in unions. Starting with the dual premises that workers are an indispensable part of the production process and that those in management will pay them as little as they can get away with, he argued that only unionized workers acting collectively can force managements to pay wages that reflect the workers' essential roles in production. As the *Shipyard Worker* was often handed out to everyone leaving a shipyard, Brown in fact used his column to recruit members for the Industrial Union.

Brown's actions during the 1940 presidential election, when Franklin D. Roosevelt ran for a third term, reveal something of his character. In a letter to the secretary of the Industrial Union, Brown stated that an election in September won by the Republican candidate for Congress by more than seventy thousand votes had made clear that in November Maine would be solidly for Wendell Willkie's Republican ticket. Despite the odds, as a committed Democrat and as a fighter, Brown "wasn't for handing it to them." After working hard in what he knew was a losing cause, he had to be content with believing that his efforts helped win Sagadahoc County, his home county, for the Democrats and helped keep the Republican majority across the state to less than ten thousand.[33]

Late in the evening of 19 June 1941, Brown sat on the back door stoop of his house in Woolwich working on his hunting rifle. Somehow it went off in his face, wounding him so severely that he died within the hour. He was seventy-four years old. At the Bath Iron Works at noon the following day, a spokesman for the Industrial Union, in announcing Brown's death over the public-address system, observed that "he was a great and good man, an outstanding American. His spirit still lives on and John Brown will remain an immortal in the ranks of American labor."[34]

By the time MCE Hull 312 was ready to be launched, she weighed about thirty-two hundred tons. As a prelude to launching, the first step was to transfer her from the keel blocks, shorings, and cribbings that still supported her to a movable cradle that would slide her into the river. This complicated process usually began a week or two before the launch date with carpenters installing "ground ways" if they were not already in place. Ground ways are two three-foot-wide parallel wooden tracks placed about twenty to twenty-five feet on each side of the row of keel blocks and extending the length of the shipway into the water. The carpenters coat the ground ways with heavy grease and place the "sliding ways" on them. As their name indicates, these slide the ship into the river. The sliding ways extend the length of the ship and are attached to the land end of the shipway by a strip of steel plate with perforations spaced about an inch apart. Using the sliding ways as a foundation, carpenters then build a heavy wooden cradle snugly around the length of the ship's bottom. When the ship is ready to launch, the carpenters knock away the keel blocks, shorings, and cribbings, leaving the ship resting on the cradle. The cradle in turn rests on the sliding ways, which are kept from moving down the ground ways by the strip of perforated steel attaching them to land. At launch time welders with acetylene torches burn through the steel plate to the perforations and then cut through the perforations until the weight of the ship causes the steel plate to tear apart. At this moment when the ship first begins to slide toward the water, the sponsor breaks a bottle of champagne against the bow.[35]

Although the major task in launching is to transfer a hull weighing thirty-two hundred tons from land to water, there are innumerable less weighty details that must also be attended to. Perhaps the least weighty is the preparation of the champagne bottle. Bethlehem-Fairfield always provided the best available champagne for launching ceremonies—a nice touch since the least expensive would serve as well—but the problem was that when the bottle was smashed on the ship's bow, the highly charged champagne could explode and spray the sponsor and anyone else nearby not only with champagne but also with slivers of broken glass. To prevent the bottle from exploding, a Bethlehem-Fairfield worker had the job of covering it with bronze mesh to hold in the broken glass, and then as an added precaution sewing several layers of canvas around its neck, where the sponsor would grip it. Now safe for smashing, the bottle was next sent to a flag shop for decoration. There a seamstress first covered the bronze mesh and canvas with sateen and then sewed a silk flag around the upper half of the bottle and red, white, and blue bunting around the lower half. She finished by tying red, white, and blue ribbons around the bottle to add a festive, patriotic note.[36]

By the time Labor Day dawned, the sponsors had been realigned so that Mrs. Green would now christen the *Brown*, as was appropriate, and Miss Daugherty the *Mitchell*. There had been a very light rain on Sunday, 6 September, and some sprinkles on the 7th, but at least the temperature during the launching ceremonies was a pleasant seventy-two.[37] Although the Labor Day program was to begin at 11:00 A.M., the first launching of the day at Bethlehem-Fairfield was at 10:00 A.M., when the *Benjamin Hawkins* slid down the ways. Named for the first senator from North Carolina, the *Hawkins* was launched thirty-nine days after her keel was laid, a new Atlantic Coast record.[38] In keeping with the Bethlehem-Fairfield practice of having one of every three Liberty ships sponsored by the wife, mother, daughter, or sister of a shipyard worker, Mrs. Leila M. Knight, the mother of a driller in the fabricating shop, sponsored the *Hawkins*. As this launching was not part of the Labor Day program, only the approximately fifteen thousand workers in the yard at the time had a chance to witness it.[39]

The crowd in the yard increased to more than twenty thousand when the main gate was opened shortly before 11:00 to admit guests to the Labor Day ceremonies. As workers and guests found places around the speakers' platform, Bob Iula's band entertained them with patriotic numbers and popular dance music. Meanwhile the sponsors and their families, the speakers, and other special guests had arrived in a procession of twenty-five black sedans.[40] The program began when Miss Daugherty at 11:00 smashed a champagne bottle across the bow of the *John Mitchell* and the band played the "Star-Spangled Banner."[41] Some speeches followed, but not the one by Maryland Governor Herbert R. O'Conor listed in the program. The governor had overbooked his schedule for the day and couldn't make it to the Bethlehem-Fairfield Shipyard. He gave the main address at the Annapolis Yacht Yard, where his wife sponsored one of the two naval vessels launched there, and later in the day he and Mrs. O'Conor joined dignitaries including the Brazilian ambassador and Lt. Gen. Leslie McNair on the reviewing stand at Fort Meade to watch thirteen thousand men of the 76th Infantry Division pass in review.[42]

John Green in his address recognized that "on us in the shipbuilding industry a terrible burden has been placed. The naval ships and the cargo vessels form the link between our production lines and the fighting fronts of the world. That link must be maintained, it must be strengthened. On its strength depends the defeat of the enemy." After noting that "our brothers, fathers and sons in the armed forces are already under fire," he made perhaps his most important point when he predicted that "very soon, in speaking to shipyard workers, I shall be able to add *husbands* to that list because women are undoubtedly going to supply a lot of labor required in the shipyards."[43] The *Baltimore Evening Sun* in an editorial the next day enlarged on this point, stating that too few women had gone to work in essential war industries and concluding that "the realization that this is a woman's war, too, must spread more widely among them. When it does, the 'lot of labor' which Mr. Green foresees will be supplied."[44]

With the speeches and other items on the program finished shortly after noon, Mrs. Green and her daughters Muriel and Alice gathered in Shipway 12 by the bow of MCE Hull 312. Taking a vigorous swing, Mrs. Green smashed a bottle of champagne across the bow of the ship and named it SS *John W. Brown*. As the *Brown* slid into the Patapsco River at 12:15, Bob Iula's band played "Stars and Stripes Forever."[45] This ended the ceremonies, and the sponsors, dignitaries, and other platform guests left for an elaborate reception at the elegant Belvedere Hotel in downtown Baltimore. The shipyard workers, however, went back to work because this first Labor Day of World War II was not a holiday.

One hundred and seventy-four vessels were launched in shipyards across the country on 7 September 1942. Among the destroyers, submarine chasers, PT boats, tugs, minesweepers, seaplane tenders, landing craft, and the like were sixteen merchant ships, six of which were Liberty ships named for labor leaders.[46]

After launching, the *Brown* was shifted to one of the two outfitting piers at the Bethlehem-Fairfield Shipyard. Although the ship was 90 percent complete by this time, the 10 percent of the work remaining involved as many as five hundred workmen from twenty-five departments installing about five thousand items.[47] The riggers completed such jobs as setting the standing rigging and installing the lifeboat davits; the sheet metal workers finished installing ventilators, ducts, insulation, and galley equipment; the carpenters took care of gangways and ladders; the joiners put up the paneling and

Mrs. John Green smashes a bottle of champagne across the *John W. Brown*'s bow. *Project Liberty Ship Archives*

The *Brown* slides down the ways. *Project Liberty Ship Archives*

trim and installed the furniture in the living quarters; the electricians finished work on the lighting and power circuits and installed the electrical communications and navigational systems; and so it went in department after department for a total of about two thousand separate operations. Since only about 15 percent of the necessary painting had been done before launching, the painters continued at the outfitting pier so that by the time of trials the painting was 95 percent complete.[48]

On 15 August, three weeks before the *Brown*'s launching, the Maritime Commission had written to States Marine Corporation, the company selected to operate the ship, concerning the assignment of officers. Anticipating a 16 September delivery date, the commission noted that its regulations required that States Marine assign the master, chief mate, chief engineer, and first assistant engineer to the ship about a month before delivery, and the other mates and engineers, the chief steward, and the radio operator about two weeks before delivery. Although the officers were to spend this time getting

The *Brown* plows into the Patapsco River stern first. This photograph gives an idea of the amount of work remaining to be done at the outfitting pier. *Project Liberty Ship Archives*

the *Brown* ready for immediate operation after being turned over to States Marine, they were to "assume no authority and [were] . . . not to interfere with the progress of the work."[49] If the stipulations of this letter were met, Capt. Matt R. Coward, Chief Mate Gerald W. Griffin, Chief Engineer Leroy C. Poole, and First Asst. Engineer Raymond McMahan soon arrived in Baltimore to do what they could on the *Brown* during her final weeks in Shipway 12 and at the outfitting pier. Meanwhile, four cadet-midshipmen who had completed basic training at the Merchant Marine Academy at Kings Point on Long Island were ordered to report "with gear" to the States Marine office in New York on 11 September. There they were ordered to Baltimore to join the *John Mitchell*. The confusion over names still persisted at the States Marine office, and it was not until they arrived in Baltimore that the cadets learned that their ship was the *John W. Brown*. Since the *Brown* was still at the outfitting pier when they arrived, they had a chance to observe the final stages of construction and to go with her on bay trials.[50]

On 14 September 1942 the *Brown*'s boilers had been lighted off and the machinery operated during dock trials to demonstrate her readiness for official trials, which were conducted on the Chesapeake Bay south of the Patapsco River four days later.[51] Copies of the report of the *Brown*'s trials are either lost or destroyed, but since there was a specific procedure for conducting trials of Liberty ships, one can reconstruct what she did from a report that did survive. The Liberty ship SS *Santiago Iglesias* was launched at the Bethlehem-Fairfield Shipyard on 30 March 1943 and underwent trials on 8 April, about seven months after the *Brown*. The only difference in the trials was that the six-hour endurance run that was required at the time of the *Brown*'s trials had been reduced to four hours.[52] Aboard the *Brown* on 18 September were Bethlehem-Fairfield's Trial Capt. T. E. Ness, Trial Mate John W. Hart, and other members of the deck and engine departments necessary to operate the ship.[53] Also on board were the officers and cadets assigned by States Marine Corporation and representatives from the Maritime Commission, Bethlehem-Fairfield Shipyard, the American Bureau of Shipping, and the U.S. Coast Guard Inspection Service. If the *Brown*'s tests were in the same order as the *Iglesias*'s, the first was the full-astern crash stop. While steaming at full speed ahead, 76 rpm, the ship's engine was thrown to full astern to find out how fast the ship could come to a full stop. The *Iglesias* required three minutes and thirty-seven seconds. Then came the astern steering gear test. As the ship steamed astern at about 65 rpm, the inspectors determined how long it took to move the rudder from amidship to hard left, then from hard left to hard right, from hard right to hard left, and then back to amidship. The ship continued steaming astern for about another half hour and then performed the full-ahead crash stop test to find out how long it took to bring the ship to a full stop by going from 65 rpm astern to full ahead. While the ship was stopped, the anchor windlass test was conducted by dropping one of the anchors, letting out 60 fathoms (360 feet) of chain and then timing the recovery, about seven and a half minutes on the *Iglesias*. Next came the ahead steering gear test, identical to the astern steering gear test except that the ship was steaming at full ahead. The *Brown* probably performed this test during the six-hour endurance run at full ahead. As part of the endurance trial, which may have taken her as far south on the Chesapeake as Poplar Island, the *Brown* ran the Kent Island measured mile course in both directions. By determining how long it took to cover a mile, the inspectors could calculate her exact speed. While all this was going on topside, inspectors in the engine room monitored and recorded the performance of the boilers, main engine, condenser, auxiliary condenser, generators, and pumps. By the end of the trials, the inspectors had surveyed the entire ship and from their investigation had compiled a list of "Unfinished and Unsatisfactory Hull Items"; the list for the *Iglesias* illustrates the thoroughness of the inspection, as it contained 292 items, mostly such minor ones as "paint chart room," "ease drawers under settee in Captain's state room," "weld bad rivets in Officer's toilet," and "lower lockers in Bos'ns state room so that life preserver can be stowed."

At 11:00 A.M. on 19 September, the day after the *Brown's* successful trials, the Maritime Commission delivered her to the War Shipping Administration, which in turn delivered her to States Marine Corporation for operation. Although still at the Bethlehem-Fairfield Shipyard and not yet quite ready to sail, her maiden voyage officially began the same day with the signing of articles by the crew.[54] By signing articles a seaman contracted to work aboard the ship in a specified job for which he would be paid at the end of the voyage when he signed off. Later in the day the *Brown* was shifted to dry dock at the Bethlehem–Key Highway Shipyard, where surveyors from the American Bureau of Shipping, the Maritime Commission, and States Marine inspected her bottom to make sure that she was fit for sea.[55] On the 22nd she shifted from the Key Highway Shipyard to Pier 5 Pratt Street in downtown Baltimore, where shipyard workers worked through the 28th taking care of "Unfinished and Unsatisfactory Hull Items" uncovered during bay trials. Now ready for sea, the *Brown* on the 29th took on 3,516 barrels of fuel oil (147,672 gallons) and prepared to leave Baltimore that evening.[56] Her mission was to deliver Lend-Lease supplies to the Soviet Union via the Persian Gulf, an assignment made on 18 September replacing an earlier one to carry coal to New England.[57] Even though she was leaving Baltimore, however, she was not yet ready to load a cargo and head toward the Persian Gulf.

The *Brown's* Merchant Marine crew on her first voyage was typical for a Liberty ship. The crew was under the command of the master—the captain or "old man"—who had overall authority and responsibility for everything having to do with the ship except for her defense and the internal affairs of the Armed Guard. The actual day-to-day running of the ship was handled by the deck, engine, and steward's departments. At sea the crew members who stood watches worked seven days a week, and those on "day work" worked five and a half days.

The chief mate, as head of the deck department, was second in command under the master. In port he was in charge of loading and unloading cargo. At sea he stood the 4:00–8:00 A.M. and P.M.[58] watches in the wheelhouse or on the "monkey" bridge above it, making certain that the ship maintained her course and, especially in convoys, didn't get dangerously close to other ships. In addition to standing watch, the chief mate was responsible for the general condition of the ship and supervised the bos'n in keeping her properly maintained. He also instructed the two deck cadets and assigned them to jobs that, in theory at least, would contribute to their training. The second mate stood the noon to 4:00 P.M. and midnight to 4:00 A.M. watches and served as navigating officer. The third mate stood the 8:00 A.M. to noon and 8:00 P.M. to midnight watches and looked after the lifeboats, rafts, firefighting equipment, and the like.

The unlicensed deck personnel consisted of a boatswain (bos'n), six able-bodied seamen (ABs), and three ordinary seamen. The bos'n, under the direction of the chief mate, planned the repairing or overhauling of deck equipment, chipping, painting, cleaning, and other routine maintenance and supervised the ordinary seamen and ABs on "day work" in carrying out the assignments. The ABs assigned to watches followed the same "four on, eight off" schedule that the licensed mates did. At night during a four-hour stint the AB generally stood bow lookout for two hours and steered the ship for two; during the day, if not needed for lookout duty, he worked on deck for two hours and steered for two. The deck department was rounded out by ordinary seamen, usually three, who as "beginners" at sea were assigned to "day work" scrubbing, chipping, painting, and the like while learning the skills necessary to qualify for AB papers. Ordinary seamen were also used as lookouts.

The chief engineer was generally responsible for the operation of the ship's machinery and for keeping records of fuel and water consumption and so forth, but unlike chief mates, chief engineers did not stand watches. The first assistant engineer was the engine room equivalent of the chief mate. In addition to standing the 4:00 to 8:00 watches supervising the engine room crew and checking to make sure that the engine and machinery were functioning properly, the first assistant was responsible for the maintenance of the machinery, supervised the "day workers," and trained the engine cadets. The second assistant engineer stood the 12:00 to 4:00 watches. With a specific responsibility for the boilers, as part of his routine he chemically analyzed the boiler water for impurities and, if necessary, added chemicals to neutralize them. Periodically he operated the soot blowers to clean the boiler tubes. The third assistant engineer stood the 8:00 to 12:00 watches and looked after the auxiliaries and the electrical equipment. Besides a licensed engineer, an oiler and a fireman/watertender were assigned to each watch. The oiler periodically felt the engine and shaft bearings to make certain that they were not running hot, oiled the piston rods and valve stems on the main engine, and checked the auxiliaries. The fireman/watertender managed the boilers to maintain proper steam pressure by keeping the burners clean and making certain that the water in the boilers was at the proper level. Three wipers completed the engine department. Beginners on "day work" like ordinary seamen, wipers spent their days scrubbing, chipping, painting, and "wiping" the engine room to keep it safe and clean.

Although not licensed, the chief steward was considered one of the ship's officers. In charge of food, linen, and living quarters, the chief steward on the *Brown*'s first trip supervised a staff consisting of first and second cooks and an assistant cook; two utilitymen to wash dishes, help in preparing food, and assist in general cleaning up in the galley and the officers' living spaces; and at least three messmen to serve food in the officers' saloon and in the Merchant Marine and Armed Guard messes and, between meals, to assist the cooks in the galley and to help in maintaining the officers' quarters.

The *Brown*'s basic crew was rounded out by a radio operator and, instead of the more usual purser, a clerk/typist. Although always on call, the one radio operator assigned to most Liberty ships stood an eight-hour watch in the radio room. When off duty he set an alarm that automatically sounded in his bedroom and on the bridge if a distress call came in. Since during the war a radio operator was allowed to transmit while sailing alone only if attacked or torpedoed and while in convoy only in brief acknowledgment of orders from the convoy commodore, he spent his time on watch listening. He was especially alert to Broadcasts to Allied Merchant Ships (BAMS), which sent messages to a ship by first sending her secret call sign and then a ciphered message, which the radio operator turned into plain

English using cipher books and codebooks.[59] The purser kept the ship's financial records and operated the slop chest, the ship's store where the crew could buy cigarettes, candy, shaving equipment, soap, some clothing, and the like. Some pursers were given basic medical training so that they could look after the crew's minor health problems. On Voyage 1 the *Brown* also carried four cadet-midshipmen, a maintenance man in the deck department, and a junior engineer in the engine department.

As the *John W. Brown*'s "Official Log-Books" show, the size of a Liberty ship's crew could change according to mission, availability of personnel, and such other variables as the expected duration of the voyage and whether she carried passengers. On the *Brown*'s second voyage, when she carried troops and POWs, her enlarged steward's department included a chief cook, two second cooks, a third cook, a night baker, and four messmen. On Voyage 4 she had, for the first time, three radio operators. The two Merchant Marine radio operators and the Navy radioman third class assigned to the *Brown* for this trip made it possible to have someone on watch in the radio shack at all times. Voyage 4 was also the first on which the *Brown* had a carpenter in the deck department. On Voyages 5, 6, and 7, radio communications were entirely in the hands of three Navy radiomen. With the end of the war in Europe, radio responsibilities on the *Brown* once again reverted to Merchant Marine operators, but on Voyage 8 and the others when she carried troops home from Europe she always had three. The steward's department, however, experienced the most dramatic change on Voyage 8: in addition to the usual staff, it included a second steward, a storekeeper, two cooks for the Army, a chief and second baker, a chief butcher, troop officers' messmen, and several additional utilitymen. The general pattern of Voyage 8 was repeated with a few variations on Voyages 9 and 10, during which the *Brown* continued to bring troops back home. The sixty-two Merchant Mariners on Voyage 10 comprised the *Brown*'s largest crew. With the resumption of straight cargo-carrying duties for Voyages 11–13, her last three, the *Brown*'s crew was reduced to thirty-eight, approximating the pattern of Voyage 1 but somewhat smaller because she had no cadets.

The men who crewed American merchant ships during World War II were civilians hired through the various unions by the private shipping companies that operated the ships for the War Shipping Administration—the *Brown*, for example, by States Marine Corpora-

tion. Men subject to the draft under Selective Service received defer-
ments while they served at sea in the Merchant Marine; without
risking reclassification to 1-A, they could stay ashore between trips
on a formula of two days ashore for every seven at sea up to a maximum of thirty days.[60] Most of the unlicensed crew were members of
such unions as the National Maritime Union and the Seafarers International Union. The National (now International) Organization of
Masters, Mates, and Pilots represented the deck officers and the Marine Engineers Beneficial Association the engine officers. Merchant
Marine crews were notable for their diversity, and their motives for
going to sea during the war were just as diverse. Many, of course,
were professionals for whom manning ships was their livelihood;
consequently, unlike in the Navy, men in their fifties, sixties, and
sometimes even seventies could be found working aboard merchant
ships. Since the physical requirements for the Merchant Marine
were much more flexible than for the armed forces, many men who
were classified 4-F by their draft boards were able to join. One can
hope, however, that the standards were usually higher than those applied to George Spittel, who recalls that his Maritime Service physical examination consisted of the physician saying, "You got two
arms, you got two legs, I suppose they're all right, drop your pants,
you got a peter—O.K., you're in."[61] Spittel was one of many who
went into the Merchant Marine because they wanted to be a part of
the war effort but didn't qualify for the armed forces. Others felt
pressures in their communities to get involved in the war but for various reasons did not want to serve in the armed forces; still others
were motivated by the desire to find adventure away from home; and
some no doubt joined in the belief that they could earn more money
at sea than ashore. Another significant group was comprised of men
from countries under Nazi domination who wanted to participate in
the fight against Hitler.

This diversity is well illustrated by the crew that signed on the
Brown in April 1944 for Voyage 4. The forty-one men who served
under Capt. George N. Brown ranged in age from eighteen to the
sixty-six-year-old chief engineer. The bos'n and first assistant engineer were in their late fifties, and the steward was fifty-four. Five men
were in their forties, six in their thirties, twenty-two—slightly over
half the crew—in their twenties, and four were teenagers. The
twenty-year-olds included three officers: the chief mate at twenty-
nine, the third mate at twenty-three, and the third assistant engineer

at twenty-seven. The twelve crew members born outside the United States came from the British West Indies, the Cape Verde Islands, Czechoslovakia, Finland, Greece, Latvia, Norway, Russia, and Sweden. Eleven—over 25 percent—were married.

Unlike the armed services, which assigned blacks and whites to separate units, the crews supplied by the National Maritime Union, the union on the *Brown,* were fully integrated. On Voyage 4 the carpenter, one of the ABs, the steward, and the first and second cooks were black. White Firemen/Watertender George Spittel's two roommates on Voyage 5 were both black, and one was sixty-two years old.[62] On the *Brown*'s last voyage in 1946 there were five black crew members—the carpenter, two ABs, the deck engineer, and a utilityman.[63]

During World War II, U.S. merchant ships were equipped with guns manned by Navy Armed Guard crews. Their mission was simply stated: "to defend merchant ships and transports from enemy air, surface, and submarine attacks." Thus their "primary duties" were standing watch and manning and maintaining the guns. More specifically, they were to "open fire in the direction of an attacking submarine, even if the enemy could not be seen,"[64] in an attempt either to sink it or at least make it submerge without attacking.[65] As to aircraft, they were instructed "to open fire on any unidentified plane outside the Western Hemisphere which flew within 1,500 yards of the ship or flew directly toward the ship."[66] Sinking an attacking submarine or shooting down an enemy plane was, of course, defense at its best, but preventing an attack on the ship by driving the enemy away with gunfire also counted as success.

As with crew size, the armaments on merchant ships in World War II varied with mission and availability. When the *Brown* sailed on her maiden voyage she was armed with a 5"/51 on the stern, a 3"/50 on the bow, two 20-mm guns on the deckhouse, and two 20 mm's aft. The 5"/51 was a pre–World War I gun—the one displayed in the Navy Museum in Washington, D.C., for example, dates from 1913. The 5"/51s made up the standard secondary battery of battleships in World War I and of some of the older battleships like the *Arkansas, Nevada,* and *Texas* that were still around in World War II, but they had been largely replaced by the more versatile dual-purpose 5"/38 that the Navy had developed in the early 1930s. Because she was armed early in the war, when there were not enough 5"/38s to meet demand and the Navy's needs came first, the *Brown* did not get a 5"/38. Unlike the newer gun, the twenty-one-foot-long 5"/51, which loomed menacingly over the *Brown*'s stern railing, could not be elevated enough to fire at planes; however, at a rate of fire of at best four or five rounds a minute, it could hurl 50-pound armor-piercing shells at a muzzle velocity of 3,150 feet per second (about 2,150 miles per hour) toward surface ships and submarines. The 5"/51 was so powerful that its shells could penetrate armor an inch and a half thick on targets five miles away and three and a half inches thick on targets two miles away.[67]

The 3"/50 on the bow was twelve and a half feet long and could be used against both aircraft and surface vessels. At a rate of twelve to fifteen a minute, the gun could fire 13-pound shells about six miles horizontally; when elevated to its maximum eighty-five degrees, its vertical range was about four miles.[68] Although a highly effective weapon, the 3"/50 had two characteristics that caused problems for the gunners: when fired it made a sharp, loud crack that could cause discomfort if not pain and damage to the gunners' ears, and after firing it ejected the spent shell with such force that it was difficult to catch and many men were injured trying.[69] These problems were compounded by the fact that the gun fired every four or five seconds during combat.

Unlike the 5"/51 and the 3"/50, the 20-mm Oerlikon gun was an automatic weapon. However, since the 20 mm's effective range was only about half a mile at high elevation and a little over a mile horizontally, it was used primarily against low-flying planes at close range. The 20 mm was also much smaller than the 5"/51 and 3"/50: its barrel was only fifty-eight inches long, and it fired armor-piercing or explosive shells weighing about a quarter of a pound. However, the rapid rate of fire more than made up for its lack of size in fighting off attacking planes. A skilled gunner backed by a loader, usually a volunteer merchant seaman,[70] could fire as many as 320 rounds a minute. The gun theoretically was capable of firing many more rounds a minute, but the gunner was slowed because the magazine that holds the ammunition had to be changed every sixty rounds and the barrel replaced after 120 rounds of continuous firing to prevent overheating.[71] Obviously there was constant activity around the gun during action: the gunner not only had to concentrate on aiming and firing the gun, but after every sixty rounds, that is, every twelve seconds, he had to stop while the loader took off the empty magazine and replaced it with a full one, and at twenty-four-second intervals he had to stop to change barrels.

Although the captain of a ship had overall command of the ship, the Armed Guard commander had exclusive authority over the Navy gun crew. Even if the captain gave the order to abandon ship, the Navy crew had to stay aboard until the Armed Guard commander gave the order, and his instructions read that "there shall be no surrender and no abandoning ship so long as the guns can be fought."[72]

Consisting of a lieutenant (junior grade) in command of twenty enlisted men, the Navy Armed Guard crew on the *Brown*'s first trip was typical for a Liberty ship in the later months of 1942. The highest-ranking enlisted man, a boatswain's mate second class, was in charge of the one seaman first class and seventeen seamen second class who comprised the gun crews. Seaman second class was the rank automatically attained after four months' service in the Navy. These men had all completed basic training, "boot camp," and perhaps some of them had had a bit of gunnery training at one of the Armed Guard centers. A signalman third class rounded out the Navy crew. Competent to send and receive messages by semaphore, blinker, and flag hoists, the signalman was an essential link in communications when the ship was in convoy or near other ships because radio operators during the war could transmit only under conditions of extreme emergency.

The size of the Navy crew increased as the *Brown*'s armament increased during the course of the war and her missions changed to include transporting troops as well as carrying cargo. During Voyages 5, 6, and 7, when the *Brown* was armed with one 5"/51, three 3"/50s, and eight 20-mm guns, the Navy crew reached a peak of forty-one, about double that of Voyage 1. During these voyages the Navy crew was comprised of two gunnery officers, both lieutenants; a communications officer with the rank of ensign; a boatswain's mate second class; a radioman second class; a coxswain; four gunner's mates third class; a signalman third class; two radiomen third class; and twenty-eight seamen first class. Just because there were no seamen second class as on Voyage 1 does not mean that the seamen first class on these voyages were necessarily more experienced. Effective 5 November 1942, the Bureau of Naval Personnel, presumably for a good reason, had ordered that seamen second class assigned to Armed Guard units be automatically advanced to seamen first class, thereby creating two kinds of seaman first class on merchant ships, those who earned the rating and those who didn't.[73]

In his "Log" for Voyage 5, Lieutenant Argo, the ranking Navy offi-

cer, has left a description of the normal routines at sea and in port. At
sea the Armed Guard crew rotated watches on the same four hours
on, eight hours off pattern that the Merchant Marine crew did except
that the nature of the watches was determined by the military situation. At the start of a typical twenty-four-hour period beginning at
midnight, the only men of the Armed Guard on duty were those
standing the midnight to 4:00 A.M. watch at their guns under Condition III—the normal watch when the ship was not under attack or
expecting attack. At 3:30 the 4:00 A.M. watch was called. The men
didn't really need a half hour to get ready, but since it was still dark
outside they did need the extra time to accustom their eyes to the
darkness by arriving at their stations fifteen minutes early or by
wearing red glasses for fifteen minutes. Since U-boats liked to attack
at dawn and dusk, a half hour before dawn the off-watch gun crew
was called to join the men on watch at battle stations to bring the
ship to full battle readiness (Condition I, General Quarters). As soon
as it was full daylight the crew secured from Condition I and resumed the normal watch (Condition III), with the men on duty
standing watch at their guns.[74] However, if enemy attack was imminent, the Armed Guard commander set Condition II, in which the
Armed Guard crew was arranged in two divisions standing "watch
and watch," that is, four hours on and four hours off. During each
four-hour watch, each man stood two hours lookout duty and two
hours at his gun station.[75]

Under Condition III the gun crews off watch ate breakfast at 7:30.
The watch changed at 8:00. There was, however, much more to the
Armed Guard's responsibilities than standing watch. From 9:00 to
11:15 the men off watch checked and cleaned the guns; made certain
that the temperature in the powder magazines was within the proper
range; painted the guns and tubs as needed; cleaned their living
quarters and heads; and studied training courses published by the Bureau of Personnel to qualify for advancement. Dinner began at 11:30,
and a new watch took over at noon. During the afternoon the men
off watch continued work details and studied training courses until
the watch changed at 4:00 P.M. Supper began at 5:30. As at dawn,
Condition I was set at dusk until full darkness. The day ended with
an 8:00 P.M. to midnight watch. Although this regimen may sound
simple and monotonously repetitious, one Armed Guard officer observed that his men were "endlessly under strain, a strain . . . only in-
frequently relieved by action."[76] His point was that the men were

wearied by constantly being ready to fight and by everlastingly searching the seas and skies for an enemy who rarely justified their preparation and alertness by making an appearance. Endlessly waiting for something to happen became a torment.

The "General Orders" posted by Lieutenant Argo also suggest something of the Navy sailor's life in a merchant ship. In an attempt to keep the Navy and Merchant crews from encroaching on each other in the confined living spaces on a Liberty ship, the orders stress that the two crews were forbidden to enter each others' quarters and messrooms. This regulation did not stop the men from getting to know each other, and since some of the Merchant crew assisted with the guns, they not only knew each other but worked together as teams. In practice, indeed, the regulation was often ignored completely. If, for example, all the seats in the Armed Guard mess were taken, the Navy men sometimes ate at unoccupied seats in the Merchant Marine mess. Off duty, the men in the two crews talked and joked together, and sometimes a Navy man or two would join the Merchant crew in working around the ship.[77]

The daily routine called for the Armed Guard crew to be up and have bunks made before the 7:30 call for breakfast, except that the midnight to 4:00 watch had until 11:00 A.M. to make their bunks. Even they had to get up an hour earlier on Saturdays, however, because at 10:00 A.M. Lieutenant Argo inspected the Armed Guard quarters, heads, and lockers to see if the weekly "field day" (cleaning up day) on Fridays had produced satisfactory results. At 10:00 P.M., "Victrola playing" in the sleeping quarters had to stop and the overhead lights be turned off. Even though it seated only twelve men with no extra floor space, the Armed Guard messroom served as a lounge between meals. The men could play records there between 8:00 A.M. and 10:00 P.M., but they had to keep the noise down so as not to disturb the Merchant crew off watch sleeping in their rooms just a few steps aft along the port passageway. Everyone except the standbys of the watch section had to be out of the messroom by 10:00 P.M., and the standbys on each watch were responsible for having the messroom cleaned by the end of their watch.

The fact that civilian Merchant Mariners and men sworn into the Navy had to live together in close quarters provided the potential for conflict. Fearing that hard-won gains in pay and working conditions in the 1930s would be lost and that Navy protocol, uniforms, saluting, and the like would be imposed on men who valued their civilian status, the maritime unions had successfully resisted attempts at the beginning of the war to incorporate the Merchant Marine into the Navy.[78] Despite this victory, however, some Merchant seamen continued to feel—and sometimes articulate—a strong antimilitary bias. Although a tiny minority, they sometimes caused hard feelings between the two groups.

For their part, some Navy men were understandably envious when they compared their disciplined lives to the freedom that off-watch Merchant seamen enjoyed. The greatest potential for discord, however, had to do with salaries, with many Navy men believing that Merchant seamen were grossly overpaid. Because the seamen's unions in negotiating salary increases at the beginning of the war had opted for war-risk bonuses rather than increases in base pay,[79] the discrepancy between the base salaries of Merchant Marine and Navy personnel was not great during World War II. A third mate on a merchant ship, for example, was paid $193.75 to $200.00 a month; a Navy ensign received $150.00 to $157.50 a month plus rental and subsistence allowances between $81.00 and $117.00, plus 10 percent additional for sea duty. An ensign earning the maximum thus received $290.25.[80] When Merchant Marine bonuses are added, however, the difference in income becomes vast. From the time of departure from the United States on a foreign voyage until arrival back, each Merchant Marine crew member received a monthly bonus of 100 percent of base pay, but not less than $100.00. Crews on ships operating in the Mediterranean received an additional $5.00 a day, and if there was an air raid while the ship was in port an extra $125.00 was added. According to this formula, in October 1943 the third mate on the *John W. Brown* earned between $537.50 and $550.00, almost $250.00 more than a Navy ensign and slightly more than the monthly pay of a Navy captain on sea duty receiving maximum rental and subsistence allowances. Actually, since they do not take into account overtime pay averaging about 30 percent of base,[81] these figures for the Merchant Marine are minimums. It so happened that in October 1943 the enemy did not attack the ports the *Brown* visited; otherwise the third mate would have received even more, in increments of $125.00 times the number of attacks.[82]

Among the unlicensed crew, the lowest paid was the ordinary seaman, earning $82.50 a month. A seaman second class in the Navy received a base pay of $54.00 plus a 20 percent increase while on sea duty. There were also allowances for dependents, but assuming a seaman second class on sea duty without dependents, the salary would be $64.80, not quite $20.00 less than the ordinary seaman's base pay. However, the ordinary seaman at sea received a bonus of $100.00 a month and in certain areas a supplementary bonus of $5.00 a day. Not counting overtime, an ordinary seaman on the *Brown* in October 1943 earned $332.50, about $30.00 less than a Navy lieutenant on sea duty with maximum allowances and about the same as the base pay of a Navy captain with less than three years' service.

On the other hand, a Merchant Mariner received pay only while under articles. When he signed off at the end of a voyage, his pay stopped and didn't resume until he next signed on a ship. With this system, average Merchant seamen received pay for ten months of the year,[83] whereas Navy men received pay all twelve months of the year. Furthermore, unlike his counterparts in the Navy but like any other civilian, he had to provide his own clothes and while between ships had to pay for his housing and food and the costs of transportation. Also, he received no additional compensation for dependents. The Navy man had a much wider and more generous variety of benefits than the Merchant seaman, dealing with such matters as allowances for dependents, access to medical care for dependents, disability pay, amounts paid to dependents in the event of death, eligibility for national service life insurance, and the like. Perhaps the differences can be epitomized by an example from insurance coverage: since the Merchant seaman is covered by insurance only while aboard ship, if he is "hit by a truck while ashore, he receives no compensation for being incapacitated. . . . A Navy man's insurance is applicable in such a case."[84] When these considerations are factored in, it is clear that the size of paycheck each month does not present a clear picture. It was the size of paycheck, however, that fueled perceptions.

Except for a couple of occasions during the first voyage, there were no recorded instances of significant conflict of any sort between the Merchant Marine and Navy crews on the *John W. Brown*. On the contrary, the evidence in the following chapters points to friendliness, close cooperation, and mutual respect.

With this background, it is now time to return to the *John W. Brown* in Baltimore on the evening of 29 September 1942 as the crew prepared to get her under way on her maiden voyage to the Persian Gulf.

2

The Maiden Voyage

WHEN the SS *John W. Brown* left Baltimore on her maiden voyage on 29 September 1942, the United States had been at war with the Axis powers for ten months. In August, U.S. forces had taken their first offensive action in the Pacific with landings on Guadalcanal, starting a battle that would last six months. There was no similar offensive action in Europe. The situation in fact was grim: Germany and Italy controlled most of the continent, and across the Mediterranean in North Africa, Field Marshal Erwin Rommel was pressing east toward Alexandria, Egypt. In Russia, Germany's ferocious attack on Stalingrad, now in its thirty-eighth day, had succeeded to the point that the Germans controlled parts of the city. The defenders, however, continued to fight back heroically. The outcome of this battle could determine what the *Brown* would find when she arrived in the Persian Gulf, because if Stalingrad fell the Nazis would be in position to cut the supply lines to Russia through the Gulf.

On the night before sailing, crew members who wanted to go ashore to see a last movie had many choices, including Red Skelton and Ann Sothern in *Panama Hattie*, James Cagney in *Yankee Doodle Dandy*, Greer Garson and Walter Pidgeon in *Mrs. Miniver*, and Cary Grant and Joan Fontaine in *Suspicion*.[1] In bars, diners, and soda fountains, for five cents a song they could listen to the jukeboxes playing such top-ten recordings of the week as the Andrews Sisters' "Strip

Polka," Bing Crosby's "Be Careful, It's My Heart," Sammy Kaye's "Stage Door Canteen," and Vaughn Monroe's "My Devotion."[2]

The weather was pleasant, with "gentle" winds, clear skies, and the temperature in the middle fifties,[3] when at 6:43 P.M. on Tuesday, 29 September, the *John W. Brown,* under the command of Capt. Matt R. Coward, started to maneuver through the tangle of ships jamming Baltimore harbor to begin a trip to Norfolk.[4] Captain Coward, a wiry man about five feet, eight inches tall and weighing about 140 pounds, was "very quiet but efficient, calm, didn't smile a lot, but a man's man that exuded confidence."[5] He displayed all these qualities one day when the chief cook and the assistant cook got into a loud and angry argument that quickly escalated from words to flashing galley knives. The Armed Guard officer and Second Mate Robert Bloxsom happened along, but wary of the menacing knives and angry shouts, both just stood there and did nothing. Captain Coward suddenly appeared, and as Robert Bloxsom finishes the story, "he walked right into the galley and right between those two cooks; he was only about 4' away from me and his voice was so quiet that I couldn't hear what he said. He spoke to the two of them for less than a minute and then turned on his heels and walked out of the galley and that was the end of the fighting and those two never fought again that I know of. I did notice that when Captain Coward walked past me into the galley that he had one hand on his back pocket and he had a 38 cal pistol in that pocket."[6] It was clear to everybody that Captain Coward was in complete control of his ship.

The Armed Guard had reported aboard on the day of departure and had settled in their quarters, with Lt. (jg) Charles Calvert, the twenty-six-year-old[7] Armed Guard commander, on the boat deck starboard side, the boatswain's mate second class and the signalman third class on the bridge deck, and the others in the six spaces available on the main deck starboard side amidships and the fourteen spaces aft under the 5"/51. At this time, besides the 5"/51, the *Brown* was armed with five 20-mm guns. The guns had been installed at the Bethlehem–Key Highway Shipyard, but because the gun crew had not yet joined the ship, no ammunition had been put aboard.

With the engine turning 62 rpm to produce a 10.5-knot average speed, the *Brown* covered the 192 miles to an anchorage in Hampton Roads in a little over eighteen hours. On 1 October she left the anchorage to run the degaussing course at the Wolf Trap Range along the western shore of the bay between the mouths of the York and Rappahannock Rivers, and on the 2nd she spent nine hours in the Norfolk area being depermed at the Lambert Point Deperming Station in the Elizabeth River. Designed to reduce the magnetism the ship acquired during construction, deperming involved wrapping the ship in a solenoidal coil through which a succession of varying currents were passed. On the degaussing course technicians determined how much current was needed in the ship's degaussing cable installed inside the hull to offset the magnetism generated by her moving through the water.[8] Unlike deperming, the degaussing had to be recalibrated from time to time because the earth's differing magnetic fields in different parts of the world influence the magnetism that a ship generates.[9] These measures to reduce magnetism made it less likely that the ship would trigger the firing mechanisms of magnetic mines laid by the enemy in channels and shallow water.

After deperming and degaussing and after having ammunition for her guns put aboard, the *Brown* shortly after midnight on 3 October began the return trip up the Chesapeake Bay on the way to New York. Nineteen hours later she joined a large number of other ships at anchor off Annapolis. Early the next morning she left the Annapolis anchorage, headed north up the Chesapeake, spent two and a half hours passing through the Chesapeake and Delaware Canal, and that evening anchored off the Brandywine Light Vessel in Delaware Bay. She spent the night at anchor because at that time coastal convoys between the Delaware capes and New York ran only during daylight hours so that U-boats could not easily sneak up on them.[10] Just before dawn the next morning, the 5th, the *Brown* left the Brandywine anchorage in a convoy consisting of four merchant ships, three escort vessels, and a Navy blimp searching for U-boats from above. The introduction of such convoys six months before and a strictly enforced blackout at night in coastal towns and cities had put a stop to the German U-boats' massacre of ships sailing along the East Coast.[11] Thus the *Brown* enjoyed an uneventful trip up the coast of New Jersey and anchored just before midnight off Red Hook in Brooklyn, New York.

Early the next morning, 6 October, she moored at Pier 17, less than a mile down the East River from the Brooklyn Bridge. Her hatches were opened immediately and she began loading. On the 9th loading was interrupted so that she could spend half a day on the degaussing and compass-adjusting ranges, and on the 11th she went to the nearby Atlantic Basin Iron Works in Brooklyn to have a 3"/50 gun mounted on the bow in place of one of the 20 mm's. The *Brown*'s armament on her first voyage thus consisted of one 5"/51 mounted on the stern, one 3"/50 on the bow, two 20 mm's on the deckhouse, and two 20 mm's aft. The ship returned to Pier 17 and at 2:30 A.M. on 13 October completed loading there. A few hours later she shifted across Upper New York Bay to Caven Point in Jersey City, almost literally in the shadow of the Statue of Liberty, and began loading an additional 915 tons of ammunition and 608 tons of deck cargo. By 10:00 the next night the *Brown* was completely loaded and ready to sail.[12]

Of the 8,380.9 long tons of cargo, 8,084.3 were for Russian Lend-Lease, 233.7 for purchases by the British, and 62.9 for British Lend-Lease. A few details about the cargo illustrate just how crucial a role the Merchant Marine played in winning the war. In her holds the *Brown* carried motorcycles, trucks of various sizes ranging from 10-ton Mack trucks to 1.5-ton Fords, armored scout cars, jeeps, canned pork lunch meat (Spam?), dried beans, steel, railway car axles, .45-caliber submachine guns, smokeless powder, various kinds of ammunition—the list goes on and on. Lashed on the decks were two P-40 fighter planes, ten Medium M4 (Sherman) Army tanks, and ten

The *John W. Brown* in New York harbor on 9 October 1942 returns to Pier 17 in Brooklyn after a run on the degaussing and compass-adjusting ranges. *U.S. Coast Guard*

Canadian-built Valentine VIII medium tanks.[13] Besides the implements of war and food for fighting men, the cargo also included twenty-two sacks of U.S. Army mail and ten sacks of regular overseas mail.

Shortly before sailing, Captain Coward and Lieutenant Calvert attended a convoy conference for convoy NG-314 from New York to Guantánamo Bay, Cuba. Chaired by Capt. F. G. Reinicke, USN (Ret.), the port director of the Third Naval District, or by his representative, convoy conferences were normally attended by the convoy commodore, the escort commander, the commanding officers of the other escort vessels, the masters and Armed Guard commanders of the merchant ships, and representatives from the Coast Guard and several other official bodies. They were given information about dates, times, and routes, and each master received his specific sailing orders with details about exactly when he should leave, which ship he was to follow out of the harbor, his position in the convoy, the flag hoists he was to use for identification, and the like.[14] The convoy commodore for NG-314 was Comdr. G. B. Wooley, USN (Ret.), in the SS *Monroe*; the master of the SS *Carbella* served as vice commodore and Captain Coward in the *Brown* as rear commodore.[15] A U.S. Navy task unit under the command of Lt. Comdr. E. J. Burke, USN, in the USS *Simpson* was assigned to guard the convoy. Besides the *Simpson*, a four-stack "flush-deck" destroyer built in 1919, the task unit included the 193-foot Canadian corvettes *Sudbury* and *Frederickton*, the U.S. Navy corvette *Fury*, the 165-foot submarine chaser *PC-556*, and, for part of the trip, a blimp patrolling from above.

The roles of the convoy commodore and escort commander were carefully delineated in "United States Fleet Anti-Submarine and Escort of Convoy Instructions." Because the convoy commodore almost always outranked the escort commander, the "Instructions" unequivocally identify the escort commander as the officer in charge: "The Escort Commander commands both convoy and escort even though there may be present in a ship in the convoy an officer senior to him." The commodore's responsibilities as commander of the convoy focused on such internal matters as assigning ships to stations, issuing instructions and interpreting regulations, controlling the convoy tactically "under normal conditions," and above all else seeing to the "safe navigation" of the ships. The escort commander's main responsibility, of course, was to defend the convoy by the effective deployment of his escort vessels, but "when exigencies of the situation warrant," he was authorized to order evasive course changes, "if practicable," after consulting the convoy commodore. Since the escort commander was the judge of what was "practicable," in effect he could issue whatever orders he thought appropriate without discussing them with anyone.[16]

At 9:00 A.M. on Thursday, 15 October, the *John W. Brown* left Jersey City with a Merchant crew that now numbered forty-five plus the master[17] bound for Guantánamo Bay on the first leg of a voyage that would take her to the Persian Gulf via the Panama Canal. The ships assigned to the convoy had to leave their berths and anchorages in Upper New York Bay at specific times to form a single column with the ships spaced five hundred yards apart. The column steamed at seven knots through the swift currents of the Narrows and just beyond Gravesend Bay through the gate of the submarine net that prevented enemy submarines from sneaking into the harbor.[18] The ships then entered the seven-and-a-half-mile-long Ambrose Channel and continued steaming at seven knots until abeam Gedney Buoy at the end of the channel about three and a half miles east-northeast of the tip of Sandy Hook. Although now out of Ambrose Channel and with plenty of room to maneuver, the ships still could not form into convoy because "the danger of magnetic mines in such shoal water could not properly be safeguarded against."[19] Since it was impossible to sweep the entire area of mines, the best that could be done was to maintain a swept passageway further out to deeper water.

When abeam Gedney Buoy the ships slowed to four knots for five minutes to drop their pilots. The masters then had to take over following the somewhat complicated plans for departure, made easier for ships in NG-314, however, because leaving during daylight hours allowed them to keep an eye on each other. The ships increased speed to eight knots to a designated point where they went down to six knots while maneuvering to assigned positions in a "staggered double column" called "column open order."[20] In this formation the ships then steamed at eight knots through the rest of the swept channel to a point some thirty miles at sea where "deep water was available safe from mines."[21] In deep water at 4:30 P.M., more than seven hours after getting under way, the ships formed themselves into a convoy with a front of seven columns.[22] The first five columns contained three ships each and the sixth and seventh two each. As the first ship in the seventh column, the *Brown* was on the starboard side of the convoy.

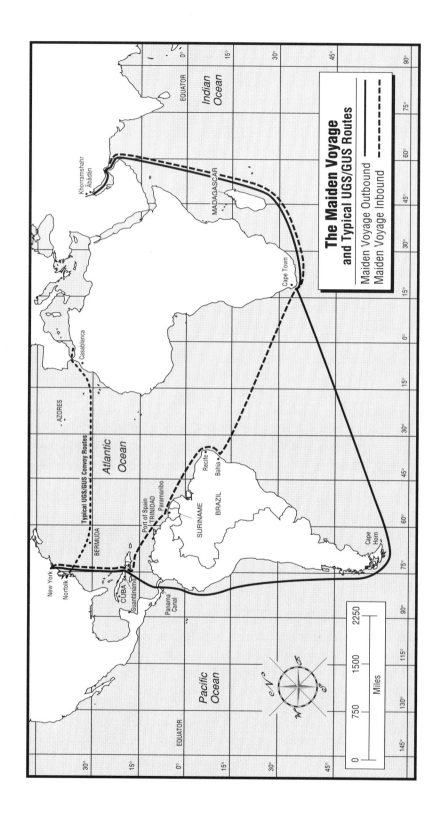

The Maiden Voyage
and Typical UGS/GUS Routes

Maiden Voyage Outbound
Maiden Voyage Inbound

Indian Ocean

EQUATOR

Khorramshahr
Ābādān

MADAGASCAR

Cape Town

Casablanca

AZORES

Atlantic Ocean

Typical UGS/GUS Convoy Routes

Recife
Bahia

BRAZIL

Port of Spain
TRINIDAD
Paramaribo

SURINAME

BERMUDA

New York
Norfolk

CUBA
Guantánamo

Panama Canal

Cape Horn

Pacific Ocean

EQUATOR

Miles

0   750   1500   2250

According to Samuel Eliot Morison, the official historian of U.S. naval operations in World War II, "sailing along the East Coast in convoy . . . was [by this time] no longer dangerous," and the interlocking system of convoys, "by which ships were run almost like trains," had proved so successful that during October, November, and December 1942 no losses to enemy submarines had occurred along the East and Gulf Coasts and the area around the Panama Canal.[23] The situation in the Caribbean Sea, however, was quite different. Although not as dangerous as the worst month, August 1942, when forty-six ships were sunk in the Caribbean, still twenty-five ships were sunk in September, and fifteen in October, when the *Brown* sailed through the Caribbean.[24]

Although the number of sinkings was declining, the terse statement in the sailing orders for NG-314 emphasized that there was no cause for complacency: "Enemy mine fields have been laid in U.S. coastal waters. Enemy submarine activity may be expected in U.S. coastal waters and CARIBBEAN SEA." Hence on the first full day at sea, 16 October, Lieutenant Calvert at 8:30 A.M. muster instructed the Armed Guard crew to sleep in their clothes, wear whistles around their necks, carry knives, and either carry or wear life jackets. The precautions at 3:30 A.M. on the 17th extended to "extra lookouts on watch," specifically, Lieutenant Calvert and one extra man on the flying bridge, two extra men on the forward gun platform, and four on the after gun platform. As the convoy progressed at eight knots, the *Simpson* steamed at fourteen knots patrolling a station some five to six thousand yards ahead.[25] Along with these important defensive measures, there were also prosaic housekeeping chores to attend to, as on the 21st when Captain Coward, at the steward's request, surveyed a hundred pounds of canned meat and, finding it "unfit for consumption," ordered it thrown overboard.

Sailing at speeds varying from eight to ten knots, the convoy reached Guantánamo Bay on the southeast corner of Cuba around noon on 22 October. After twenty-four hours at anchor in the bay off the strategically important U.S. Navy base at Guantánamo, the *Brown* on the 23rd left for the Panama Canal in convoy GZ-9, consisting of eleven American, three British, and two Norwegian merchant ships escorted by the "four-piper" destroyers *Barry* and *Borie* and by five submarine chasers.[26] Among the merchant ships was the *Thomas T. Tucker*, bound for Suez and, like the *Brown*, a Liberty ship on her maiden voyage. The *Brown*'s crew would see her again under much different circumstances later in the voyage.

The convoy was about halfway between Guantánamo Bay and the canal the following day when, just as the men off watch on the *Brown* had begun their noon meal, there was suddenly the sound of frantic screaming and someone pounding along the passageway shouting "He's been shot! He's been shot!"[27] Fearing that the ship was under attack, men poured out of the midship house. Dodging around the tanks lashed to the deck, they rushed aft toward a group of Armed Guard sailors clustered around a cot on which lay a sailor whose face and hair glistened with blood gushing from wounds in his head. They soon learned that the sailor had been shot by another member of the Armed Guard. Lieutenant Calvert's dispassionate account in his "Log" cannot mask the horror of the scene: the sailor was "lying on a cot aft, on the port side, just forward of the rear gunners' compartments. One hole was in the head just above the right eye and another hole one and a half inches to the right. Blood was streaming out and brain matter could be seen." The sailor who had shot him was "by his side with arms about him . . . sobbing and saying, 'I didn't mean to do it. He was my chum.'" The sailor was ordered away, first aid applied, and a doctor signaled for. Less than an hour later, Lt. (jg) Andrew W. Orlowski, a Navy physician, arrived from the *Barry*, but the wounded man was beyond help. Lieutenant Orlowski pronounced him dead at 2:20 P.M. from intercranial hemorrhage, a fractured skull, and shock. Although the sailor who had done the shooting had been given two doses of morphine, in his grief and guilt he twice attempted suicide during the next hour, "once by choking himself with his hands and once by an attempt to jump overboard." To prevent further attempts, Lieutenant Calvert ordered a shipmate to stay with him constantly. Although very different—the dead man had been reserved, almost a loner, whereas the other man "was always pulling pranks and joking around"—the two had been close friends as civilians and had enlisted and gone through boot camp together.[28] The incident itself stemmed from thoughtless horseplay. Thinking his pistol unloaded, the sailor who did the shooting had playfully pressed it against the other man's head and pulled the trigger. The pistol clicked and he again pulled the trigger. This time it fired and the bullet made two holes in tearing through his friend's head.[29]

Obviously the death had to be investigated, and later in the after-

The "flush deck" destroyer *Barry,* built in 1919–20, was one
of the escorts for convoy GZ-9. *Naval Institute*

noon a preliminary "investigating party" headed by Ens. Richard W.
Habersat boarded the *Brown* from the *Barry.* The *Barry,* which
stayed nearby, picked up Lieutenant Orlowski, Ensign Habersat, and
the other members of the "investigating party" about two hours later
and then returned to her assigned station in the convoy.[30] Early the
next morning, 25 October, a board of investigation headed by Lt.
Comdr. S. B. Colt and consisting of two other officers, one a physician, and three enlisted men was convened aboard the *Borie.* The
board then transferred to the *SC-746,* a 110-foot wooden submarine
chaser, and left "with instructions to make the Commodore's ship to
pick up embalming equipment and then to proceed to the S.S. John
W. Brown to hold an investigation into the causes of death and to
embalm the remains." The *SC-746* delivered the board of investigation to the *Brown* at 10:20 A.M.[31] Meanwhile, Lieutenant Orlowski,
Ensign Habersat, and one enlisted man left the *Barry* to join the
board on the *Brown.*[32] After taking testimony, the board concluded
that the shooting was accidental and hence that no disciplinary action should be taken. By the time the investigation was finished and

the two physicians had embalmed the body, most of the day had passed, and it wasn't until late afternoon that the *SC-746* came by the *Brown* to take off the board of investigation and return its members to the *Barry* and the *Borie.* In transferring to the *SC-746,* which was rolling wildly and plunging up and down in heavy seas as she tried to stay alongside the *Brown,* Lieutenant Orlowski injured his right foot so severely that he had to be admitted to the hospital when the *Barry* got to the Canal Zone.[33]

At 8:00 P.M. on 26 October, the day after the investigation, convoy GZ-9 arrived at Cristobal. The *Brown* dropped anchor but was soon ordered to shift to Pier 8A, where the body was taken ashore. The sailor who had done the shooting was detached the same night, and the next morning, the 27th, two replacements reported aboard. A few hours later, however, the sailor who had been detached was ordered back to the *Brown,* but he was soon sent off again, perhaps because of Captain Coward's insistence to the Navy authorities that "he didn't want the man aboard his ship as each time the man saw the place where he had killed his buddy he would be affected and sooner or later it would drive him out of his mind."[34] That afternoon, with members of the Navy Armed Guard from the *Brown* serving as pallbearers, the dead sailor was buried in Mount Hope Cemetery, Cristobal. As it turned out, this death that shouldn't have happened was the only one to occur on the *Brown* during her seagoing years.

Meanwhile, between 12:30 A.M. and 4:15 P.M. on the 27th the *Brown* took on 9,265 barrels of fuel and 150 tons of water. She then shifted to an anchorage, which she left early the next morning to pass through the Panama Canal. Nine and a half hours later she took departure from the Pacific side of the canal and started to sail independently down the west coast of South America, headed for Cape Town, South Africa, by way of Cape Horn. Because the Allied navies did not have enough ships available for escort duty at this time, the long, roundabout route to the Persian Gulf was used to keep ships as far as possible from the areas frequented by German U-boats. Since ships using this route were not in convoys, they had the advantage of being able to steam at full speed instead of at the speed of the slowest vessel in a convoy. However, the vast distance that had to be covered negated much of this advantage. There was the further disadvantage that if attacked by the enemy a ship was completely on her own, and, if sunk, there were no nearby rescue ships to pick up survivors.

During the run down the west coast of South America there were the usual fire and lifeboat drills plus antisubmarinc and antiaircraft drills and practice with the guns by the Armed Guard crew. But there were no emergencies of any kind to interrupt the routines of shipboard life at sea. The loneliness and lack of anything unusual during the first two weeks of this leg of the voyage are emphasized by Lieutenant Calvert's finding it worth recording in his "Log" that on 12 November "a tanker proceeding north was observed one point on the starboard bow a long distance away. It passed the beam five or six miles away." The next day, however, he could report the exciting news that "we will round the Horn today." Deck Cadet Kenneth Nielsen was the first to see the grey, forbidding silhouette of Cape Horn through a cold rain driven by blustery winds. On watch in the crow's nest about seventy-five feet above the water, as the *Brown* rolled heavily in the surging seas around the Horn he was swung out over the water as if he were the weight on a giant inverted pendulum. Some men working on deck yelled up to him to "'take a good look—you'll probably never see that again.' So I took a good look and . . . I've never seen it since."[35] Ralph Nilsen, one of the engine cadets, remembers that at times the *Brown* rolled so far over that the sea swept across the starboard side of the midship house on the main deck and he could "see solid green water" through the porthole in his cabin.[36] At about this time the *Brown* picked up an SOS from a Liberty ship that had rounded the Horn a day or two earlier. Under orders to ignore calls for help for fear that U-boats might be lurking in the area, the *Brown* plowed ahead without responding.[37]

Like the trip down the Pacific coast of South America, the seventeen days in the South Atlantic between Cape Horn and South Africa were uneventful and only three other ships were sighted, two a great distance away and one just "a couple of thousand yards to our port." The seas during this time continued to be extremely heavy. Lieutenant Calvert recorded in his "Log" for 17 November that the "main deck [was] being swept by a starboard sea," and on the 23rd he ordered the lookout stationed on the forward gun tub back to his quarters because the seas crashing over the *Brown*'s bow threatened to sweep him away. As the ship rolled, waves surging over the bulwarks damaged some barrels lashed to the main deck. The tons of water hurled by a particularly huge and vicious wave smashed with such force into one of the lifeboats on the boat deck that its sides were dented.

As the *Brown* fought her way forward, she received an order by radio to go to Saldanha Bay instead of Cape Town, probably because Cape Town's harbor was choked with ships. When she approached the areas off South Africa where U-boats might be patrolling, she began zigzagging to make it more difficult for submarines to track her. Although the *Brown* made no enemy contact, two bales of hay sighted in the water on the 26th were perhaps evidence that the enemy had recently been successful in the area. Shortly after 8:00 A.M. on 29 November, thirty-three days after leaving the Panama Canal, the *Brown*'s crew sighted land on the port bow. Four and a half hours later the ship was safely anchored and "finished with engine" behind the minefields that protected the entrance to Saldanha Bay.

Early the next morning the *Brown* was again under way on the short trip south to Cape Town. At 2:30 P.M. she "arrived at the roadstead outside Capetown," spent about an hour on the degaussing range, and shortly afterwards tied up at a pier to take on water and fuel. For the first time in over a month, the men on the *Brown* could go ashore. The four cadets—George Kurtz, Kenneth Nielsen, Ralph Nilsen, and Warren Wagenseil—spent part of their eight-hour shore leave seeing the movie *For Me and My Gal*,[38] a musical starring Judy Garland, George Murphy, and Gene Kelly in his first film.[39] They also went to a restaurant where they dined on huge antelope steaks, but they still had room sometime later for ice cream sodas.[40] Second Mate Robert Bloxsom, Third Mate Jerome Mamo, and Clerk/Typist Joseph Whelan went swimming at an indoor pool but had to return to the ship early because Bloxsom, while horsing around in the pool, slightly injured his shoulder.[41] There is no record how others in the crew amused themselves, but a hint is implicit in one of Lieutenant Calvert's "Recommendations" turned in at the end of the voyage that "a large number of . . . condoms should be provided."

The *Brown* sailed from Cape Town the next afternoon. A short time later she passed by a grounded Liberty ship that turned out to be the *Thomas T. Tucker*, which had sailed with her in convoy GZ-9 at the end of October. The *Tucker* had run hard aground in a fog a few days earlier and was a total loss.[42] While ashore in Cape Town some of the *Brown*'s crew had heard stories about a ship that owed her escape from a pursuing U-boat to fog but then got lost in the fog and ran aground. Obviously the stories were about the *Tucker*, whose good luck had suddenly turned bad.[43]

As the *Brown* continued around the Cape of Good Hope, the crew

The four cadet-midshipmen on Voyage 1 pose for a picture (*left* to *right*):
George Kurtz, Kenneth Nielsen, Warren Wagenseil, Ralph Nilsen.
Project Liberty Ship Archives

became intrigued by red patches that appeared in the deep blue
water. Robert Bloxsom remembers that the patches "began getting
bigger, until at last we were sailing on a red sea, it was blood red."
The red disappeared in a day or two, but discussions about it continued for some time: "Some said that it was dust from the Sahara Desert, others said that a volcanic eruption had caused it, my guess was
minute growth in the water caused it, similar to the red tides that we
hear about in the Florida area. It was pretty but weird, I've never
experienced it again and we did not see it on our return trip that
way."[44] But at least the phenomenon provided a break from the routine and gave the men something besides their escapades in Cape
Town to talk about.

Among the recreational possibilities in Cape Town was the opportunity to get drunk, and at least one crew member brought some
brandy aboard so that he wouldn't have to stop drinking when liberty
ended. About six hours after leaving port, Lieutenant Calvert learned
that one of his men could not stand watch because he had passed out

in his bunk after drinking half a bottle of brandy, probably the notorious Cape brandy that Chief Mate Griffin called "fire water."[45] Lieutenant Calvert put the man under a shower to try to sober him and as punishment ordered him to scrub the crew's shower with a toothbrush, a punishment that wouldn't deter most thirsty sailors.

Because of the possibility that magnetic mines had been laid in the shallow water near Cape Town, the *Brown*'s degaussing system had been turned on at departure on 1 December. On the 3rd, when it was turned off, the ship began zigzagging in case U-boats were lying in wait. Sailing in the Indian Ocean on the third day out from Cape Town, the men on the *Brown* got a vivid reminder that their precautions were well taken when they sighted an empty lifeboat off the starboard bow. Hence there was some nervousness on the 5th when the *Brown* had to stop for forty minutes while the engineers replaced a gasket on the auxiliary feed pump, which pumps water from the auxiliary condenser to the boilers. Problems continued on the 6th when rough seas, whipped by winds of about thirty-four to forty knots, poured over the *Brown*'s bow with such force that they dented the splinter shield on the forward gun platform about ten feet above the main deck.

Otherwise most of the voyage up the Indian Ocean was routine, although at the time the *Brown* sailed through it U-boats sank four ships.[46] Some of the action was along the route the *Brown* took. On 28 November, two days after leaving Cape Town, the SS *Jonathan Elmer* was ordered by radio to change her course "to miss path of vessel that had just been torpedoed."[47] Five days later the *Brown* crossed the same area but saw nothing of the enemy.

On 9 December the crew sighted the southern tip of Madagascar on the port bow. One morning at about the same time a lookout saw smoke on the horizon. Because there had been reports that a German commerce raider was operating in the area, Captain Coward was immediately notified. In appearance like merchant ships but in fact heavily armed and fast, commerce raiders preyed on Allied merchant ships steaming alone. Captain Coward could not have known that the raider *Michel* patrolling off the southeast coast of Madagascar had sunk the American Export Line's *Sawokla* during the night of 29–30 November and the Greek freighter *Eugenie Livanos* on 7 December,[48] but as soon as he saw the smoke he changed course at full speed away from the other ship. Second Mate Robert Bloxsom recalls that while still in sight of the other ship he was just able to make out her masts through the binoculars, "and to this day I believe that it was another Liberty Ship south bound and that he did the same thing that we did and turned tail and ran away from us as fast as we were running from him. But in time of war it is best to take no more chances than . . . necessary."[49]

About two weeks later, on 22 December, the lookouts sighted land on the port bow, signifying that the outbound voyage was almost over. Soon afterward the *Brown* entered the Persian Gulf. She could now stop the zigzagging that had been considered necessary in the Atlantic and Indian Oceans, but the degaussing was turned on because of the possibility of mines. The crew soon found out that they were no longer alone on a seemingly endless ocean: a two-engine monoplane flying low and fast crossed several hundred feet astern of the *Brown* on the 22nd; the next morning they passed a convoy of twenty-six merchant ships and three escorts heading south; and twice that afternoon they were challenged by patrol boats.

At 9:41 A.M. on a partly cloudy Christmas morning with the air temperature in the upper sixties, the *John W. Brown* finally arrived at her destination in the Persian Gulf. A few hours later, as she approached the group of ships crowding an anchorage off the mouth of the Shatt-al-Arab River, the crew were surprised to see each ship flying a four-flag hoist and a five-flag hoist. Four-flag hoists normally give a ship's call letters, but what puzzled the men on the *Brown* was that five-flag hoists didn't exist in the signal code. Finally the *Brown* got close enough for Second Mate Bloxsom to make out the code: "I got M, E, R, third repeater, Y, then X, M, A, S. All the anchored ships were flying Merry Xmas. I thought that this was great and as soon as we had our anchor down we hoisted Merry Xmas."[50] Appropriately, Christmas Day ended "fine & clear."

The trip from New York to the Persian Gulf had lasted almost two and a half months and covered about 15,400 miles.[51] The *Brown* was to spend an additional two and a half months in the Gulf area before starting home because the ports were choked with shipping—in January 1943, for example, a total of forty-two War Shipping Administration (WSA) ships spent time there.[52] At the beginning of February, Maxwell Brandwen, a WSA administrator, noting that the December 1942 discharge rate of cargo was 56,192 tons, remarked that "if the December rate continues, it will take about 3 months to discharge the cargo in the WSA vessels already in the Persian Gulf."[53] And of course more ships were constantly arriving. The reasons for this congestion included inadequate facilities, a limited number of berths for ships with deep drafts, inexperienced port battalions unloading the ships, administrative confusion caused by the U.S. Army's taking over operations from the British Army, and the priority given to unloading supplies needed by the British Army in the field, to mention just a few of the major problems.[54] Furthermore, more and more pressure was being put on the area, especially after the Russian victory at Stalingrad at the end of January 1943 eliminated the enemy threat to the Middle East from the north. Thereafter, more and more cargo for the Russians was routed through the Gulf, so much in fact that the Persian route became second only to the Far East route in tonnage handled.[55]

At the time the *Brown* was in the Gulf, the ports were undergoing rapid development. Khorramshahr, a major port sixty-seven miles up the Shatt-al-Arab River from the Gulf,[56] was being transformed from "a sleepy native village . . . connected with the interior only by a desert road fit for camels, to a vital port of entry for millions of tons of war material destined for the USSR."[57] A hard-surface two-lane highway north was still under construction, and not until March 1943 did trucks begin to carry appreciable amounts of freight to the USSR. Until truck transport was available to share the burden, trains carried the freight from Khorramshahr to the railroad junction at Tehran, where it either went northeast to Bandar-e Shāh on the Caspian Sea or northwest to the end of the rail line at Miāneh, about a hundred miles south of the Soviet border. From Miāneh, trucks took the freight the rest of the way.[58]

In Khorramshahr itself construction continued on a narrow pier that already had berths for five ships and when completed would handle seven. The pier paralleled the beach about fifty yards offshore and was connected to land by trestles for trains and trucks. With no room on the pier to store cargo, ships discharged directly into railway cars or trucks, although unloading into trucks had to stop whenever it rained because water transformed the yet-unpaved roads into impassable muddy quagmires.[59] Because only fifteen-ton cranes were available at the pier, the ships' cargo-handling gear and mobile cranes did most of the unloading.[60] On 15 February 1943, the day before the *Brown* moored there, WSA representative Eugene Seaholm reported that five berths were in use at Khorramshahr and that construction on the sixth and seventh was "well advanced."[61] In February 1943 these facilities handled fourteen ships in addition to the

This photograph shows the completed pier at Khorramshahr. When the *Brown* was there, two of the seven berths were still under construction. The trees in the foreground are date palms. *Library of Congress*

Brown. An average of 9.6 working days were spent on each ship to reach a total discharge of 57,906 tons of cargo.[62] Although the total discharge was a slight improvement over December's, a huge backlog of ships continued to clog the port while the *Brown* was there.

Thus the *Brown* spent week after week after boring week at anchor: "There was not a lot to do, we swam off the ship at times. . . . Some of our best excitement was when fighter planes would come down over the anchorage and go through all sorts of maneuvers, loop the loop, barrel rolls, and sometimes they would fly through the ships at mast top level. Evidently some of the planes that we had given the Russians were being demonstrated by our pilots or were being tested by the Russian pilots."[63] For the period between Christmas 1942 and late January 1943, Lieutenant Calvert recorded no unusual activity except the visit of a "merchant marine physician" from the SS *President Buchanan* to examine a sick sailor. The ship's "Deck

Log" for this period consistently records "Anchored as before awaiting orders," but also provides a few details about what was going on.
On New Year's Day, for example, with the weather clear and a high
temperature of sixty-four at noon, a boat drill was held at 1:30 P.M.
The "Official Log-Book" explains that number 3 boat, the aft boat on
the starboard side, was launched "in command of 2nd officer to exercise crew at oars and sail."[64] Both the "Deck Log" and "Official Log-
Book" record that at 4:30 number 3 boat returned and was hoisted in
and secured. Neither, however, explains that during the three hours
between launching the boat and hoisting it back in, Second Mate
Bloxsom, Third Mate Mamo, Third Assistant Engineer Whiteford,
and about five crew members had used it to visit a British gunboat in
the anchorage. The captain of the gunboat invited the three officers
aboard for a couple of rounds of Scotch to welcome the New Year.
Meanwhile, the crew members had been invited by the gunboat's
crew to share some bottles of Canadian Black Horse Ale. After visit-
ing the captain, the three officers from the *Brown* joined the crew's
party, which had picked up considerable momentum: "You would
get a bottle about 3/4 finished and someone would give you a fresh
bottle. There was singing and talking and all sorts of carrying on. . . .
We must have drunk gallons of Black Horse Ale." The men finally
tore themselves away from the party and somehow managed to get
back to the *Brown* on this first day of 1943.[65]

Nothing much happened during the early part of January, except
that on the 6th an Army physician came aboard to examine Clerk/
Typist Joseph Whelan and found that he had acute appendicitis.
Whelan was taken ashore on a British ship to go to Ābādān Hospital,
where he stayed for almost three weeks before rejoining the ship. On
the 18th it appeared that the *Brown* at last was going to move when
she was told at 11:30 A.M. to have steam up, but the order was canceled three hours later. On the 22nd there was a little flurry of activity. In the morning an Army tug came along the starboard side to
pick up twenty-two sacks of Army mail, and early in the afternoon
antiaircraft, fire, and boat drills were conducted. That night at 10:30
the *Brown* was suddenly ordered to get steam up immediately. This
time it appeared that the *Brown* was really going to move because at
11:00 a sick man from another ship was brought aboard to be taken
ashore to the hospital, and at 11:55 a pilot came aboard.

After routine testing, examining, and finding in "good order" the
"steering gear, whistle, telegraph, running lights & all voice com-

munications," the *Brown* got under way on 23 January at 12:20 A.M. She soon found, however, that the tide was too low for her to enter the river. She therefore had to return to the anchorage, but with permission to enter on the next high tide. Shortly after noon the *Brown* received orders to "proceed in," and five and a half hours later she was anchored off Ābādān, Iran, some eleven miles down the Shatt-al-Arab River from Khorramshahr. Late the next morning she moored at Ābādān to discharge eleven tanks and the two P-40s[66] and to deliver ten sacks of mail to the Iranian postal authorities. Early that evening she left Ābādān and went across and downriver a short distance to an anchorage at Harta Point.

Not much happened over the next ten days, except that on the 29th and 30th the *Brown* experienced the kind of exasperating administrative mixup that contributed to the long delays in unloading. During the morning of the 29th nineteen stevedores came aboard and remained until the following afternoon. However, as no lighters were brought out to the ship, no cargo was discharged. With nothing much to do to keep busy, some members of the crew looked for diversion ashore. After paying outrageous fees to get to Khorramshahr on local boats, they found that the town was filthy and run-down and had little to offer except some squalid prostitutes. Although dirty, smelly, and unkempt, they nevertheless succeeded in attracting a few men. The two crew members who reported their sexual intercourse with "natives" at least had judgment enough to use condoms and immediately after contact to rush to the Army's 19th Station Hospital for chemical prophylaxis.

Early in the morning of 3 February the crew got ready to move the ship, and at 7:20 A.M. with a pilot aboard, the *Brown* at slow ahead tried to turn in order to go in to a pier in Ābādān, but "the ship refuses to maneuver because of contact with silt." In other words, she was aground. It took a little over two hours for the tide to rise sufficiently for the ship to turn, and it was almost noon before she headed downriver on the way to the oil docks, which were actually upriver but could not be reached by a direct route from the anchorage. Shortly before 2:00 P.M. the crew "let go Port Anchor to turn ship up river," and after swinging around on the anchor, the *Brown* started upriver. By 3:30 she was moored in Ābādān to take on fuel. Early the next morning, 4 February, the *Brown* went back to an anchorage at Harta Point. While there she discharged seven tanks onto a barge on 7 and 8 February and discharged the final two on the 13th. Starting in the afternoon of the 15th and continuing until early the next morning, 160 tons of smokeless powder were unloaded from number 5 'tween deck (the area between the main deck and the lower hold) onto a British Inland Water Transport (IWT) barge, and in the afternoon of the 16th ammunition was unloaded onto another barge. It was a slow process, but at least something was happening.

Still later on the 16th the *Brown* shifted upriver a short distance to another anchorage, and the next afternoon she moved to Berth 2 on the new pier at Khorramshahr. Almost immediately an IWT tug brought five lighters alongside. By 7:00 P.M. stevedores were aboard discharging from numbers 1, 2, 3, and 5 hatches into the lighters and onto the pier. Unloading continued for the next two and a half weeks, often on almost a twenty-four-hour basis seven days a week. Late in the afternoon of 5 March the *Brown* left her berth and steamed upriver a short distance to an anchorage from which stevedores unloaded cargo onto barges while the crew cleaned the forward deep tanks and secured the tank tops and the bos'n supervised "a gang of coolies" preparing the ship for sea. The *Brown* was finally "entirely discharged of cargo" at noon on 9 March, seventy-five days after arriving at the Persian Gulf on Christmas morning. During the three weeks she was berthed at Khorramshahr, about seventy-five hundred tons of cargo were discharged from the ship, obviously at a very slow pace. Ralph Nilsen recalls that the "local natives" who did the stevedore work at Khorramshahr were so slow that the Armed Guard crew voluntarily pitched in, making it possible to leave Khorramshahr several weeks earlier.[67] It was also during this time that the *Brown* lost two of its crew members: an AB was sent to the 19th Station Hospital for observation and a fireman/watertender for medical care. The Army doctors concluded that the AB was insane and the fireman/watertender too ill to return to the ship. Their pay vouchers and personal belongings were then turned over to the authorities at the 19th Station Hospital.

The *Brown* finally departed Khorramshahr in the afternoon of 9 March to start her homeward voyage via Cape Town with a stop at Paramaribo, Suriname, for bauxite.[68] After a brief stop at about 6:00 P.M. to wait for high water and after the routine search for stowaways and contraband, the *Brown* once again headed downriver and just before midnight was abeam the Rooka Light Vessel at the river's mouth. A little over three hours later the *Brown* dropped the pilot and began steaming at full ahead.

In the morning of 11 March, when the *Brown* had gone a little over two hundred miles down the Persian Gulf, a pilot boarded to guide her to a dock at Bahrain Island to take on 10,655 barrels of fuel. At the same time, stevedores transferred fifty-six drums of gold precipitates weighing 12,577 pounds[69] from a barge into the *Brown*'s main mast house. Meanwhile one of the Armed Guard crew took advantage of the stop at Bahrain to go ashore to the American Mission Hospital to have a tooth pulled. Departing early the next morning, the *Brown* proceeded to Clarence Strait (now called the Strait of Hormuz), near Bandar 'Abbās, Iran, where she anchored in the early afternoon of Saturday, 13 March, to await orders. On the 14th, while waiting, the *Brown* took aboard a bag of British mail; the next day Captain Coward and Lieutenant Calvert "attended a master's conference aboard a station ship"; and on the 16th the *Brown* departed in combined convoys PA-29 and PB-31, consisting of twenty-two merchant ships and five escorts steaming at 8.5 knots.[70]

As the *Brown* was the only ship going from the Persian Gulf to Cape Town, the others bound either for Aden (the PA convoy) or Bombay (the PB convoy), she stayed with the convoy for only two days, until the morning of 18 March, when she increased speed to full ahead and began steaming independently for Cape Town. That evening she began zigzagging, and five days later she crossed the equator. Late on the 24th the sea began to get heavier, introducing ten days of the kind of extremely rough weather that tosses men around in their bunks as they try to sleep and makes eating from a plate almost impossible because one hand is needed to hang onto something for support and the other to hold the plate. The narrowness of the passageways, however, became an advantage in such weather by limiting the distance the crew bounced back and forth between bulkheads while lurching forward like desperate drunks.

By the morning of the 26th the sea had become so heavy that the *Brown*'s engine began racing. Because she was sailing light—her draft on leaving the Persian Gulf was 8'9" forward and 17'7" aft—the turbulent seas caused her to pitch so much that her propeller lifted out of the water. Without the resistance of the water to bite into, the propeller did not load the engine, thus making the engine run so fast that it risked damage or possibly even destruction.[71] Captain Coward stopped zigzagging to get on a course that would reduce pitching, and down in the engine room someone stood by the throttle to cut steam to the engine whenever it began to race. Two days later the sea had moderated sufficiently for the ship to resume zigzagging. The next evening, however, she again had to stop zigzagging, and after resuming at midnight she had to stop again the following morning. During the night of 30 March speed had to be reduced to 70 rpm to stop the "pounding" that occurs when the sea lifts the forward part of a ship high out of the water and she then "belly flops" down so hard that she shudders along her whole length and the rigging bangs and rattles above the howling wind.

This pattern continued for the next several days. Friday, 2 April, was especially bad. The *Brown* had resumed zigzagging at 4:30 A.M. but had to stop after four hours because of the rough seas. By 10:50 A.M. the seas and a heavy southwesterly swell had made the *Brown* pitch and roll so heavily that she began to pound again and the engine began to race. Speed was reduced to 65 rpm, but an hour and a half later more pounding made it necessary to go down to 50. At 5:50 P.M. it was possible to increase to 60 rpm and at 8:20 to 70, but early the next afternoon it was again necessary to go back down to 50. On the 4th the seas finally moderated sufficiently for the *Brown* to increase to 75 rpm, full speed, and maintain it until arrival in Cape Town. The next day the men on the *Brown* sighted a convoy going in the same direction. It was not often that a Navy officer aboard a Liberty ship could then go on to report that we "left it astern," but of course the *Brown* was steaming independently at full speed and a convoy can go no faster than its slowest ship, which in practice often meant eight or nine knots, sometimes even slower.

Arriving in Cape Town on the morning of 6 April, two weeks after crossing the equator, the *Brown* ran into fog, which necessitated sounding fog signals for about an hour and lying to until the fog lifted to avoid grounding. On entering the harbor at noon the crew passed the *Queen Mary* at anchor. According to rumor, she had stopped for supplies en route to England with a load of troops. Too large for the pier in Cape Town, the *Queen* had to be provisioned from barges. Because the anchorage was open to the sea, two destroyers circled her continuously to protect her from submarines.[72] After passing by the *Queen Mary*, the *Brown* with tugs alongside continued in and by early afternoon was secured at a pier. She then took on fresh water, steward's stores, and other supplies. On 7 April, 125 bags of mail were put aboard the ship, and the next morning, just about forty-eight hours after arrival at Cape Town, the *Brown* took departure.

Before the Brown arrived in Cape Town, Lieutenant Calvert had recorded in his "Log" that sometime after leaving the Persian Gulf the Armed Guard crew discovered that the gas ejector pump on the 5"/51 had become erratic. He took up the matter with First Assistant Engineer McMahan, who explained that the air compressor for the gas ejector system, which flushes the gun's bore of hot gases after firing, is powered by steam supplied to the steering engine but that the amount of steam kept on the steering engine was insufficient to ensure that the pump would keep going. He promised to increase the steam pressure to the steering engine to eliminate the problem. According to Lieutenant Calvert, the first assistant "deliberately failed" to keep his promise. The basis for Lieutenant Calvert's accusation is not clear, but it is the first of a number of remarks in his "Log" that suggest that his relationships with some of the Merchant Marine officers had begun to unravel by this stage of the voyage. The upshot of the first assistant's failure to increase the steam pressure to the steering engine was that the gas ejector pump stopped once on 2 April and twice on the 3rd. Lieutenant Calvert's next step was to go to Chief Engineer Poole, who told him that the rolling of the ship made it impossible to do anything about the problem at sea but that when they arrived in port he would replace the steam connection to the pump with a larger one that would increase the steam pressure. The chief, unlike the first assistant, obviously kept his promise, as Lieutenant Calvert commented in the "Log" after leaving Cape Town that the pump "has now been repaired and is functioning perfectly."

Others besides Lieutenant Calvert, including the second and third assistant engineers, apparently found it sometimes difficult to deal with the first assistant.[73] Hence Lieutenant Calvert's experience with him does not necessarily imply an undercurrent of friction between the Navy and the Merchant Marine crews. On the contrary, at least to this point in the voyage, the two groups got along well enough on the *Brown*,[74] and Lieutenant Calvert in his "Report of Outward Trip" dated 11 February 1943 stated that "the Master and officers of the ship carried out fully 'Instructions for Naval Transportation and U.S. Merchant Vessels in Time of War.' There was complete realization of the risks involved in wartime merchant shipping. I commend heartily Captain Coward as being fully aware of his responsibilities and duties, and alert to carry them out. It is a pleasure to a naval officer to be in joint operations with this patriotic American."

It is also true, however, that the deck officers had little affection

for Lieutenant Calvert, finding him aloof and sometimes even un-
friendly. He certainly didn't endear himself to them when he implied
that Merchant Mariners were unpatriotic.[75] One day at about the
same time as the problems with the gas ejector pump, one of the
mates notified Lieutenant Calvert that a member of the Armed
Guard crew had been disrespectful. According to Lieutenant Calvert,
all the sailor had done was to assert—correctly—that the mate had
no authority to give orders to the Armed Guard crew. Whatever the
facts may have been, the mate's charges were sustained and the
sailor given extra duty. Lieutenant Calvert then went on in his "Log"
to analyze the mate's character at some length, explaining that the
mate's behavior stemmed from resentment over having no authority
over the Navy men on the ship. As examples, Lieutenant Calvert
stated that "one of his favorite pastimes is sneering at men in the
military services, as 'national heroes'" and that "several days ago
[he] . . . deliberately stepped into the way of the gunnery officer on
the bridge, forcing him to step aside." In summary, according to
Lieutenant Calvert, the mate "resents the presence of Naval personnel on the bridge and implies that anyone present there but the Captain is there on his tolerance. He is becoming convinced that the
gunnery officer's attempts to keep peace are a sign of weakness. Further insolent interference with Naval personnel can be expected. At
such a time, a showdown with the Captain can be expected, or,
rather, will be necessary." Since no such showdown was reported in
the "Log," apparently there were no further incidents serious enough
to prompt Lieutenant Calvert to go to Captain Coward, or perhaps he
decided on reflection that it might be wiser to overlook such incidents to avoid an open breach between the Navy and Merchant Marine crews.

After leaving Cape Town on 8 April, the *Brown* became part of
convoy CN-16, consisting of thirteen merchant ships and four British escorts.[76] Because one of the oilers missed the ship when it left
Cape Town, Ralph Nilsen and George Kurtz, the other engine cadet,
had to take turns doing his job for the rest of the voyage.[77] On 10 April seven ships left the convoy, and in the late afternoon of the 11th
the convoy broke up, the *Brown* heading northwesterly at full speed.
Later in the evening she began zigzagging.

At about 8:00 the next morning the *Brown* had to reduce speed so
that the engineers could work on the engine. It is impossible to tell
from the "Deck Log" whether what happened over the next ten

hours was the result of failed attempts to fix the problem or whether it simply took that long to do the job. Apparently able to resume speed after fifteen minutes, the *Brown* steamed for about four and a half hours and then had to stop completely. Thirty-five minutes later she again began steaming at reduced speed, but after another four hours she once more had to stop. Obviously the engineers then succeeded in solving the problem, because twenty-five minutes after stopping the *Brown* was again able to go to full speed ahead. Despite being stopped for about an hour and steaming at reduced speed at other times, the *Brown* averaged 10.08 knots for the day. While the engine was stopped Lieutenant Calvert assigned extra men to the guns, a necessary precaution, especially since the crew got a pointed reminder of their vulnerability when an empty raft "with oars strapped on side, paint worn, and seaweed clinging to it floated by. It resembled a raft from a liberty ship." Fortunately the enemy did not appear, but one can't help wondering whether it was coincidental that the Armed Guard crew practiced with the 5"/51 the next afternoon.

About a week later, on 19 April, the *Brown* again had to stop, this time because the quadrant gear on the steering engine broke while the ship was zigzagging. Although the ship was an easy target if the enemy happened by, Ralph Nilsen recalls that there was an element of sport in the competition that arose between the deck and engine departments: "The engine crew, including two cadets, started repairs at the same time the deck crew, including two cadets, started to rig a steering system with block and tackle from the poop deck. We finished in a tie, so the deck crew had a good work out."[78] The repairs took almost four hours.

Chief Engineer Poole told Lieutenant Calvert that the deep gouge in a worm gear that caused the steering malfunction could have been the result of sabotage. Discounting the possibility that the problem was caused by "the rudder being brought hard over," he guessed that someone had deliberately jammed a piece of metal into the gear. To prevent further such incidents he locked the door to the steering engine room, but he gave Lieutenant Calvert a key because one of the entrances to the magazines was through its forward bulkhead. Lieutenant Calvert reported the incident to Naval Intelligence after the *Brown* anchored at Bahia (Salvador), Brazil, a few days later. However, after leaving Bahia, Chief Poole told Lieutenant Calvert that he had changed his mind about the origin of the trouble and had come to believe that it was caused after all by "too hard rudder." If the chief gave an explanation for his revised opinion, Lieutenant Calvert failed to record it in his "Log."

On 20 April the *Brown* started zigzagging and apparently continued to do so until the 22nd, when she reduced speed to 60 rpm. The "Deck Log" gives no reason for reducing speed, but the sea and the weather were not the causes as the sea and swell were "small" and the sky overcast with occasional rain. Possibly the reason was to time the ship's arrival at Bahia. At all events, after increasing speed to 75 rpm at 7:35 A.M. on the 23rd, the *Brown* anchored at Bahia four hours later.

The *Brown* left Bahia the next morning, Saturday, 24 April, in convoy BT-11 bound for Trinidad. On the leg from Bahia to Recife the convoy consisted of sixteen ships and three Brazilian escorts.[79] The escort commander was Comdr. C. Penna Botto on the *Rio Grande do Sul*, a thirty-three-year-old cruiser with a main armament of ten 4.7"/50s.[80] The *Brown* was the last ship to leave the harbor, as she was assigned position 24 in a convoy arranged 0, 4, 3, 3, 3, 3. This meant that the *Brown* was the fourth and last ship in column two, but since there were no ships assigned to column one, she was in fact in the first column on the port side. As the last ship in this column and the only ship in the convoy with a number four position, the *Brown* was in "coffin corner," so called because a ship sticking out in this position was more exposed to submarine attacks than the other ships in the convoy. An additional escort joined the convoy on the morning of the 25th, bringing the total to four, and the next morning the convoy slowed as it approached the waters off Recife. At this point three ships left the convoy, three others joined it, and later in the day the "four-piper" *Goff* took over as escort commander from the *Rio Grande do Sul*.[81] USS *Siren* and three PCs (submarine chasers) replaced the other Brazilian escorts.[82] The following day a tanker joined the convoy, thereby increasing its size to seventeen vessels. The tanker filled one of the empty number four positions, but the *Brown*, as the last ship in the port column, was still in "coffin corner." The convoy was protected not only by the escort vessels but also from time to time by air cover, as on 27 April when there were "numerous flights of planes around the convoy," once including "three together in the sky." There were, however, no contacts with the enemy.

Since convoy BT-11's destination was Trinidad, the *Oakley L. Al-*

exander, bound for Georgetown, British Guiana, and the *John W. Brown, Charles Goodyear,* and *Archbishop Lamy,* all headed for Paramaribo, Suriname (Dutch Guiana), broke off from the convoy on 4 May.[83] The *Brown* anchored at the mouth of the Suriname River and later shifted to an anchorage at Paramaribo.

On the morning of 5 May a foreman and twenty-two laborers boarded the ship to remove dunnage and shift the mail in preparation for taking on cargo. At midnight six of the laborers went ashore, and a few minutes after 2:00 A.M. on the 6th a pilot, five U.S. Army men (possibly hitching a ride), and a customs official boarded the *Brown.* She then started upriver in the darkness, and two and a half hours later tied up at Paranam to load 4,804 tons of bauxite ore, the basis of aluminum. The bauxite, which looked like brown sand, was loaded by hoppers and chutes[84] into numbers 2, 3, and 4 holds. On arrival at the pier the *Brown'*s draft forward was 7'9" and aft 14'2"; after taking on a total of 4,804 tons of bauxite, her draft forward was 20'0" and aft 20'4". She could not take on a full load because a bar at the mouth of the Suriname River prevented ships drawing more than seventeen feet from entering or leaving at low tide. To make up for this restriction, smaller ships shuttled bauxite ore from British Guiana and Suriname to Trinidad, which could accommodate ships with deeper drafts.[85] Thus ships like the *Brown* would take on a partial load of bauxite in the Guianas and then sail to Trinidad to complete loading.

Having loaded as much as she could at Paranam, the *Brown* returned downriver at full ahead but then had to anchor to wait for the tide to rise enough to allow her to cross the bar at the mouth of the river. Kenneth Nielsen remembers that as the ship sailed down the river "the jungle was so thick on either side of us that we could reach out and touch the wide green leaves of the trees and other plants. It was quite beautiful, really, and reminded me of the descriptions of South American jungles I'd read when I was young. The air was humid and smelled rank. We watched as monkeys leaped from the trees and swam freely in the river."[86] By early evening on 7 May, the *Brown* had left the river and was at sea steaming at full speed, followed closely by the *Charles Goodyear.* By the end of the next day, however, the *Brown* had left the *Goodyear* behind.

In the morning on 9 May the *Brown* entered the channel at Port of Spain, Trinidad, British West Indies, stopped at the examination station for five minutes, and then moved to an anchorage to await quarantine and immigration officials. Satisfied that the crew was free of communicable diseases, the medical authorities granted pratique—permission to use the port—and the *Brown* immediately notified the Alcoa Steamship Company of her "readiness to load." Late in the afternoon she moved to the bauxite dock of the U.S. Navy Air Station, located some eight miles from Port of Spain. Loading began almost immediately after arrival and continued through the night until completed early the next morning. This time the *Brown* received 3,776 tons of bauxite, bringing the total to 8,580 tons. The bauxite was consigned to the "Aluminum Co. of Canada, New York, for trans-shipment to Arvida, P.Q."[87] The *Brown* next went to an oil dock near San Fernando for fuel and water and then shifted to a mooring at the Port of Spain anchorage, where she remained for three full days. After loading and bunkering, her draft was 26' 10" forward and 29' 10" aft.

Not much happened during the first of the three days at anchor: two sacks of mail were taken ashore and ship stores were taken aboard; otherwise the "crew [were] variously employed about vessel." On the 12th, Lieutenant Calvert made a report of the trip to Naval Intelligence. Ironically, on the day after the lieutenant's report Chief Engineer Poole told him that twice since leaving Cape Town grease apparently mixed with either ground glass or emery had been discovered in the reversing engine. He showed the lieutenant a matchbox filled with grease that "tended to show small bits of glittering matter." On learning that the second assistant engineer had missed the ship when it left Port of Spain, the chief remarked that he was glad because "he suspects he may be guilty of sabotage. The 2nd Assistant did not like the 1st Assistant and may have been trying to spite him." As this is the second time that Chief Engineer Poole talked to Lieutenant Calvert about sabotage, and on both occasions a bit oddly, one wonders whether the chief was pulling the lieutenant's leg. If so, the lieutenant was unaware of it.

At all events, the second assistant was in fact gone, and George Kurtz and Ralph Nilsen, the two engine cadets, then took on the duties of the second assistant in addition to those of the oiler who had left in Cape Town.[88] Also on the 13th, Captain Coward and Lieutenant Calvert attended a convoy conference at the Naval Operating Base in Port of Spain for a briefing on convoy TAG-60 bound for Guantánamo to join GN-60 to New York.[89] On leaving Trinidad on 14 May the convoy was to consist of thirteen ships in seven columns, to be joined on the 16th by nine ships from Curaçao and four from Aruba, thereby reaching its full strength of fifteen cargo ships and eleven tankers. The convoy commodore was Lt. Comdr. J. M. Field, USN, on the Liberty ship *Charles Goodyear,* and there were four escorts, the 181-foot-long Netherlands patrol ship *Jan Van Brakel,* the flush-deck destroyer USS *Leary,* and *PCs 1123* and *1191.* Lieutenant Calvert noted in particular that at the convoy conference the ships in the convoy were ordered to fire on all submarines "without regard to endangering friendly ships." This order underlined the priority given to sinking U-boats, which in April 1943 sank forty-four Allied and neutral merchant ships in the Atlantic and Arctic region, and in May, when the *Brown* was in the region, forty-one.[90]

The *Brown* left Port of Spain on 14 May. While at sea on the 17th an incident occurred that suggests further testiness in the relations between Lieutenant Calvert and the Merchant Marine officers. As the end of the voyage neared, quite possibly some of the men no longer felt it necessary to repress antagonistic feelings that had developed along the way. According to Lieutenant Calvert's account in his "Log," he was told at 3:55 P.M. by the chief mate that a gun drill would take place in ten minutes. However, when the time came, there were fire and boat drills, but no gun drill. There seems to be a note of belligerence and the assumption that he was deliberately misinformed in his statement that he "protested to the captain against receiving false information." One wonders whether he was reading too much into the incident or whether he was in fact being taunted.

On 19 May TAG-60 reached Guantánamo. In his report on Convoy Form "D," Lieutenant Commander Field implicitly rebuked the masters and deck officers of the *Brown* and the *Archbishop Lamy* for poor station keeping by noting that both vessels were "continually out of position." The rebuke was no doubt well deserved, as there is nothing in the "Deck Log" about the weather and the seas that would account for their straying from their assigned stations. Perhaps it was another indication that the length of the voyage was taking a toll on the men.

At Guantánamo the convoy broke into two parts. Without stopping, the part that included the *Brown* then joined other ships to become convoy GN-60,[91] with Lieutenant Commander Field continuing as convoy commodore in the *Charles Goodyear.* This convoy consisted of twelve U.S. cargo ships, five U.S. tankers, six British cargo ships, three British tankers, one Norwegian, one Dutch, and one Panamanian cargo ship, and two Panamanian tankers, for a total of thirty-one vessels. The escort consisted of the corvette *Fury*, which had been part of the escort when the *Brown* left New York seven months earlier, the corvette *Brisk*, and PCs *484, 554,* and *565.*

During this last leg of the homeward voyage, the men on the *Brown* faced as troubling a mystery as the ground glass in the reversing engine. The issue arose when one of the Armed Guard crew told Lieutenant Calvert that he had seen a swastika chalked on the ship's railing and another traced in bauxite dust on the bow. The bos'n, Matts Oman, confirmed the story, stating that he too had recently seen swastikas chalked on the ship. The bos'n suspected a wiper who had joined the *Brown* in Cape Town. Lieutenant Calvert's statements in his "Log" suggest that the wiper's unusual habits were the only grounds for this suspicion: "The Bosn. mentioned that . . . [the wiper] continually walks about the ship at night . . . [and] sleeps on a cot aft [when he's not continually walking?] next to the companionway leading down to the shaft alley. On several occasions the Bosn. has tried to induce him to move elsewhere in order that the Navy would have full use of the small amount of room available aft on deck for sleeping . . . [but he] refused. The Bosn. has a feeling that [he] may be much shrewder than appears on the surface." Apparently, Lieutenant Calvert believed that he had stumbled across a truly suspicious, and perhaps dangerous, person; otherwise it is difficult to explain the detail with which he continued his account: the wiper "came aboard the John Brown in Capetown. He had no seamans papers, and the American consul reported that they had been lost. He was reported by the consul to be an ordinary seaman who did not wish to ship as a wiper. Nevertheless he came aboard the John W. Brown as a wiper in the engine department. According to information he gave Captain Coward . . . he is New Hampshire born, 23 years old, and five feet, ten inches tall." Obviously, Lieutenant Calvert discussed the wiper with at least the captain and the bos'n, and quite likely with others as well. He also talked to the man himself: "On one occasion he told the gunnery officer that he had spent some time in the Civilian Conservation Corps in Minnesota and Oregon. He has a noticeable hesitation of speech, and his phrases are sometimes noticeably disjointed."

From the perspective of fifty years later, Lieutenant Calvert's attention to the wiper simply because of his personality seems excessive, but one must remember that the men on the *Brown* were sailing through dangerous waters in a war against an enemy adept at sabotage and subversion. Thus anything or anyone out of the ordinary might appear threatening to them. In that context, Lieutenant Calvert probably felt that he was recording information that might one day be important. However, there is no mention in subsequent entries in the "Log" that anyone was able to connect the wiper with the swastikas that had mysteriously appeared. It is also quite possible that the man who first reported the swastikas had drawn them himself to vex Lieutenant Calvert, perhaps in retaliation for being punished twice by the lieutenant during the previous month, once for being disrespectful to one of the Merchant Marine officers and once for disobeying orders.

Meanwhile, the *Brown* was making her way toward New York. As part of the preparations for arrival, the ship on 23 May was again "searched for stowaways and contraband," but none was discovered. In the afternoon the seas turned rough, and until they moderated two days later the ship was frequently "laboring & pitching & shipping heavy spray." On the morning of the 26th several ships left the convoy, probably to go to Norfolk, Baltimore, or Philadelphia. Then at about 4:00 P.M., less than a day out of New York, the convoy encountered dense fog. On the *Brown* the bridge rang "standby" on the engine room telegraph, and to reduce the risk of collision the crew streamed the fog buoy. When towed behind a ship, this device causes a fountain of water to spurt into the air. If the bow lookout on the following ship can see the fountain, he knows his ship is getting dangerously close. The heavy fog lasted for about six hours.

The morning of Thursday, 27 May, broke "fine & clear" with the air temperature in the sixties as the *Brown* at 9:06 arrived "abeam [the] first channel buoy in harbor approach," some thirty miles out. At 12:50 P.M. she passed the Ambrose Light Vessel and shortly afterwards took a pilot aboard. After passing through the submarine net, she steamed for almost an hour before dropping anchor to await immigration and quarantine authorities. They arrived at 4:00 P.M. and granted pratique a half hour later. Shortly after 5:00 the *Brown* started up the Hudson River to her assigned pier. A pilot came aboard at about 7:00, and with two tugs alongside to assist, the *Brown* moved into the pier. The tugs cleared at 7:30, and ten minutes later the lines were secured to the north side of Pier K, Weehawken, New Jersey, across the Hudson from midtown Manhattan. The *John*

W. Brown was home again after a voyage of about eight months and thirty-three thousand miles.[92]

There was much work yet to be done, however, commencing at 8:00 the next morning when a gang of stevedores came aboard to remove sacks of mail from number 5 hatch. This task took a little over an hour, and the stevedores then worked another hour discharging the fifty-six drums of gold precipitates from the main mast house. Early in the afternoon the *Brown* shifted a mile north of Pier K to Pier 9, Weehawken, where she discharged bauxite from numbers 4 and 5 hatches until 7:00 P.M. Discharging cargo resumed the next morning, Saturday, 29 May, and continued every day, including Sunday, until finally completed on Wednesday, 2 June. Saturday, 29 May, was also the day the crew were paid off by W. B. Nagle of States Marine Corporation,[93] although from references in the "Deck Log" it is clear that at least two ABs and one ordinary seaman stayed aboard. Captain Coward signed the "Deck Log" for the last time on 5 June, Chief Mate Griffin left the *Brown* after being paid off on the 7th, and Third Mate Jerome Mamo left on the 9th.

Saturday, 29 May, also marked the first appearance of shipyard workers on board to start overhauling the cargo gear, the high-pressure and intermediate-pressure cylinders of the main engine, the gauges in the engine room, the reversing engine, the sea valves, and the like—the list is a long one—and to fix a crack in the steam line to the bilge pump and repair the lifeboat that heavy weather had damaged the previous November.[94] These men didn't work on Sunday, but they came aboard again on Monday in a routine that lasted until 11 June. On 1 and 2 June cleaning gangs came aboard to clean the holds. Sometime before the job was finished, the mate on watch turned in to U.S. Customs three leather coats that had been found during cleaning. These coats were part of the Soviet Lend-Lease shipment and had been stolen and hidden aboard ship while the *Brown* was discharging cargo in the Persian Gulf. The loss of three coats isn't much, but there is no way of knowing how many other items may have been successfully stolen. Pilferage had in fact become enough of a problem during loading and unloading operations that the U.S. Army Transportation Corps in October 1942 made provisions for an Army officer to sail as a cargo security officer on ships carrying Army cargo.[95] On 3 June, Lieutenant Calvert and his Armed Guard crew were detached, and because there had to be Navy men aboard armed merchant ships at all times, they were immediately replaced by a partial crew of fifteen enlisted men commanded by Lt. (jg) Arley T. Zinn. Late that afternoon four tugs came alongside the now empty *Brown* to tow her to a dry dock at the Bethlehem Shipyard in Hoboken, New Jersey, about two miles downriver. During the time the *Brown* was being worked on in dry dock, two surveyors from the American Bureau of Shipping inspected the hull. One examined it to ascertain what damage had been done when the *Brown* struck a submerged object while leaving the Persian Gulf. He found four plates indented and three buckled, but since the hull was still tight he recommended that the ship "be retained in her present class with this Bureau" and that permanent repairs be made whenever convenient to the owner.[96] The other surveyor made a routine examination of the bottom, rudder, propeller, sea valves, and the like, noted that the bottom had been freshly painted and the sea valves overhauled, and likewise recommended that the classification be retained.[97] On 3 June the dock was flooded. A pilot and four tugs then shifted the *Brown* to Bethlehem's Hoboken yard for another eight days of repairs and alterations.

While the *Brown* was steaming along the Pacific coast of South America seven months earlier, in November 1942, the Allies made their first offensive strike in the European theater by invading North Africa. By the middle of May 1943 they were in complete control of North Africa and getting ready for their next move, Operation Husky, the invasion of Sicily, scheduled for 10 July 1943. The planners worried, however, that a sufficient number of troopships might not be available to transport the needed American personnel overseas, thereby threatening to delay long-range operations.[98] This situation influenced decisions that affected the *Brown.*

In May 1943, Maj. Gen. Charles P. Gross, chief of transportation, decided to meet the shortage of troopships by converting some Liberty ships to limited-capacity troop carriers with the dual functions of taking troops overseas and bringing POWs back.[99] One of the 222 Liberty ships selected, the *John W. Brown* was thus fitted out at Bethlehem's Hoboken yard to carry about 350 troops in addition to cargo.[100] The alterations to accommodate these men in numbers 2 and 3 'tween decks (the decks beneath the second and third forward hatches, also called the second deck) included installing port and starboard covered companionways (stairways) immediately aft of number 2 hatch to provide access to the 'tween decks, adding a large deckhouse for head and washroom facilities on the main deck aft of number 2 hatch, installing additional facilities on the second deck, and installing fittings to set up standee (removable) bunks. The total cost for the repairs and alterations was $106,363.48. Because of her new function, the *Brown's* armament also had to be increased. Four additional 20-mm guns were installed, two forward just aft of the 3"/50 and two atop the after end of the midship deckhouse. The *Brown* now had one 3"/50, one 5"/51, and eight 20-mm guns.[101]

On 7 June at 9:30 A.M., Chief Mate Griffin witnessed with W. A. Shepard of the American Bureau of Shipping the test of the number 4 port boom; this was one of his last official acts on the *Brown*, and at 5:00 that evening he was paid off and left the ship. From then on until the next crew took over, States Marine provided a standby mate to watch over the ship during the day in addition to the night mate who had been on duty at night since the second day in port. On the 9th, Third Mate Jerome Mamo was paid off and the name of Joseph Melendy, chief mate on the second voyage, appears for the first time in the "Deck Log." On the 10th two tugs shifted the *Brown* away from the pier so that another ship could take the berth, after which the *Brown* tied up to the new ship. This arrangement lasted less than twenty-four hours, as shortly after noon on the 11th four tugs moved the *Brown*, at the time a dead ship, down the Hudson River, around the southern tip of Manhattan, across the mouth of the East River, to Pier 24, Brooklyn, about a mile downriver from the Brooklyn Bridge. Tied up by 2:00 P.M., she began taking on stores a half hour later. Obviously, since there are no shops around the corner at sea, ships must have supplies on board to take care of every conceivable need. Hence the list of supplies put aboard the *Brown* is a long one, more than 250 separate items for the deck department alone, including, to give a hint of the range, 300 pounds of brown laundry soap, 2 toilet seats, a "Verys pistol and colored rocket for convoy emergency signals," 200 gallons of grey hull paint, 6 dozen seventy-five-watt lightbulbs, a Heath sextant, 12 four-by-nine blotters, and 350 cartons of Camel cigarettes.[102]

At about the same time that the first shipment of supplies arrived, a cleaning gang came aboard to work on the holds, a surveyor from the American Bureau of Shipping arrived to test the heavy lift boom at number 2 hatch,[103] and 300 tons of ballast were loaded in number 5 hatch. On the 12th, the first day of the second voyage according to a note in the "Deck Log," 375 tons of ballast were loaded in number 4 hold and 600 tons in number 3, bringing the total to 1,275 tons. At

11:30 A.M., Arnold Zambik, the new chief mate, and Robert Armstrong, the new third mate, reported aboard. The "Deck Log" for the first voyage ends with the information that between 5:00 and 7:15 P.M. the ship took on two thousand barrels of fuel from a barge that had come alongside.

After two busy weeks in port, the *John W. Brown* was just about ready to begin a new assignment.

3

Voyages 2 and 3

The Mediterranean Theater

Except for Bos'n Matts Oman and AB Abe Ostrusky, an entirely new crew signed on the *John W. Brown* for Voyage 2 with Capt. William E. Carley, the new master, in command of a Merchant Marine crew of forty-seven.[1] A big, handsome man in his fifties, Captain Carley wore his hat crushed in the manner of Army Air Force pilots, giving him the flamboyant air of a Hollywood actor playing the part of a captain.[2] Despite his devil-may-care appearance, however, Captain Carley was a forceful and conscientious leader whose overriding concern was always the safety of his crew and his ship. Lt. (jg) Arley T. Zinn and the fifteen Navy Armed Guard enlisted men who had joined the *Brown* on 3 June were increased by twelve more before sailing, making a total of twenty-eight Navy men on Voyage 2.[3] The *Brown* was assigned to the Army Transport Service for this voyage to carry food[4] and troops to Algiers in the Mediterranean theater. Accordingly, on Sunday morning, 13 June 1943, she shifted about four miles down the Upper Bay from Pier 24 to Pier 4 Army Base[5] at the foot of 59th Street in Brooklyn. During the *Brown*'s stay at the Army base, Lieutenant Zinn assigned men to the bridge to cover the "hot loop" phone that connected the ship to the Aircraft Warning Center in the New York area. Set up by Navy Ordnance in late 1942, the "hot loop" circuit was a special communications system designed to add armed merchant ships moored at the Army base to New York's permanent antiaircraft defenses. In the event of an air attack on New York, the ships would receive orders over the "hot loop" phones on how to use their firepower to supplement that of the permanent antiaircraft batteries.[6] Fortunately, the system never had to be put to the test.

Although the *Brown* was fully loaded with 5,023 long tons of cargo[7] by Saturday, 19 June,[8] she had received no orders to sail and hence remained at Pier 4. Meanwhile, Convoy and Routing administrators at the New York offices of the Tenth Fleet were making arrangements for her to sail in convoy UGS-11. To determine the *Brown*'s readiness, on 21 June an officer from Convoy and Routing interviewed Captain Carley to get specific information about crew size, armament, equipment, and the like. Among other details, the interview revealed that the *Brown* carried one Merchant Marine and one U.S. Navy radio operator, was equipped with four lifeboats and fifty rafts, had 12,500 barrels of fuel (Bunker C) aboard, and would not require fuel, water, stores, or repairs at her next port of call.[9]

Captain Carley and Lieutenant Zinn attended a convoy conference on 23 June, and at 2:00 A.M. on the 24th the *Brown* left Pier 4 Army Base to begin the voyage. Captain Carley recorded in his "Secret Log" that at 5:00 A.M. she passed Gedney Channel Light at the end of Ambrose Channel as she steamed out over the same route she had followed eight months earlier at the beginning of Voyage 1. During the war, masters of merchant ships kept "Secret Logs" provided by the Navy to report such items of interest to the Navy as conditions in ports visited and sightings of enemy submarines, ships, and planes. They could also use the logs to record the information about positions, courses steered, ports of call, and arrival and departure dates and times normally included in deck logs but prohibited for security reasons during wartime. The master was instructed to store his "Secret Log" in a weighted bag during a voyage so that it could be thrown overboard in an emergency to prevent the enemy from getting it. At the end of the voyage the master turned it in to the Navy routing officer. In practice there was considerable variation in the amount of information that masters provided. Captain Carley made detailed notes in the "Secret Logs" for Voyages 2 and 3, but subsequent masters of the *Brown* rarely did more than note noon positions and the times and dates of arrivals and departures.

On leaving the port area, the *Brown* became part of the New York section of convoy UGS-11, bound for Hampton Roads to join the main body of the convoy. The New York section consisted of thirty-seven merchant ships deployed in nine columns. The *Brown*'s number, 64, indicates that she was the fourth ship in column six. The convoy was escorted by the destroyers *Hobby, McCook, Barker,* and *Bulmer.*[10] On the *Brown,* Captain Carley posted four extra lookouts so that there were a total of five Merchant Marine lookouts on duty at all times during the trip in addition to the Armed Guard lookouts. In assigning five, Captain Carley exceeded the requirement that in dangerous waters four lookouts must be posted.[11] This minor detail, as we shall see, was typical of Captain Carley's constant concern for the safety of the ship.

Early in the afternoon on the first day at sea, the first of the seven fire and boat drills on the outbound voyage was held. These drills were especially important because besides cargo the *Brown* was carrying 5 officers and 145 enlisted men of U.S. Army Military Police detachments who on arrival in North Africa would be assigned to guard POWs. Also aboard were Capt. Larry D. Rider, an Army physician, three medical corpsmen, and 2nd Lt. A. Sankowski, the cargo security officer assigned by the Transportation Corps. Since merchant ships did not ordinarily carry a physician, having Captain Rider aboard was a luxury for the Merchant crew, thirteen of whom he treated for a variety of illnesses and injuries during the voyage.[12] Lieutenant Sankowski's primary responsibility as cargo security officer was "to prevent pilferage or mishandling of military supplies."[13] Besides the Army personnel, the *Brown* carried 3 Royal Navy officers and 150 Royal Navy enlisted men,[14] survivors of a torpedoed ship on the first leg of their trip home for reassignment.[15]

Lieutenant Zinn organized the Armed Guard unit into three watches consisting of one petty officer and five men each, on a rotation of three hours on and six off. Two Army MPs also stood watch on the after gun platforms, one on each side during each watch, and two Royal Navy sailors did the same on the forward gun platforms. When the five Merchant Marine lookouts are added in, a total of fifteen pairs of eyes searched the sky and sea for signs of the enemy and, at night, for other blacked-out ships in the convoy suddenly looming out of the darkness.

At 4:00 A.M. on 25 June the convoy arrived at the seaward entrance to the sixty-three-mile-long, thousand-yard-wide swept channel to the Chesapeake Bay.[16] After maneuvering into a single column, the ships in the convoy followed the channel into the bay, accompanied by Navy patrols looking for enemy submarines trying to sneak in. Security was extremely tight throughout the area. Of the ten-mile-wide entrance to the bay, only the two-and-a-half-mile-wide channel just north of Cape Henry was used. A controlled minefield that could be deactivated to allow friendly ships to pass through guarded the channel, and contact mines that exploded on impact guarded the rest of the entrance. As secondary lines of defense, antimotorboat booms and antisubmarine nets secured Hampton Roads and the entrance to the York River, and a controlled minefield near Thimble Shoals Light provided additional protection.[17]

It took almost ten hours for the *Brown* to reach her assigned anchorage in Lynnhaven Roads just inside Cape Henry. About an hour before she anchored, a stray bolt had been discovered in her steering engine—in Lieutenant Zinn's opinion either an "accident or if sabotage probably placed there from 1030–1230." Captain Carley unequivocally stated that "an attempt was made . . . to disable the steering gear" and reported the incident to Naval Intelligence in Norfolk. Since, however, neither Captain Carley nor Lieutenant Zinn mentioned the incident again, apparently there was no significant follow-up investigation and resolution. But clearly the men on the *Brown* on Voyage 2, like those on Voyage 1, were alert to the possibility of sabotage.

On 26 June, Captain Carley and Lieutenant Zinn attended a convoy conference to learn the details of UGS-11,[18] which was the first UGS (U.S. to Gibraltar, Slow) convoy originating in Hampton Roads—earlier ones had originated in New York[19]—and the first to use Liberty ships as troop carriers.[20] The procedure for departure, as described at the conference, called for the *A. C. Bedford*, the convoy commodore's vessel and the first to leave the harbor, to sound a fifteen-second blast at 4:30 A.M. on the 27th to signify "Departure Commences." The *Bedford* would then weigh anchor and adjust speed in order to pass Cape Henry at 5:00 A.M. The second ship was scheduled to pass at 5:02, the third at 5:04, and so forth until the sixtieth and last passed at 7:00.[21] Scheduled to pass Cape Henry at 6:02 as the thirty-second ship, the *Brown* with a pilot aboard weighed anchor at 5:20 and left the Lynnhaven anchorage. She dropped the pilot about an hour and a half after passing Cape Henry and increased speed to full ahead. She then steamed in single file through the swept channel for about another sixty miles to UGS-11's rendezvous position, which she reached at 2:00 P.M. After the convoy formed up, the convoy commodore, Capt. H. V. McCabe, USN, in the *Bedford* or-

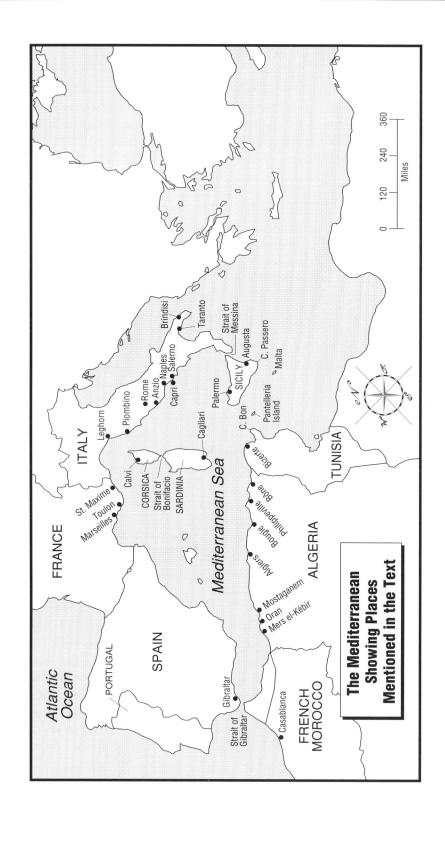

The Mediterranean
Showing Places
Mentioned in the Text

dered a speed of 10.0 knots as a trial and then reduced speed to 9.5 knots for the night of 27–28 June.[22]

Bound for various North African ports, the ships were organized into five sections so that they could easily leave the convoy in groups at different times; for example, the ships in section one were bound for Algiers, those in section two for Oran. The *Brown*, in section five, was bound for Bône (now called Annaba), Algeria. The ships were spread out in thirteen columns across the front, with no more than five in any column. Since the distance between columns was seven hundred yards and the distance between ships in column five hundred yards, the convoy was almost five miles across and slightly over a mile long. As number 43, the *Brown* was the third ship in column four, between the Liberty ships *George H. Thomas*, number 42, and *Lambert Cadwalader*, number 44. The USS *Hobby*, under Comdr. C. L. Winecoff, USN, continued as flag of Task Force 62, which had been increased to total ten destroyers and destroyer escorts, and of Task Unit 21.12, consisting of the auxiliary aircraft carrier (ACV) *Core*, soon to be redesignated the escort carrier (CVE) *Core*, and her four escorts.

Escort carriers provided air cover for convoys while they were out of range of land-based escort planes, but more important, they initiated offensive action against U-boats. Unlike the usual convoy escorts, which were purely defensive and went into action only when the enemy appeared, the CVEs, guided by intelligence derived from decrypted German naval codes, sent their planes out searching for U-boats. The result was that during the two years from May 1943, when they first began significant action, until the end of the war in Europe in May 1945, they had more than fifty "kills."[23] The *Core*, a converted Maritime Commission C-3 merchant ship now fitted with a 442-foot flight deck and armed with nine TBF torpedo bombers (Avengers) and six F4F fighters (Wildcats), was making her first trip into action.[24] Assigned position 63 in the convoy, she was about fourteen hundred yards directly to starboard of the *Brown*. Except for the column leader, the *Elihu Yale*, column six was kept empty for the *Core* so that she could easily and quickly drop astern of the convoy to launch and recover her aircraft and then rejoin it when her patrols were completed. On 28 June, for example, from a position some seven thousand to ten thousand yards astern of the convoy the *Core* "routinely" launched and landed two TBFs and two F4Fs on antisub-

The USS *Core,* one of the escort carriers on the UGS\GUS convoy routes,
accompanied UGS-11 in late June and early July 1943. *Naval Institute*

marine patrol and didn't return to her station in the convoy until the
evening of the 29th.[25]

Shortly after midnight on 28 June, Captain McCabe reacted to a
"suspicious contact" by ordering "an emergency turn to port," a maneuver in which the ships in the convoy turn forty-five degrees to
port in unison and hold the course until ordered to resume base
course, in this instance for forty minutes. Since the convoy had been
formed less than twelve hours earlier, Captain McCabe had not yet
had a chance to have the ships practice evasive tactics. Thus there
was confusion on some ships about what they should do, creating a
dangerous situation because with sixty blacked-out ships maneuvering together in the middle of the night, the possibility of collision is
high unless each ship does exactly what she should. Consequently,
starting at 8:30 A.M. Captain McCabe drilled the convoy in emergency turns for almost two and a half hours, using whistles and flag
hoists to issue his orders. Part of the problem, he discovered, was that
the crews on many of the ships had little prior convoy experience.[26]

Besides practicing convoy maneuvers, on the *Brown* it was also
necessary to set shipboard schedules for the passengers. Water for the
troops was turned off during certain periods of the day, and they were
fed only two meals, breakfast at 10:00 A.M. and supper at 3:00 P.M.
The menu for 6 July was typical: for breakfast, stewed fruit, oatmeal
and milk, scrambled eggs and bacon, rolls, butter, peach marmalade,
and coffee; for supper, frankfurters and sauerkraut, navy beans, rolls,
butter, coffee, tea, and stewed fruit—a combination that certainly
did nothing to settle the stomachs of the many who were seasick.[27]

The *Core* carried six F4F Wildcats like this one. *Naval Institute*

A TBF Avenger of the type on the *Core* releases its torpedo. TBFs could carry either a torpedo or bombs. *Naval Institute*

The passengers were restricted to the forward deck, the unlicensed Merchant and enlisted Navy crews to the aft deck, and officers were free to go where they wished. In practice, however, there was frequent contact between the passengers and crew. Wiper Wes Arrance, for example, didn't stay aft as ordered, but instead spent much of his free time on number 3 hatch among the passengers and often slept there in hot weather.[28]

On 29 June, Lieutenant Zinn instructed the Merchant crew, the MPs, and the Royal Navy sailors on using the 20-mm guns. Perhaps so that Lieutenant Zinn could follow up on his instructions and also give the Navy gun crews practice, the next morning Captain Carley requested and was granted permission from Captain McCabe to leave the convoy for gunnery practice. Each of the eight 20-mm guns fired ninety rounds into the bursts of six shells fired from the 3"/50. The 5"/51 also got a workout, firing five times just before the session ended. After about an hour, the *Brown* returned to her station in the convoy. Captain Carley thought the practice "very good." Shortly afterwards the men on watch on deck and anyone else who happened to be topside were treated to a good view of the *Queen Elizabeth* as she and her seven escorts passed about a mile astern of the convoy.[29] Steaming at about three times the speed of the convoy, they were soon out of sight.

Sometime during the night of 29–30 June several boxes of dried salt fish were discovered missing from number 4 hatch, "apparently thrown overboard." Captain Carley did not explain why he thought someone would steal boxes of fish and then throw them overboard, but two possibilities are that the thief planned to sell them on the black market in North Africa but on second thought decided to get rid of them to avoid being caught, or that he was a saboteur leaving a trail to lead U-boats to the convoy. As the presence of a cargo security officer indicates, however, pilfering was always a problem, and Captain Carley pointed out that a "strict watch is kept" to prevent it. The captain questioned a number of men about the theft but, not surprisingly, found "no one who knows anything about it."

During this same night the destroyer escort *Wyffels* was busy patrolling some six or seven miles off the starboard bow of the convoy. At 1:20 A.M. she started to leave her station to investigate a radar contact, but almost immediately turned back when the "radar contact [was] identified as cloud." As it turned out, most of the contacts on the convoy routes to the Mediterranean stemmed from something other than enemy U-boats. The Germans throughout the war assigned relatively few U-boats to these routes, preferring to concentrate their strength on the routes to northern Europe. However, there could be no relaxation of vigilance, for the Germans might at any moment change their tactics. Shortly after daybreak the *Wyffels* sighted an unidentified ship and again left her station to investigate. Again there was no action as the ship turned out to be a British LCI (landing craft, infantry) from Bermuda on her way to join the convoy. Late in the afternoon the *Wyffels* investigated an oil slick that the *Core*'s patrol planes had reported and found that it came from one of the ships in the convoy, number 52,[30] the *E. G. Seubert*, a tanker carrying fuel oil. Presumably the *Wyffels* informed the crew of the *Seubert*, who then tried to stop the leak, for no one except a saboteur would knowingly leave a trail of oil for U-boats to follow.

To instruct the *Brown*'s Merchant Marine crew, Navy Armed Guard, and passengers in their duties in an emergency, Captain Carley held a fire and boat drill at 1:00 P.M. on 1 July. Not satisfied with the drill, the next morning he held another one, which he found acceptable. It is typical of Captain Carley that he would not tolerate sloppy performance when the safety of the men and the ship in his care was at issue.

Late that night the men on the *Brown* felt three or four "slight jarring" motions, apparently caused by depth charges, followed by orders for a forty-five-degree emergency turn to port and a half hour later for a forty-five-degree turn to starboard. This evasive action was taken because of radar and sound contacts, presumably from a submarine that had been "reported as cruising off Bermuda."[31] Apparently Captain McCabe was again dissatisfied with the way the ships in the convoy executed the emergency turns, because the next day he ordered another practice session. Captain Carley no doubt approved of Captain McCabe's insistence on precise maneuvering, as both obviously were careful leaders who did everything possible to make certain that important safety procedures were executed correctly. Meanwhile, the *Core* operated her planes during the daylight hours and the escort vessels patrolled the waters around the convoy, leading Captain Carley to observe that "the efficient & very able destroyer Escort & Plane protection gives one the feeling of absolute security." Clearly the various parts of the convoy, even though spread out over more than five square miles, were working harmoniously together to ensure a safe crossing. The harmony stemmed from careful planning and scrupulous attention to details.

On 3 July, for example, Captain Carley noted that escort vessels were refueling two at a time from the Navy oiler *Enoree* assigned to UGS-11. Two Merchant Marine tankers, the *Seubert* and the *Gulf Disc,* were designated as standbys to give fuel from their cargoes to escort vessels if the *Enoree* ran out. On the *Brown* that morning Captain Carley spent the better part of an hour inspecting the Merchant Marine, Navy, and passenger quarters and found them all in "satisfactory condition."

That night, in reaction to apparent U-boat contacts, the escorts dropped depth charges whose explosions caused reverberations felt on the *Brown.* With U-boats suspected in the area, Captain McCabe ordered the ships in the convoy to begin zigzagging. Apparently the threat persisted, for the ships continued zigzagging throughout the night. Shortly after 1:00 A.M. on 4 July "an explosion was heard on the starboard flank followed by lights and rockets," indicating that the *John P. Mitchell,* the first ship in the starboard column, had been hit by a torpedo. The indications, however, were misleading. The *Mitchell* was one of four ships in the convoy equipped with Mark 29 gear to stream paravanes to which cables with microphones and explosives were attached. The idea was that the microphones would pick up the sounds of an approaching torpedo and automatically detonate the explosives to blow up the torpedo before it reached any of the ships.[32] While the *Mitchell* was streaming the Mark 29 in the darkness of early morning, the second assistant engineer on watch, following normal routine, blew the boiler tubes to clean them. The noise caused by blowing the tubes apparently activated the Mark 29 to cause the explosion.[33] After a busy night and the threat of U-boat attacks, the morning of the Fourth of July brought the more mundane request from the captain of the *Wyffels* that the *Brown* give her some meat. Accordingly, for about an hour provisions were transferred from the *Brown* to the *Wyffels* while both vessels continued at standard speed, about 8.5 knots. The *Brown,* it appears, like the *Seubert* and *Gulf Disc,* stood by to supply escort vessels from her cargo if necessary.

Captain Carley's entries in his "Secret Log" for 5 July begin with the information that the convoy was engaged in "evasive steering & courses" and that the *Thomas Pinckney* in position 51 "broke down" and "drifted astern." With evidence of U-boat activity in the area, it was a bad time for the *Pinckney* to leave the convoy, but as it turned out nothing happened to her. Late that afternoon, however, an incident occurred that caused considerable concern over the next several days. During his watch, Richard Schiff, the Merchant Marine radio officer on the *Brown*, "heard a series of dots, the letter E. This was not some radiation from a radio, but hand administered transmission signals" of a kind not normally permitted in convoys. Schiff immediately took a bearing with the radio direction finder and notified Captain Carley, who in turn had a Navy signalman report the position by blinker to Captain McCabe. Schiff's opinion at the time was that the signals were "homing signals from an enemy submarine tracking the convoy." Others must have had the same opinion, because shortly afterwards several escorts raced astern of the convoy and launched depth charges.[34] Captain McCabe ordered the masters of the ships in the convoy to take bearings and to search their vessels for unauthorized transmitters and for personal radios, which were forbidden aboard ship because they can radiate signals that the enemy could pick up.[35] Comdr. C. L. Winecoff in the *Hobby* attempted to locate the source of the transmissions by using the direction finders on five escorts and, like Captain McCabe, alerting all merchant ships with direction finders to take bearings. Nothing came of the use of the direction finders because the "situation [was] complicated by heavy rain and darkness" and by the strength of five transmissions from two merchant ships from neutral Sweden, no doubt doing everything they could to make their identities known to any U-boats in the area. Commander Winecoff concluded that although treachery was possible, "if so [it was] poorly timed and not followed up effectively." More likely someone was "stupidly careless."[36]

However, it was necessary to be sure that the transmission wasn't deliberate, because just a few weeks earlier during UGS-10's crossing "some of the ships failed to keep station, showed lights, had one bad collision, and broke radio silence with a transmission of such character as to indicate that an enemy agent was concealed on board one of the merchantmen."[37] Thus the incident in UGS-11 was thoroughly investigated and additional precautions were ordered. On the *Brown*, Radio Operator Richard Schiff "stood [an] all night D/F watch as per Commodore orders" on the night of 6–7 July. During the day on the 7th the *Brown* was searched for private radios, and the three found were confiscated and locked up. On the 9th, responding to Captain McCabe's order that all ships in the convoy be thoroughly searched again, Chief Mate Arnold Zambik and Lieutenant Zinn on the *Brown* led search parties to inspect the cargo spaces, quarters, iceboxes, storerooms, and so forth. The U.S. Army troops and Royal Navy sailors had "bag inspection." Nothing was found on the *Brown*, and there is no report that the origin of the transmission was discovered elsewhere. Although Commander Winecoff was probably correct that someone had been "stupidly careless," sabotage was a constant threat and even a remote hint of it had to be looked into.

On the same day the ships' officers were searching their ships, Hyman Katsoff, an ordinary seaman on the *Gulf of Venezuela*, died aboard the USS *McCook*, to which he had been transferred for medical treatment. He was buried at sea at 5:10 that evening; in tribute to their shipmate, "Convoy and Escort half-masted colors during ceremony."[38] Earlier in the day, two men of the *Brown*'s Armed Guard unit were brought before captain's mast for "leaving watch without being properly relieved" and "not showing up for general quarters," two especially serious offenses in view of the apparent danger the convoy was in. As punishment the men had to paint the amidships shower and clean the covers of the 5"/51 and 3"/50. This very light sentence for serious breaches of discipline contrasts sharply with the sentence of ten days in solitary confinement on bread and water with a full ration every third day imposed on a sailor on a Navy ship who had been absent without leave for about nine hours and had been insolent to an officer.[39] Apparently Lieutenant Zinn wished to make his point with as light a sentence as possible, but he did warn the men that if they didn't do the work properly or required supervision while doing it, he would impose an additional sentence of four days in solitary confinement on bread and water. The fact that nothing further is said suggests that Lieutenant Zinn knew what would work with his men. Problems with personnel arose again a few days later when Lieutenant Zinn had to handle a complaint that the Armed Guard was discourteous to officers, particularly an Army lieutenant "who has complained about everything on ship and who is very unpopular due to overbearing personality." In this case, however, Lieutenant Zinn clearly felt that the officer provoked whatever discourtesies may have occurred.

An ugly incident from about the same time emphasizes that bigotry never rests, even though the men involved were on the same side risking their lives fighting a vicious and dangerous enemy. The incident arose after the Merchant Marine officers had generously invited the Army officers to take their meals in the saloon. During dinner one day an Army officer sitting with Richard Schiff suddenly said to him in a loud voice, "I guess y'all one of those New York Jews. I don't sit and eat with Jews." All conversation in the saloon stopped immediately. As the officer rose, Schiff quickly reached over and grabbed him by the shirt. The two men scuffled a moment or two before other officers separated them. When Schiff took his place at the table again the Merchant Marine and Army officers sitting there got up and left him to eat alone. Angered and deeply hurt, he "felt I was now fighting not only the Nazis, but a virulent group of American bigots. . . . I have forgotten much of that voyage, but I will never forget that incident of Anti-Semitism."[40] Schiff endured other "unpleasant affairs" from time to time throughout the voyage, some during the return trip when the *Brown* carried German POWs to the United States. He noted the bitter irony in a letter to Marilyn Shapiro, whom he later married: "Imagine being on a ship with 500 Nazi prisoners and Jew haters in your own crew!!!"[41]

Perhaps because he was dissatisfied with the convoy's performance when it had to make emergency maneuvers at dawn the previous day, Captain McCabe once again ordered the convoy to practice emergency maneuvers on 13 July. That he was by no means overzealous in insisting on practice is emphasized by his observation in his "Brief Narrative" that a few days earlier the "Core's planes attacked a submarine 150 miles away from the convoy."[42] On the 12th Captain Carley had noted that he had not seen the *Core* during the day. He of course could not know that after dropping back to launch her planes, the *Core* did not rejoin the convoy because she had been ordered to leave it on the 12th to escort westbound GUS-9. At the time the convoys were some six to seven hundred miles south of the Azores.[43] Incidentally, on the day after the *Core* left UGS-11, her planes sank the German submarine U-487, a "milk cow" used to supply U-boats with fuel and provisions, and she had another kill on the 16th.[44] On the 13th Captain Carley noted seeing a seaplane at 5:00 A.M., and from time to time throughout the 14th, 15th, and 16th he again saw planes, indications that as the convoy approached the west coast of Africa the responsibility for air cover had passed from the *Core* to land-based planes.

On the 14th the *Brown* shifted from position 43 in section five to position 73 in section one because her destination had been changed from Bône to Algiers. Although the convoy was getting close to Africa, the fact that "planes [were] over & around [the] convoy throughout [the] day" meant that protection against enemy submarines was still essential. It is not surprising, therefore, that for an hour before noon on the 16th Captain McCabe once again—and for the last time—drilled the convoy in emergency turns.

During the afternoon of 17 July, twenty days after leaving Hampton Roads, the *Hobby* sighted the British corvette *Teviot* and four other corvettes that shortly afterwards officially relieved the U.S. Navy escorts.[45] At this time the convoy was just off the coast of Morocco and west-northwest of Casablanca. While the change in escorts was taking place, the convoy assumed a four-column formation to detach the ships in section four bound for Casablanca.[46] Going from twelve to four columns sounds simple enough on paper, as all it involves is that certain columns maintain speed and course as the rest reduce speed until they can fall in behind the "leaders." In practice, however, given the large area covered by the convoy and the need for radio silence, not to mention the vagaries of the weather, the maneuver was anything but simple.

After detaching the ships bound for Casablanca, the main convoy reversed the procedure in order to form a twelve-column front again and steamed ahead to join convoy KMS-20 on its way from Britain to the Mediterranean, at the time about three hours ahead of UGS-11. At 1:30 A.M. on 18 July the convoy again went from a twelve-column front to a four-column front, this time in preparation for passing through the swept channel of the Strait of Gibraltar. At 5:00 A.M. the convoy arrived off Europa Point at the east end of the strait, sighted KMS-20 ahead, and "closed up" to the rear. The now combined convoy formed a twelve-column front and then zigzagged throughout the day. When Captain McCabe aboard the *A. C. Bedford* went to Gibraltar, Capt. George L. Woodruff, USN, aboard the *M. M. Guhin* assumed command of the forty-six ships remaining in UGS-11,[47] which was now linked astern of the thirty-six ships in convoy KMS-20.[48] The convoy steamed through the Mediterranean at 7.5 knots, protected by the five British corvettes that had joined UGS-11 off Casablanca, by the four escorts accompanying KMS-20, and by fighters, bombers, and observation planes.[49] This degree of protection was even more necessary in the Mediterranean than in the Atlantic at this time because the convoys off the coasts of Algeria and Tunisia were harassed not only by U-boats operating out of Toulon but also by *Luftwaffe* planes based in southern France.

On 19 July about thirty-four ships left the convoy to go to Oran.

The *Brown* was moored in Algiers when this photograph of the port
was taken on 23 July 1943. *National Archives*

The following morning the Algiers section of the convoy, which now
included the *Brown*, left the convoy and headed into Algiers, arriving
at noon. However, another five hours passed before the *Brown* was
"all fast to dock." She had steamed for a total of twenty-two days and
twenty-two hours to cover 4,664 miles at an average speed of 8.48
knots. Four hours after the *Brown* tied up, the Royal Navy passengers debarked.

The port was in excellent condition, not having been damaged by
bombs or blocked by sunken ships. It could accommodate more than
thirty ships at piers and an additional twenty at an "ample anchorage." However, although both military personnel and local labor
were used, there were too few stevedores available at this time to
take full advantage of the port's potential.[50] Thus the *Brown* was
berthed outboard of another ship for four days before shifting to an
inside berth to begin discharging cargo. Although she discharged
cargo from 8:00 A.M. to 6:00 P.M. every day, it took eleven days—until 4 August—before she was completely empty.

While the *Brown* was tied up, the crew were free to go ashore. Algiers was a bustling, interesting city, but it also had a seedy side that attracted some of the men. After an evening of carousing on 26 July, one of the *Brown*'s crew succeeded in weaving his way back to the ship until he came to the flight of steps from the main road to the waterfront. He apparently tripped or passed out, for some British seamen later found him lying injured and unconscious at the foot of the steps. Concerned about his condition and safety, they moved him inside the dock gate and reported what they had done to Third Mate Armstrong on watch on the *Brown*. Armstrong got several soldiers on board to go with him with a stretcher to carry the man back to the ship. Captain Rider, the Army physician, examined him and took three stitches in his cut lip.[51] The injury, however, turned out to be more serious than Captain Rider first thought, and the man had to be hospitalized ashore. Because he still had not recovered sufficiently to rejoin the ship when the *Brown* left Algiers more than a week later, he was paid off through the American Consulate.[52]

By 28 July all but three officers and thirty-five enlisted men of the Army passengers had debarked.[53] The MPs left behind constituted the guard for the 500 POWs who embarked on 4 August. Because 500 prisoners were crammed into accommodations designed for about 350, a rotation scheme was worked out whereby about 150 men slept on blankets on the decks of the 'tween decks each night while the other men slept in bunks. The men sleeping on the deck changed each night, so that for every night on the deck they slept three nights in bunks.[54] The POWs, from Rommel's Afrika Korps, ranged in age from fifteen to fifty. According to Wes Arrance, "the only thing that they were afraid of was that they would not live long. They were so Brain-Washed that they believed that we would not make it across the Atlantic. They 'knew' that the German subs had complete control of the Atlantic. So much for German Propaganda."[55] Richard Schiff's recollections are similar except that he heard that the Germans were certain that they would be rescued by U-boats. He also remembers being issued a pistol to defend the radio room in case the prisoners tried to take over the ship, a precaution that fortunately turned out to be unnecessary.[56]

As if contending with the enemy and the usual hazards of the sea were not enough, the crew of the British merchant ship *Fort La Montee*, also at Algiers, had to fight a fierce fire that broke out in her number 1 hold on 4 August. Captain Carley on the *Brown* could see "flames belching up through dense smoke" as the stricken ship was towed out of the harbor. A destroyer had pulled alongside to help fight the fire, which had started in an area of number 1 lower hold where smoke bombs were stowed. Suddenly, explosives in number 2 hold ignited and blew up with such force that the "fore part of the S/S Fort La Montee went straight up in the air" and the back of the destroyer was broken. The forward part of the *Fort La Montee* sank, and the stern section was later sunk by gunfire.[57] Captain Carley does not speculate on how the fire started, but sabotage must have been uppermost in his thoughts. He tried to find out how many men were killed, but when he questioned survivors of the destroyer, "all they would say was, It was ghastly."

Captain Carley did not say how he was able to talk to the survivors, but presumably he was ashore sometime during the afternoon of the 4th to attend a convoy conference and make last-minute preparations for sailing. The next morning, the *Brown* turned on the degaussing system before leaving the pier and by midafternoon cleared the outer harbor. Bound for Oran, she joined convoy GUS-11, which was developing as it sailed westward in the Mediterranean. The convoy had started in Alexandria, Egypt, on 28 July, and before the *Brown* joined on 5 August it had picked up ships while passing Tripoli on the 1st, Bizerte on the 3rd, and Bône on the 4th.[58] Between 7:00 and 8:20 P.M. on the 6th the convoy was on alert while the escort vessel on the starboard side of the convoy and some ships astern of the *Brown* fired on two planes. Lieutenant Zinn noted that "they may or may not have been Axis planes," implicitly acknowledging the practice of firing at planes not immediately recognized as friendly if their maneuvers seemed potentially threatening. Less than a half hour after the alert ended, the *Brown* anchored with the rest of the convoy in Oran harbor. Early the next morning, she weighed anchor and left Oran in convoy GUS-11. Sailing in ballast, her draft was 8'9" forward and 21'1" aft.[59] Capt. H. V. McCabe again served as convoy commodore, this time aboard the *M. M. Guhin.* While in the Mediterranean there were fifty-six ships in the convoy, with British escorts providing protection.[60] On 8 August, Captain Carley gave his noon position as "East End of Straits of Gibraltar," and Captain McCabe in his "Brief Narrative" noted that eighteen ships were detached for Gibraltar and that fifteen ships from Gibraltar were attached. The U.S. Coast Guard cutter *Bibb,* which had joined the convoy from Gibraltar, "passed orders to Commodore via line throwing gun" as the convoy moved through the strait at four knots.[61]

The passage through the strait, made difficult enough by the number of ships steaming together in convoy and by the need to be constantly looking for the enemy, was made even more difficult by a large number of Spanish fishing boats working the area, some of which, despite the efforts of the escorts to keep them away, sailed "in and out of the Convoy's columns." These boats may in fact have been seeking information about the convoy rather than fish, for it was known that many fishing boats from neutral Portugal and Spain carried agents who reported to the Germans. The convoy succeeded in getting by this group, but when it happened upon a large fleet of similar boats that night, the added complication of darkness required even greater vigilance to avoid running them down.[62]

On 9 August, when the convoy was off the coast of Morocco not far from Casablanca, the British escort was officially relieved by the American escort under the command of Comdr. R. L. Raney, USCG, aboard the *Bibb*, accompanied by the Coast Guard cutter *Ingham* and seven U.S. Navy vessels.[63] Additional merchant ships from Casablanca also joined GUS-11, bringing the convoy up to its full strength of fifty-seven ships. Because two of the ships had torpedo holes below the waterline, the convoy could not go faster than 8.6 knots. To compensate for the slow speed, Captain McCabe agreed with Commander Raney's suggestion that diversion courses be executed "only upon existence of a definite emergency such as being trailed by submarines." As he did with UGS-11, however, Captain McCabe emphasized practice in emergency maneuvers, conducting drills early in the voyage during all three watches to give each mate a chance to execute. Consequently he was able to report that maneuvering was "better than average . . . during the numerous contacts reported by . . . [Commander Raney] during the voyage."[64]

Among other activities on the *Brown* on 10 August, there was a fire and boat drill during which the line-throwing Lyle gun was fired and the Army MPs had a target practice session. As some of the ship's officers had been issued sidearms,[65] the men on the *Brown* were prepared for enemy aggression from without or from the POWs on board. Although low-lying clouds and darkness hindered visibility, late that night Lieutenant Zinn discerned three planes flying about in the vicinity of the convoy. Unable to identify them, he assumed they were hostile. Fortunately, the clouds prevented action because the planes were Navy PBYs (twin-engine flying boats called Catalinas) providing air coverage during the hours of darkness.[66]

Earlier that evening the USS *Bogue,* an escort carrier like the *Core,* had joined GUS-11, moving into position 64. The *Bogue* and her three escorts had accompanied eastbound convoy UGS-13 to a point about five hundred miles west of the Strait of Gibraltar, close enough for land-based planes to take over the responsibility for air cover. The carrier's escorts took up stations nine thousand yards from the convoy, one on each quarter and one directly astern.[67] The *Bogue* continued with GUS-11 for a week, sometimes at her station within the convoy, sometimes close by, sometimes a considerable distance away. She left the convoy on 17 August.

On 13 August the *Brown* dropped astern of the convoy to practice firing, demonstrating, in Captain Carley's opinion, "excellent shooting." Just as the gun crew finished practice, four destroyers sped past in the opposite direction to hunt down a submarine further to the rear of the convoy. The *Brown* immediately increased speed to full ahead to get out of the way and to regain the relative security of her place in the convoy. One of the *Bogue*'s planes had discovered the submarine about four miles astern of the convoy and had attacked, but even with the help of the escorts had not been able to destroy it.[68] Apparently the U-boat was not deterred by the attack, because less than two hours later escorts dropped a series of depth charges some distance off the *Brown*'s port beam, and late that night, after being alerted by the escorts that submarines were in the area, the convoy executed emergency turns. There was, however, no engagement. Three days later at about 6:00 P.M., a favorite time for submarine attacks, suspected U-boats in the vicinity necessitated a ninety-degree emergency turn to starboard while the escorts dropped depth charges. Captain McCabe in his "Brief Narrative" summarized the situation in noting that up to the fiftieth meridian submarine contacts "were had almost daily. . . . The presence of the aircraft carrier Bogue and her planes . . . undoubtedly had its effect on the convoy's freedom from submarine attack." Actually there were several reasons besides the *Bogue,* most significantly the German decision to concentrate U-boats on the northern routes to Europe, leaving too few on the UGS/GUS routes to be much more than an annoyance. Consequently, of the almost three thousand ships that sailed in fifty-five UGS/GUS convoys in 1943, only four were sunk in convoys in the Atlantic. That five stragglers sailing independently were sunk during the same period attests to the effectiveness of the convoy system.[69]

On the 17th Captain Carley reported sighting "a vessel to the

southward all lighted up like a Christmas tree." Probably registered
in a neutral country, the ship was ostentatiously proclaiming her
neutrality to any U-boats in the area so that she wouldn't be torpedoed by mistake. The crew on the *Brown* were having a different
kind of problem on the 17th. Lieutenant Zinn in his "Log" goes directly to the point: "Crew has shits." Captain Carley on 18 August
recorded in the "Official Log-Book" that the chief mate had informed him that some of the crew were complaining of cramps and
diarrhea. Noting that the food and iceboxes were "both in first class
condition" and "inspected regularly," the captain nonetheless told
the chief steward and chief cook to "use every precaution" to make
certain that tainted food did not cause the problems. He then noted
that while the *Brown* was in Algiers, her "domestic tanks were filled
with local water. Leaving there, some was dumped & ships evaporator made our drinking water. If there is any cause I would place
the cause on the water."[70] Since evaporator water is distilled seawater, it could not cause the sickness. Apparently, Captain Carley
means that some Algerian water was still being used for drinking. At
all events, the problems with diarrhea disappeared after a day or two
and were not mentioned again.

More significantly, 17 August 1943 was also the day that the last
German forces withdrew from Sicily across the Strait of Messina,
bringing Operation Husky to a close and opening the way for an invasion of mainland Italy. Husky had begun on 10 July with landings
on the southern and southeastern coasts of Sicily by General Pat-
ton's U.S. Seventh Army and Field Marshal Montgomery's British
Eighth Army. Although the Allied forces outnumbered the Italian
and German defenders, the Allies needed thirty-eight days of fighting
over difficult terrain to drive them out.

On the 18th and the morning of the 19th the possibility of U-boats
nearby led the escorts to drop depth charges while the ships in the
convoy executed emergency turns. During the afternoon of 19 August the convoy crossed the fiftieth meridian, from which point, according to Captain McCabe, except for a contact made on the last
day, "the area appeared to be singularly free of enemy submarines."
On the 21st Captain McCabe informed Captain Carley that the
Brown's destination was Hampton Roads. On the 23rd, three days
before making port, the convoy encountered a strong easterly current
and heavy groundswells that cut its speed in half.[71] As a result the
convoy steamed only 115 miles on the 24th after averaging 212 on

the previous three days. Conditions improved the next day, enabling the convoy to make 191 miles.

On 24 August the New York section of the convoy left the main convoy and headed north. Shortly before noon on the 25th, the last full day at sea, the commodore signaled that a submarine was close by and ordered an emergency turn. The Armed Guard units manned their guns and the escorts dropped depth charges, apparently with no success. This last alert of the voyage occurred just off the coast of Virginia. Late in the afternoon of the 25th, while there was still daylight, the convoy re-formed from a broad ocean front to a single column in preparation for entering the swept channel into Chesapeake Bay sometime after midnight. As night fell the convoy ran into fog, which got worse as the night wore on. Nonetheless, just before the convoy reached the swept channel, five merchant ships and two escorts peeled off and headed north for Philadelphia.[72] The fog on the morning of the 26th was still heavy enough to hold up the convoy somewhat, but by noon the ships had passed Cape Henry and were in the two-and-a-half-mile-wide channel at the entrance to the bay. Except for four ships continuing on to Baltimore, the convoy anchored in Hampton Roads, the *Brown* at 3:00 P.M. A few hours later the *Brown* shifted to an anchorage off Newport News, at which time twelve prisoners who had been crew members of U-boats were debarked for questioning by Navy Intelligence. Early the next afternoon the remaining 488 POWs were discharged to the tender *Mohawk* to become part of the record 10,172 POWs who went through the deinfestation plant in thirty-two and a half hours "without a loss" on 27–28 August, and part of the 18,310 POWs debarked at Hampton Roads that month.[73] Thus ended a homeward voyage during which the *John W. Brown* had steamed 3,833 miles in nineteen days and ten hours at an average speed of 8.2 knots.

Captain Carley remained aboard for Voyage 3, which officially began on 31 August 1943.[74] On 4 September the *Brown* shifted from the anchorage to Chesapeake and Ohio Railroad Pier 8 in Newport News, where beginning on the 6th the Coast Guard supervised the loading of a little over three hundred tons of explosives, inflammables, and "hazardous articles." Finished on the 9th, she shifted to C & O Pier 2 to complete loading. While the *Brown* was at Pier 2 an American Bureau of Shipping surveyor made the annual hull and boiler surveys. He found some deposits in the lower rows of the circulating tubes of the boilers, but after they were cleaned he declared the ship "in seaworthy condition and fit to retain present status with this Bureau."[75] Fully loaded on 11 September, she shifted from Pier 2 to an anchorage to await sailing in convoy UGS-18.[76] The 7,854.5 measurement tons of cargo loaded at Newport News was so varied that it required a manifest sixty-one pages long to list the more than twenty-five hundred items, ranging from TNT, Sherman tanks, and a locomotive to Purple Heart medals, cigarettes, and skirts for female officers.[77]

The *Brown* also carried 36 officers and 303 enlisted men as passengers.[78] When the *Brown* left Lynnhaven anchorage at 3:00 a.m. on 15 September, again bound for the Mediterranean, Sicily had been in control of the Allies for about a month. At the beginning of September, British and Canadian infantry had successfully invaded Italy at Calabria, the toe of the Italian peninsula directly across the Strait of Messina from Sicily, and on 9 September the Fifth Army under Lt. Gen. Mark Clark landed at Salerno. On the 8th Field Marshal Pietro Badoglio's Italian government, which in July succeeded the Fascist government of Benito Mussolini, had surrendered to the Allies. However, the German Army in Italy, commanded by Field Marshal Albert Kesselring, dug in to repel the invasion, but after a week of hard fighting the Allies succeeded in forcing the Germans to retreat to the north to establish a defensive line. The success at Salerno led to the fall of Naples on 1 October 1943.[79]

At dawn on 15 September the *John W. Brown* left the Chesapeake Bay and entered the swept channel. By 6:00 p.m. she had steamed through the channel and taken up her assigned position in convoy UGS-18, which consisted of sixty-seven ships and ten escorts. The convoy was assembled in a broad front of thirteen columns, with a thousand yards between columns and five hundred yards between ships in column. The *Brown,* in position 113, was the third ship in column eleven.[80] The convoy commodore was Capt. G. L. Woodruff, USN (Ret.), in the *Thomas Pinckney,* and the commander of the escort group was again Comdr. R. L. Raney, USCG, in the Coast Guard cutter *Bibb.* The cutter *Ingham* and eight Navy vessels, including the oiler *Housatonic,* made up the rest of the escort. The sea escort was supplemented by land-based air escorts from the time of sailing on the 15th until nightfall on the 20th, and from the afternoon of the 28th until arrival.[81]

On the night of the 16th, their second night at sea, the men on the *Brown* could hear the sounds of firing and could feel the reverberations of depth charges as the escorts responded to suspected U-boat contacts. On the 17th the convoy made 45-degree emergency turns, but apparently there were no further suspicious contacts during the next two weeks as the convoy made its way across the Atlantic. Although the enemy was not causing problems, the weather was: on the 20th heavy rains and an overcast sky made it necessary for the safety of the ships that they suspend blackout conditions for a time by showing dimmed sidelights and their blue stern light. The danger of collision in this kind of weather outweighed the danger from the enemy, because it took only two or three minutes for a ship to cross the distance between columns. Two days later the convoy again encountered heavy rain squalls, and again the *Brown* had to show light to lessen the possibility of collision, this time the blue stern light for two minutes every half hour.

After that the routine of a ship at sea was interrupted only by periodic fire and boat drills and by inspections of the passenger and crew quarters, such as the "Master's Inspection" on 25 September: "inspected crew, Navy, & troop quarters, toilets, showers, storerooms, ice boxes, messrooms, passageways, steering engine room, etc." Captain Carley conducted these inspections at various intervals while at sea and held them every day when the *Brown* was in the Mediterranean.[82]

On 28 September, Captain Carley observed that a bomber from a shore base was escorting the convoy, and from then on there was continuous air coverage during the day. That the enemy at this time was active off Gibraltar was made clear on 1 October when, for the first time since 17 September, the escorts made contact with U-boats. They dropped depth charges, and since there were no attacks on the ships in the convoy, apparently the U-boats were driven off. Shortly after noon the next day, the convoy reduced its broad front to a four-column front to get ready to pass through the Strait of Gibraltar; at about 4:00 P.M. the convoy passed Spartel Point at the west end of the strait, and at 8:00 P.M. it was off Europa Point at the east end.

It was at this time that the convoy ran into a potentially dangerous situation arising from someone's oversight in taking care of the countless details involved in organizing and operating convoys. As Captain Woodruff explained in his "Brief Narrative," Commander Raney, the escort commander, was not given the key to decode the cipher containing information about the convoy's route, the Mediterranean escort, times of arrival, and the like. With no instructions beyond Europa Point, Commander Raney decided to continue eastward through the night at six knots. The sixteen merchant ships that were scheduled to join UGS-18 at Gibraltar for the trip through the Mediterranean had gathered ahead of the convoy and stayed ahead all night until daylight made visual signaling possible. At daybreak the authorities at Gibraltar ordered UGS-18 to meet its British escort at 12:30 P.M. at a point about forty miles west—that is, to the rear—of the convoy's 8:00 A.M. position. Following this order necessitated risky maneuvering, as the eighty-three ships that now comprised the convoy—strung out in four columns, with twenty ships in one column and twenty-one in each of the other three—had to turn completely around. The escorts directed the maneuver, and when all the ships were in position the convoy steamed westward at nine knots, its maximum speed. When the convoy sighted the British escort, the ships again had to reverse direction. The British then took over from the Americans and the convoy's speed was adjusted so that it would arrive at Oran at 8:00 A.M. the following morning. Only too aware of the possibilities of disastrous collisions that the situation created, Captain Woodruff concluded his account by stating that "Comdr. Raney, USCG and all American escort are warmly commended for efficient handling of a dangerous situation, thrust upon them by bungling of communications."[83] Captain Carley's only comment in the "Secret Log," "Convoy Maneuvering," reveals that he had no idea about what was really going on. There must have been a good reason to force the convoy to go through dangerous and difficult maneuvering to meet the escorts rather than to have the escorts speed up to overtake the convoy, but it's difficult to imagine what the reason might have been.

The maneuvering necessary to twice reverse the direction of the convoy, however, did not create the only danger: at midnight on 3 October the escorts dropped a "heavy series of depth charges," a reminder that U-boats were more active in the Mediterranean than along the UGS/GUS routes in the Atlantic. As planned, the convoy arrived at Oran at 8:00 A.M. on the 4th, and two hours later the *Brown* anchored in the harbor. She had steamed 3,842 miles over a period of eighteen days and twenty-two hours at an average speed of 8.46 knots.

The *Brown* remained at anchor for two days before tying up on 6 October outside the *Zebulon Pike* at one of Oran's twenty berths. The troops debarked, and Army stevedores came aboard to discharge

This view of the harbor at Oran was taken shortly before
the *Brown*'s first visit there. *National Archives*

the deck cargo. For the next eight days, cargo was discharged twenty-
four hours a day, except for an interruption caused when tear gas in
the *Pike*'s cargo was accidentally set off. Until the gas dissipated, the
stevedores unloading the *Brown* had to wear gas masks.[84] When
stevedores finished unloading the ship on 15 October, her draft forward was 9'11" and aft 19'8". Using the "Secret Log" as a "note
book in which to record all events or observations of Naval interest,"
Captain Carley added statistics that in his opinion described the
"average condition of a Liberty vessel on final discharge":

The Weight in Vessel.
1,275 Tons Sand Ballast. #3, 4 & 5 Hatches. (L.H.)
    300   "   Permanent " #2, 3 Hatches. L.H.
1,160   "   Fuel—All D.B. Full. (Not pressed up)
    340   "   F.W: Fore Peaks, Void Tank, & #4 Full. A.P. 13'
    175   "   Stores & Spares
3,250 Tons D.W.

On 19 October, as the *Brown* lay idle, Captain Carley was aston-
ished to see three ships "flying the [German] Swastika Flag" steam

into the harbor without challenge. They turned out to be the *Djenna, Sinaia,* and the hospital ship *Aquileia* arriving at Oran from Marseilles to exchange prisoners. The following morning another German hospital ship entered the harbor and anchored offshore. By late morning the three ships that had arrived the previous day were "loaded down with German Soldiers" and had left the inner harbor to anchorages offshore. Sometime during the night all four ships left. Captain Carley was witnessing one stage of an exchange of POWs who were so severely wounded or seriously ill that they would never again be fit for combat. The Swedish Red Cross under Vice Chairman Count Folke Bernadotte administered the exchange of the American, British, and German prisoners in Goeteborg, Sweden; Barcelona, Spain; and Oran. At Oran, 3,876 Germans were transferred to the ships that Captain Carley saw.[85]

Meanwhile, sometime between 15 and 21 October the *Brown* had shifted to another berth, where the 21st was spent preparing for taking on cargo and passengers. At 7:00 the next morning loading began on all hatches and continued without interruption until the last of the deck cargo was in place two days later. Among the 274 pieces of equipment were half-tracks, motorcycles, and 61 tanks, all assigned to the 15 officers and 346 enlisted men of the First Armored Division who embarked at the same time.

On 23 October, Paul Baran, a twenty-one-year-old seaman first class in the Armed Guard unit, began a daily journal that, with only a few lapses, continued for most of the rest of the voyage. The entries were cast in the form of letters to his fiancée, but contained details that would have been censored if included in the actual letters he wrote to her. About half of the hundred-page journal is personal, while the other half gives some details but is mainly important in revealing his attitudes and moods. Even though Baran's comments are uniquely his, they also to some extent typify the feeling of his shipmates. His remarks during this period in Oran, for example, emphasize the deadening boredom that the men often experienced while they waited for something to happen. In his first entry on 23 October he complains that there is "no place to go [in Oran] & the place ain't fit for a dog. So I just stay on the ship & play ball on the dock & ride around with my friend I met from McKees [McKeesport, Pennsylvania] on an invasion barge." On the 26th he notes that "we're sitting out in the stream now waiting to go." On the 29th "we painted our guns & gun bucket & gun cover. And fixed up 2 life rafts back aft for ourselves. Just something to occupy our minds. Because all we're doing is sitting around waiting to go somewhere." Part of the next day was spent listening to records—among others, "Paper Doll," "Everything Happens to Me," "When You're a Long Way from Home," and "Smoothie Little Cutie." His comment a few days later emphasizes how the monotony eats away at men's morale: "Boy! I'm really disgusted with this war. All this laying around & not doing nothing. I wish it would hurry up & get it over with." But the next day there was a change in tone as the men prepared the ship to leave Oran. They also spent some of the time making a life jacket for their dog.[86]

In the evening of 25 October the *Brown* left her berth and anchored off the breakwater. While at anchor the next day the crew and passengers were "exercised" at fire and boat drill, and as further evidence that the ship was going into dangerous areas, some of the Merchant crew and soldiers were assigned to help the Armed Guard crew. Captain Carley did not say whether he was dissatisfied with the fire and boat drill, but for whatever reasons he held another one the next morning and a third five days later. This third drill also included instruction in using the 20-mm guns and in spotting planes and U-boats. If nothing more, the mere fact of the drills emphasized to the men that the days ahead would require that they be alert and prepared for all kinds of emergencies. Typically, Captain Carley was conscientious in preparing them.

For reasons apparently not known to Captain Carley, the anchorage off Oran was cleared of all ships during the afternoon of 27 October, the *Brown* going to an anchorage at the nearby port of Mers el-Kébir until the 31st, when she returned to Oran in time for Captain Carley to attend a masters' conference in the afternoon. The next afternoon the *Brown* and eight other ships left Oran and two hours later joined the eastbound convoy UGS-21, which at the time consisted of about sixty ships, seven British escorts, and six planes providing air coverage. The convoy stayed close to the coast, an average of about eight miles offshore on 2 November, and on the 3rd, while still close, it zigzagged between 9:00 and 11:00 A.M. and between noon and 4:00 P.M. Ships left and joined as it passed Algiers, Bougie, and Bizerte. On the 4th, after passing Bizerte, the convoy reduced its ten-column front to four columns to pass through the Tunisian War Channel. By the morning of 5 November it had passed south of Pantelleria Island, re-formed into a ten-column front, and headed east in the general direction of Malta.

Late that afternoon, as the convoy was gaining twelve ships from Malta, the convoy commodore ordered the *Brown* and the five other ships in the same column to reduce speed to five knots while the rest of the convoy pulled ahead at seven knots. Because there were no further instructions, Captain Carley, after waiting an hour, signaled the convoy commodore to find out what he should do. The not very reassuring reply was that the escort commander should have contacted them, but since he hadn't the column should "hang on to rear of convoy until daylight." They then received orders by light to "haul up" for Sicily at 2:00 A.M. the next morning, 6 November. Captain Carley again understated the situation when he observed that the convoy was "rather confused at this stage." As at Gibraltar, bungled communications caused the problem. In this instance the commodore's instructions separating the Naples section from the main convoy somehow failed to reach the ships involved.

At 2:00 A.M., as ordered, the five ships in the Naples section turned toward Augusta, Sicily, and the main convoy continued on toward Port Said. However, no doubt the result of more sloppy communications or planning, there were no escorts, although sometime before dawn the gunners on watch reported sighting one or two escort vessels that had belatedly joined the convoy. Fortunately there was no contact with the enemy. At 6:00 A.M. the lookouts on the *Brown* sighted a twenty-two-ship convoy five miles to starboard. Communicating by blinker, they learned that three of their five ships should have remained in convoy UGS-21 instead of breaking off for Augusta. Although Lieutenant Zinn correctly observed that the incident revealed "poor management" by the convoy commodore, the escorts, or the Admiralty, it was also another example of the kind of mix-up that can easily happen when a large number of ships are involved in a variety of missions.

At noon on 6 November the *Brown* arrived at Augusta, the first of twelve stops she would make there during the ensuing year. Ships bound for Naples had to stop at Augusta to await convoys and to receive orders. On this occasion orders were fast in coming, as just two hours later the *Brown* was steaming full speed ahead toward Naples in convoy VN-8,[87] consisting of twenty-four ships escorted by three British destroyers. Although Lieutenant Zinn acknowledged that the escort was "good quality," he thought it "definitely small!!!" for a convoy of that size. After clearing the three- to four-mile-wide Strait of Messina in two columns, the convoy formed into four columns for the rest of the trip. The next afternoon, 7 November, the convoy arrived at Naples in heavy squalls, and the *Brown* anchored off the breakwater. Since leaving Oran she had steamed for five days and twenty-three hours, covering 1,092 miles at an average speed of 7.63 knots.

Shortly after midnight on 8 November, while the *Brown* lay at anchor in the early-morning darkness, she experienced the first of three collisions on Voyage 3 when heavy winds and rain squalls caused the Liberty ship *Amos Kendall* to drag anchor and bang into her. Although the damage to the *Brown* was "not too bad"—in the "Official Log-Book," however, he called it "serious"[88]—Captain Carley requested a report and survey from the War Shipping Administration (WSA), wrote a report to the WSA, and sent a letter to the *Kendall*'s master "holding him responsible for damage." His initial reaction that the damage was light was no doubt correct, as nothing further was said about the incident.

During the afternoon of the 8th the *Brown* berthed at one of the three pontoon "piers" assembled at Naples, and an hour later Army stevedores began discharging the cargo. Since the tanks, half-tracks, and motorcycles had to be maneuvered off the pontoons under their own power, the drivers had to be especially careful to stay exactly in the middle of the pontoons lest they slide off.

Expedients such as using pontoons for discharging cargo were necessary because at this time, about five weeks after falling to the Allies on 1 October 1943, Naples was still in the very early stages of recovering from the massive damage inflicted first by Allied bombing and then by the Germans just before they left. Personnel from the U.S. Army Transportation Corps had arrived to assess the damage on 2 October and found a "picture of destruction . . . of such magnitude as to belie graphic description. Not a person or vehicle was moving and not a piece of equipment was in operation. . . . every building in the port area had been blasted. In one area . . . where earlier a German ammunition ship had received a direct hit from an Allied dive bomber, four city blocks had been totally obliterated. All the thoroughfares and rail lines and passages in the port area were blocked with rubble. Fires were still burning in several sections and a huge coal dump was ablaze. No utilities in the city were functioning because of the thorough destruction which the retreating Nazis had carried out. . . . [T]here was not a single craft afloat in the harbor and nearly every pier, breakwater and wharf was hopelessly jammed with partially and totally submerged remains of blasted ships. The

This picture of the destruction in Naples was taken about three weeks
before the *Brown's* first visit there. The men are part of a
British salvage crew. *National Archives*

piers and transit sheds, warehouses, grain elevators, passenger
ramps, glider cranes and other land-based equipment had been sys-
tematically destroyed."[89] Although American and British Army and
Navy restoration teams were working hard to repair the damage—
and "doing a splendid job" in Captain Carley's opinion—Naples was
still in critical shape when the *Brown* arrived a month later. At the
time the Allies took Naples only three of an estimated total of seventy-two berths could be used, but by 1 November, a month later
and a week before the *Brown* arrived, the restoration teams had succeeded in making twelve regular and three pontoon berths available
for Liberty ships.[90] Captain Carley noted that about forty ships plus
floating derricks and other heavy equipment had been sunk in the
harbor and that the waterfront was "in shambles."

Except during air raid alerts, unloading continued without interruption until completed on the 11th. During this time, in addition to
two air raid alerts, on 10 November there was one actual bombing attack, which started at 3:40 A.M. and lasted forty-five minutes. Be-

cause the *Brown* was covered by a smoke screen, the men on the ship could not see the planes. Despite dropping four bombs before the alert was sounded, and many more afterwards, the enemy caused "very little damage to the port area." The attack was met by heavy gunfire from shore batteries—"the air was filled with lead," according to Captain Carley—but, following orders from the port authorities, the Armed Guard on the *Brown* did not fire her guns. The next day a barrage balloon was added to the *Brown*'s defenses to deter enemy dive-bombers from coming in low over the ship.

The Germans stepped up air attacks on Naples during November 1943. Compared with only four alerts in October, there were twenty-eight alerts in November, very few of them false alarms. Although work at the port stopped during alerts, damage was usually light. In some instances, however, "a few buildings were wrecked, piers were damaged, ships set afire (including one British ammunition ship), and a few persons killed or injured." According to one report, 156 enemy planes attacked Naples and 15 were shot down during the eight-month period between October 1943 and May 1944.[91]

On 12 November the *Brown* left Naples empty in convoy NV-8.[92] In position 21, the first ship in the second column, the *Brown* served as vice commodore of the twenty-ship convoy. Covering 231 miles at an average speed of 8.4 knots, the convoy arrived at Augusta the following afternoon and for the next three days lay at anchor awaiting orders. During the layover some enterprising crew members found a way to swap cigarettes for Italian wine at the rate of two packs a quart. Since the crew could get as many cigarettes as they wanted, they were able to bring a large quantity of wine aboard the ship. The result in defiance of all sorts of regulations was "our first big party aboard ship. Every one . . . was plastered."[93] Although a gross exaggeration, there was obviously some drunkenness, and inevitably some trouble. One of the Armed Guard crew disrupted a union meeting of some still sober members of the Merchant crew, and another on watch in the stern tried to fire one of the guns. When Lieutenant Zinn learned what had happened, he punished the men with two days' confinement when the ship reached Oran, a strange decision since the man on watch had committed a far more serious breach of discipline. Apparently the punishment was for being drunk rather than for what was done while drunk.

On 17 November the *Brown*, with its hungover crew, and twenty-nine other ships left Augusta to join the Mediterranean section of convoy MKS-31 westbound from Port Said to Gibraltar.[94] With the addition of seven ships that joined off Cape Passero at the southeast tip of Sicily that afternoon, the number of ships in the convoy increased to thirty-seven. The convoy proceeded westward, passing nine miles north of Pantelleria Island the next day. Even though it was mid-November, the weather was so hot that day that Paul Baran stood watch in his swim trunks. Ships joined and left the convoy as it passed Bizerte on the 18th and Bône on the 19th. Anticipating on the 19th an air attack that did not in fact materialize, the *Brown* released smoke floats and made funnel smoke for half an hour at dusk.

The next day, while the convoy was fighting through a westerly gale, the *Brown*'s steering engine broke down, forcing her to stop to make repairs. Without headway and without cargo to give stability, the *Brown* rolled wildly in the surging seas. When at one point she rolled fifty degrees in a trough, hot coals spilled out of the galley stove and started a fire; several 50-pound 5" shells that somehow got loose started rolling from side to side on the after gun deck; and one of the after 20-mm guns broke loose. By late afternoon, however, after the crew had successfully struggled to restore order and to repair the steering engine, the *Brown* was again steaming at full speed. As if foul weather and a breakdown didn't cause problems enough, the men on the *Brown* also had good reason to suspect that enemy submarines were in the area because earlier in the day they had twice seen heavy sludge in the water, usually a sign that a ship had recently been sunk nearby. The enemy, however, did not appear. If they had, they would have found heavy Allied traffic along the coast of North Africa. On the 21st Captain Carley saw six ships leave the convoy for Algiers, then counted twelve troopships coming out from Algiers and heading west, and a bit later observed a fifty-four-ship convoy sailing east. Late in the day, anticipating once again an air raid that did not occur, the ships in the convoy released smoke floats and funnel smoke. The next morning, 22 November, the *Brown* and four other ships left the convoy for Oran, on the way in passing twelve heavily loaded American landing craft and three British freighters heading west.

Particularly when in port, one of the biggest gripes of men on ships like the *Brown* was the lack of mail. A system had been worked out between the Post Office and the Navy Department so that mail from the United States would first be sorted by ship, then censored, and finally forwarded by the Post Office to the Fleet Post

Office, which in turn forwarded it "by the first available transport to such port, either domestic or foreign, as will permit the most expeditious delivery to the vessel concerned."[95] In practice "most expeditious delivery" meant almost nothing, as the men on merchant ships often went months without mail and then were overwhelmed by huge accumulations arriving all at once. One such pile of mail was delivered to the *Brown* on the day she arrived in Oran; thirty-three letters were for Paul Baran, who then considered himself "the happiest guy in the world."

Another complaint, which got worse as the trip went on, was with the food. On 24 November, the day before Thanksgiving, Baran commented that "they brought some turkeys aboard today, so I guess we'll have a good meal for a change." On the brighter side, there was an opportunity for recreation ashore in Oran. Avoiding wilder kinds of entertainment, Baran spent most of his liberties ashore watching movies at the Red Cross—"I don't know what I'd do with myself if they didn't have the Red Cross." On 24 November he saw "'Ziegfeld Follies' & 'This Is the Army' two good pictures" and on the 26th "Girl Crazy" with Mickey Rooney and Judy Garland.

At Oran the *Brown* took on 241 French and American troops and 1,877 tons of cargo, which included 261 trucks, cars, and tank destroyers and 820 tons of asphalt in the lower holds of numbers 2, 4, and 5. Although loading was completed on 25 November, it was not until the 30th that the *Brown* and fifteen other ships left Oran to join convoy KMS-33 and its British escorts on their way from the United Kingdom to Port Said.[96] Captain Carley considered the escort "far superior in size & guns" to the small British escort that had taken over convoy UGS-18 at Gibraltar two months earlier. Five escort vessels, about half the total, were concentrated on the seaward side of the convoy, the port side where the *Brown,* in position 11, was the first ship. Although the escort was supported by good air cover, the threat of air attack caused the ships to release smoke at dusk. By noon the next day, the first day of December 1943, the convoy was off Algiers, and shortly afterwards Captain Carley saw another example of administrative confusion—this time, however, not involving the *Brown:* on orders from the convoy commodore, seven ships began to leave the convoy, but before going far the orders were rescinded and the ships rejoined the convoy. Although no harm resulted from the incident, it posed additional danger for the ships involved because the enemy was active in the area: just a few days earlier, thirty torpedo planes had attacked a convoy and sunk three ships.[97]

On 2 December the *Brown's* crew saw firsthand evidence of the enemy's success when they sighted heavy sludge from a recent sinking. Later on when the convoy was about eight miles off the coast of Algeria between Philippeville and Bône, a lookout on the *Brown* sighted a mine fifty yards off her starboard side, that is, in the lane between the first and second columns. Because she was the lead ship in the port column, the *Brown* notified the escort and the rest of the ships in column one. One of the escorts quickly came along and exploded the mine with gunfire. An hour later the men on the *Brown* got an even more vivid demonstration of the danger they were in when just fifty feet off the starboard side they saw the body of a man floating face up. Wearing a Navy-type life jacket and a helmet, he could easily have been an Armed Guard crew member. After seeing the body float by, Paul Baran commented that "this is really a dangerous trip. It's the only supply route up to Italy & the Jerrys are sure trying to stop the goods from getting through."

Shortly after daybreak on 3 December, thirteen ships left the convoy and sixteen from Bizerte joined it. As the convoy continued eastward it reduced its nine-column front to four to pass through the Tunisian War Channel. That night, while still in the channel, the convoy experienced another potentially dangerous situation when it was overtaken by a hospital ship. So that there could be no mistake about their identity, hospital ships were always brightly outlined with lights at night and had in addition "a broad band of green lights along the rails and a huge illuminated red cross shining on the hull plates."[98] After passing about four miles off the port side, the hospital ship suddenly cut in front of the convoy and then cut out again, thereby silhouetting part of the convoy in its lights for any U-boats lurking astern. By good luck, apparently no U-boats were in position to take advantage of this opportunity to shoot at clearly defined targets. One wonders, however, what the captain of the hospital ship had in mind when he needlessly exposed the convoy, although it is possible that he didn't know it was there because all the ships were blacked out and maintaining radio silence. Why then did he change course?

The next morning the convoy once again formed a broad front, and in the afternoon the Augusta section, including the *Brown,* left the main convoy, which was continuing on to Port Said. At about the same time, eighteen ships from Malta linked up with the Augusta section. Captain Carley didn't comment further in his "Secret Log" entry, but Lieutenant Zinn's remarks in his "Log" makes one wish that one or the other had said a lot more: Lieutenant Zinn noted only that the "skipper raised hell at British—from Malta North—only one small escort—Lend Lease etc." Captain Carley was obviously right in considering the one British escort ship inadequate for a convoy of this size, but with whom, and how, did he "raise hell," and does the reference to lend-lease mean that the British escort vessel was obtained through lend-lease? Given the fact that Captain Carley was so careful about the safety of the *Brown*, one can understand his anger, but in view of his usual detailed observations in the "Secret Log," one also wonders why he recorded nothing at all about this situation. Fortunately, the enemy missed the opportunity to attack the inadequately defended convoy.

There was more confusion the next morning, 5 December, after the convoy had passed Augusta without stopping. About eleven miles further north toward the Strait of Messina, it was suddenly ordered to return to Augusta. The convoy had to stop, turn around, and then head south, but when it got to Augusta, eight ships, including the commodore, kept on going further south. The *Brown* entered Augusta harbor and anchored until departing that evening for Naples in convoy VN-11, consisting of twenty-two vessels.[99] The convoy experienced "foul weather" until clear of the Strait of Messina shortly after daybreak the following morning. As the ships passed Stromboli, the crews could see the volcano erupting and spewing lava down its sides.[100] On the morning of the 7th the *Brown* arrived in Naples, and that afternoon Army stevedores began unloading and continued "fast and efficiently" without interruption. Two days later all the passengers and cargo had been discharged. There were, of course, air alerts while the *Brown* was in Naples. Paul Baran no doubt spoke for his shipmates as well as himself when he noted that "we're just sort of tired of being bombed & riding up & down the Med." Meanwhile, Captain Carley recorded the improvements in berthing capacity made at Naples since the *Brown*'s visit a month earlier: there were now thirty-five berths available, including pontoon berths and presumably the two ships lying on their sides whose bottoms "make a smooth surface to dock against."

The *Brown* departed Naples with eleven other ships in convoy NV-11[101] on 10 December and, traveling at an average speed of 9.08 knots, arrived at Augusta the next day. She remained at anchor until late afternoon on the 14th, when she left in a twelve-ship convoy escorted by the British trawler *Kerrera* and two motor launches. The 164-foot *Kerrera* was armed with a 12-pounder, a somewhat less powerful gun than a 3"/50, and three 20 mm's.[102] Ironically, her firepower was much less than the *Brown*'s. To compensate for the weakness of the escorts, three French bombers provided air cover for five hours during daylight hours on the 15th. At 7:00 A.M. on 16 December the *Brown* arrived off Bizerte and two hours later dropped anchor in Lake Bizerte to await orders.

After two days at anchor, the *Brown* was ordered to berth in Bizerte, but while she was maneuvering, the British tug *Empire Fred*, coming in at full speed to assist, rammed her broadside a little aft of midships, causing heavy damage to the shell plates between frames 105 and 106. It is hard to argue with Captain Carley's opinion that "gross carelessness" by the British caused the collision.[103] The damage was bad enough that Captain Carley arranged for an inspection to get a "Certificate of Seaworthiness" before feeling free to continue the voyage.

On 18 and 19 December the *Brown* took on 6 French officers and 305 enlisted men and a total of 958 tons of cargo consisting of trucks, trailers, cars, ambulances, and weapon carriers. With only slightly more than one-tenth of her cargo capacity being used, the *Brown* obviously was not being operated efficiently, but military needs outweighed any other considerations. If men and equipment were needed somewhere, a means had to be found to get them there. The troops, according to Paul Baran, were from French Morocco, "the filthiest bunch of soldiers alive. But also the best fighting bunch. They'd kill their own brother just to fight."

Baran's morale on 19 December was about as low as it could get, and he used the diary to "get it off his chest": "I'm tired of shipping soldiers, I'm tired of beach invs. [invasions] & I'm tired of bombings. I want to quit. So long Honey. Don't mind the complaining, I'm just disgusted." The 22nd, however, was brighter because some turkeys had been brought aboard for Christmas dinner, but the crew also knew that on the 27th "we start on Army K rations because we have no more food left." This prospect, of course, did nothing to help morale. On Christmas Eve, Lieutenant Zinn went aft to the Armed Guard quarters to wish the men a Merry Christmas and, perhaps more to the point as the *Brown* was about to get under way, to remind them "to keep a good sea watch & a strict black out."[104] Perhaps he also knew that the crew had planned another big party.[105]

Shortly afterwards, at 11:00 P.M. on 24 December, the *Brown* weighed anchor and left Bizerte in a convoy of thirty-eight ships with Captain Woodruff serving as commodore. Instead of going to Naples via Augusta, this convoy took a new route north of Sicily, which, according to Captain Carley, "put [the] convoy in Naples in the time it takes to go from Bizerte to Augusta, Sicily." The captain was right on the mark: this trip to Naples covered 388 miles in one day and seventeen hours, compared with the one day and fifteen hours it took to cover the 311 miles between Augusta and Bizerte the last time the *Brown* made the trip. When the slightly over one day required to travel the 245 miles between Augusta and Naples is added on, the efficiency of the direct route becomes even more obvious. This trip, however, was an exception, which, according to Radio Operator Charles Albert, was made necessary because four grounded British ships were blocking the Strait of Messina.[106] When the *Brown* traveled between Naples and Bizerte on future trips, she always went via Augusta, probably because there was no established convoy route between Bizerte and Naples and the traffic did not justify setting one up. Augusta, on the other hand, was one of the regular transfer stations on the east-west convoy routes through the Mediterranean: a ship going from Algiers to Naples, for example, would join an eastbound convoy until it got south of Augusta, at which point the ship would leave the convoy and go to Augusta to await one of the regularly scheduled VN convoys to Naples.

En route to Naples on 25 December, Captain Carley got what had to serve as his Christmas present for 1943: for four and a half hours the *Brown* steamed at 12.5 knots while turning 70 rpm, noteworthy because her top speed was supposed to be 10.5 knots at 76 rpm. Christmas for Paul Baran and the other members of the crew "was a sad & blue & lonely day. . . . We stand 4 hrs. on & 4 hrs. off. That's how we are spending our Xmas." There was one happier note, however: "Today was the first real meal I've eaten since I left the states. Yep 'turkey.'" But there was no chance of good food after Christmas because "we're all out of food supply now. Yep! we will eat the good old army C rations now."

On the 26th, half of the convoy anchored off Naples while the other half, including the *Brown,* continued on a short distance to the northwest to an anchorage in Pozzuoli Bay off Baia to await docking space in Naples. Captain Carley seemed pleased with almost everything about this trip; in his summary he commented that "our all

American convoy (excluding Escorts) was handled in a most efficient manner" and "the speed of 9.5 kts is an able & good speed for a mixed convoy," that is, one made up of loaded and light ships.

Captain Carley had only about twenty-four hours to enjoy his satisfaction. Late in the afternoon on the 27th the *Zebulon Pike* "misjudged her distance" while shifting anchorages and "rode right over" the *Brown*'s anchor chain, thereby causing heavy damage to the *Brown*'s stem, bow plates, and frames, bending the lip of her starboard hawse pipe, and scraping along twenty-five feet of her starboard side. There is a note of being put-upon in Captain Carley's final remark that "this is the third time this vessel has suffered damage through no fault of her own." Someone from the office of the WSA port engineer at Naples examined the *Brown* and, finding "no evidence of serious damage and no leakage," judged her "in a seaworthy condition and able to proceed as scheduled."[107] Therefore repairs weren't made until she returned to the United States in March.[108]

On 29 December the *Brown* left Pozzuoli Bay and moored at Naples an hour and a half later. Once moored she had only a short time to discharge her passengers and cargo because she was scheduled to sail in a convoy two days later. As it turned out, she was unable to sail on the 31st, a day marked by high winds and severe rain squalls. The delay was not caused by the weather, however, but by the Liberty ship *Walter Reed*, which had fouled her anchors and was blocking the entrance to the harbor. The 31st was of course New Year's Eve, and although a special meal wasn't served on the *Brown*—"K rations is our dish now"—the men "had a good New Years. We rang all bells on the ship. Shot our guns & shot up flares. It seemed like the war was over, over here." The men who would have preferred to welcome 1944 in a more festive manner ashore were also aboard because shore leave had been canceled due to a typhus epidemic in Naples.[109]

One of the consequences of the delayed departure was that on 3 January 1944 the *Brown* was exposed to an air raid in Naples that she otherwise would have missed. The alert was sounded at 6:46 P.M., but for reasons not given by Lieutenant Zinn, but probably having something to do with the direction of the attack, antiaircraft guns were fired from previously designated ships, the *Brown* not among them, rather than from shore batteries, which for the most part remained silent. The *Brown* at the time was anchored in the extreme southwestern part of Naples harbor toward the Isle of Capri, and it was from that direction before the firing began that Chief Mate Joseph Melendy saw one plane coming in. The firing was concentrated "on port side almost overhead." Lieutenant Zinn in the "Log" reported that a "total of about 10 flashes were seen (4 by me personally) at north end of harbor." Although he couldn't be certain whether the flashes were from the guns of the now-active shore batteries or from bombs, in his "Report" of the voyage he noted that "no bursting charges were observed following flashes, indicating flashes were [from bombs] not from port installations."

After having been delayed four extra days in Naples, the *Brown* on 4 January left empty for Augusta in convoy NV-14.[110] The eleven ships in the convoy were escorted by one British vessel and four Italian corvettes. The Italian escorts were one result of Italy's declaring war on Germany on 13 October 1943 and joining the Allied forces as co-belligerents. The rather large escort was necessary because U-boats were operating in the vicinity of the Strait of Messina, which the convoy had to transit on its way from Naples to Augusta. The possibility of a U-boat attack may have influenced Lieutenant Zinn's decision to hold firing practice on the 4th. The U-boats, however, did not attack NV-14, and the *Brown* anchored at Augusta at noon on 5 January. Five hours later she departed in convoy MKS-36, consisting at the time of twenty-five ships, an occasional plane, and four British and Greek escorts[111] identified by Captain Carley as "light destroyers." The *Brown* was in position 12, the second ship in the port column. As the convoy proceeded westward ships left and joined it, more joining than leaving, with the result that on 6 January it totaled thirty-two ships, and on the 7th, thirty-four. Also on the 7th, off Bizerte, a British destroyer equipped with an aerial torpedo deflection device joined the convoy, bringing to five the number of escorts. During this day the ships were buffeted by a "rough beam sea," causing light ships such as the *Brown* to roll "heavily." Late the next morning the crew heard depth charges exploding off the port bow, indicating the possibility of U-boats between the port side of the convoy and the coast. The ships made emergency turns to starboard while the escorts and planes looked for the U-boats. None was seen, however, and the convoy continued on its way. A few hours later a plane sighted what appeared to be a submarine about four miles from the convoy. No escorts were at that position at the time, however, and when they arrived about fifty minutes later, they could not locate the U-boat and therefore did not drop depth charges.

In his entry in the "Secret Log" for 9 January, after identifying the convoy commodore as a Royal Navy officer in the SS *English Prince*, Captain Carley cryptically remarked that "the Commodore's special [underlined twice] attention seems to be centered on the two American ships in this section," suggesting perhaps that the British officer was unfairly singling out the American ships for criticism by picking up on even the most minor flaws in their performance. In view of Captain Carley's earlier anger at a British escort and at being rammed by a British tug and of his praise for "our all American convoy," perhaps too he was revealing a bit of anti-British bias to match what he considered the commodore's anti-American bias. On the same day that he made these remarks, the captain also noted that one British and one French submarine joined the convoy and that the British destroyer with the aerial torpedo deflection device left to go into Algiers. About three and a half hours after the convoy passed Algiers, sounds of "very heavy" depth charging meant that U-boats might be nearby. A little later the ship ahead of the *Brown* fired fifteen rounds from its 20-mm guns at an "unknown object" about two hundred yards off the port bow. Neither Captain Carley nor Lieutenant Zinn recorded the outcome of all this action, no doubt because they didn't know.

At about 4:00 P.M. on 10 January, MKS-36 met a thirty-eight-ship eastbound convoy, which at dusk less than two hours later was attacked by torpedo planes. The fully loaded *Daniel Webster* was hit twice by aerial torpedoes, and although not sunk was so badly damaged that she was subsequently beached near Oran. An hour earlier the *Brown*, seven other ships, and the French submarine had peeled off to port in preparation for leaving MKS-36 to go in to Oran. Almost immediately, escorts a short distance off the *Brown*'s port beam began dropping depth charges. At about 6:00 P.M. the second ship astern of the *Brown* was suddenly attacked by a torpedo plane that came in low on the ship's port beam. It was met with gunfire from the ship's 20 mm's and then with three rounds from the stern gun as it veered to the right to cross directly astern. Both the ship and the plane apparently escaped damage. Lieutenant Zinn in describing the incident commented that the sound of the plane "strongly eliminat[ed]" the possibility that it was friendly. Obviously the gun crews fired on the plane without being absolutely certain that it was in fact hostile, but it appeared so suddenly and swooped down so fast that they had no time to make a positive identification before firing. On Lieutenant Zinn's orders the *Brown* told the shore station about the attack. Battle stations were secured at 7:15 P.M., but general quarters was again sounded three minutes later because of an air raid alert in Oran. The enemy did not appear, however, and the all clear soon sounded. Meanwhile the *Brown,* under the protection of shore batteries, had arrived at Oran and was secure at anchor in the harbor.

After three days at anchor at Oran, the still-empty *Brown* left on 13 January for a four-hour run to Mostaganem, some forty-two miles to the east. There she loaded five thousand tons of gasoline and oil in drums and in five-gallon cans. Having been confined to the ship in Naples, the crew took full advantage of Mostaganem, "one of the best liberty ports we were in on the entire trip"[112]—meaning that there was plenty of food, alcohol, and friendly women. But while the crewmen were having fun ashore, Captain Carley was having problems which he detailed in a report to the U.S. Coast Guard and the WSA offices in Oran and in a protest to the American Consulate: "while loading to a draft of 24' 5" forward, 26' 0" aft, this vessel rested on the bottom of the harbor alongside of dock at Mostaganem, Algeria." Assisted by a U.S. Navy net tender, the *Brown* got away from the pier into deeper water, but Captain Carley was concerned about the condition of her bottom. However, since bilge soundings turned up no evidence that the *Brown* was leaking, Captain Carley was satisfied that she was seaworthy and allowed her to return to Oran on the 17th.[113]

Unloading began the next day and was completed on the 24th. The *Brown* then took on a cargo of 799 tons consisting of vehicles, engineers' equipment, and supplies. Loading was completed on 25 January, and after taking on 263 passengers, the *Brown* on the 29th left Oran and joined convoy KMS-39 heading east. The convoy was made up of about fifty ships and half a dozen escorts. To make certain that the troops knew what to do in emergencies, the ever cautious and conscientious Captain Carley held two fire and boat drills on the first day at sea. Late in the afternoon, KMS-39 met a westbound convoy of British troopships escorted by eleven large British destroyers. Among the ships carrying British troops, Captain Carley was able to identify the *Highland Chieftain* and the *Lancastershire.* A short time later the convoy received a warning that unidentified planes were approaching from the north. At about 7:00 P.M. five planes flying low over the water came in from the north astern of the convoy. Apparently KMS-39 was not what they were looking for, because instead of attacking they turned west in the direction of the troop transports that had passed two hours earlier. There was of course no way for the people in KMS-39 to know what happened when the planes caught up with the troopships, but Lieutenant Zinn in his "Log" noted that news broadcasts on 3 February reported that four or five enemy planes out of a group of forty had managed to get through a protective screen to attack a convoy of troopships. Obviously he assumed that the broadcast dealt with what he had observed.

During the first four evenings after leaving Oran, the *Brown* and other ships burned smoke floats to make themselves less visible targets. In addition to smoke screens, protective measures at dusk included raising balloons to 1,500 feet so that attacking planes could not come in right on top of the ship to drop bombs. At daylight when the gun crews could see to fire at approaching planes, the balloons were lowered to 150 feet. On 31 January thirteen ships joined KMS-39 as it passed Bône, and that afternoon it formed into two columns to pass through the Tunisian War Channel. On 2 February three ships left for Malta and two joined from Malta, and in the late morning on the 3rd the *Brown* arrived at Augusta and anchored awaiting orders. The next morning she sailed for Naples in the twenty-eight-ship convoy VN-19.[114] As the *Brown* was designated the commodore ship, Commodore McClean, RNR, was aboard for the trip. One wonders how the Royal Navy commodore and Captain Carley got along. At all events, they only had to spend about a day and a half together because, after an uneventful trip, they arrived in Naples at 9:00 P.M. on 5 February. U.S. Navy, Royal Navy, and U.S. and British Army salvage teams had performed wonders in clearing the harbor and restoring facilities at Naples. In January 1944, just three months after the Allies seized the city, the port handled over ten thousand long tons of military cargo a day. More incredibly, Naples and her satellite ports—Castellammare, Torre Annunziata, Bagnoli, Pozzuoli, and Baia, all of which had been hurt like Naples—in January 1944 "handled more cargo—495,695 long tons—than even New York, and had become the greatest port in the world." By March the figure had risen to 731,889 long tons.[115] The *Brown*'s crew were no doubt gratified by the restoration of the port, but having more personal gratifications in mind, many were upset to learn that they were still restricted to the ship.[116]

On 7 February the *Brown* suffered her fifth mishap of the voyage when the U.S. Army ordered Captain Carley to berth "without the assistance of tugs, at #51, a difficult berth, being inside and having limited maneuvering space." In the course of trying to get alongside #51, the *Brown* "brushed against" the British *Manchester Exporter.* Although both ships were only slightly damaged, the collision was reported to the WSA and the damage surveyed.[117] After discharging the passengers and cargo, the *Brown* embarked 106 U.S. Army and 13 U.S. Navy passengers and loaded fifty-one vehicles and some signal equipment. She took departure from Naples on 10 February with forty-four other ships and three escorts in convoy NV-19. An hour later the convoy passed the Italian cruiser *Scipione Africano,* heading toward Naples "loaded down" with what appeared to be POWs. Arrival in Augusta was on the 11th. While at anchor on the 12th, Paul Baran wrote in his journal that "one of the soldiers we have aboard has a radio so we're listening to it now. We just heard Sally (the German girl who was born in Reading, Pa.) program. She's suppose to break down the soldiers morale. She just said N.Y. was bombed. The big B.S. But the only reason we listen to it she plays good American records. Andrew sisters and Bing Crosby." After embarking one additional passenger, a British Navy lieutenant, the *Brown* on the 12th left Augusta in a fifteen-ship convoy and "one small Escort," the British destroyer *Wheatland.* The convoy encountered bad weather on its way to Bizerte and covered the 330 miles at an average speed of 7.2 knots, arriving on the 14th.

Between 14 and 19 February the *Brown* discharged the passengers and cargo and then loaded a cargo consisting of the "personal effects of deceased soldiers" and of barrels and boxes filled with scrap metal and brass. Paul Baran was overjoyed at the sight of scrap being loaded: "Well I'm not saying it but I think we're going home. We're now loading up with scrap iron & there's only one place they take scrap iron from here & that's good old U.S.A." His deduction was correct, but there would be some tense moments before reaching the "good old U.S.A."

Departure from Bizerte was on 21 February with seven other ships, among them the *Peter Skene Ogden,* with Comdr. L. P. Wenzel, USN, aboard as "local guide" until they joined the main convoy, GUS-31, which had begun its voyage to the United States in Port Said. On the 22nd the eight ships from Bizerte formed the eleventh and twelfth columns of GUS-31, with the *Peter Skene Ogden* as vice commodore taking position 111 at the head of column eleven, followed by the *Brown* in position 112. The convoy at this time contained seventy ships plus five British escorts. Shortly after noon, when the convoy was about fourteen miles off Cape de Fer near Bône, the *Peter Skene Ogden* and the *George Cleeve* suddenly "explode[d] aft in a huge volume of smoke & water." Despite the presence of a British destroyer near the *Ogden,* German Lt. (jg) Max Dobbert, commander of U-969, had been able to sneak into position to torpedo the two ships.[118] Since the *Ogden* was only about 500 yards ahead of the *Brown* and the *Cleeve* about 850 yards off her starboard bow, Captain Carley and the crew had a good view of the action. From their vantage point it looked like the *Ogden* had been hit at number 5 hold on the starboard side and the *Cleeve* either in number 3 or the engine room on the starboard side. The *Ogden* seemed the more severely damaged and when last seen was "down at stern with main deck about 2 feet above water," but most of the crew were still aboard and the guns were manned. The *Cleeve* didn't appear to be taking much water. In fact, neither sank, but both turned out to be total losses and subsequently had to be beached and later scrapped.[119] Even though at least one escort was close by when the ships were torpedoed, no depth charges were dropped for some time—possibly, as Lieutenant Zinn speculated, to avoid harming the few men from the two ships who were blown overboard by the explosions or who abandoned ship in a panic. A more likely reason, also mentioned by Lieutenant Zinn, is that the escorts delayed dropping depth charges and then finally dropped only seven or eight simply because they couldn't find the U-boat.

Meanwhile the "convoy proceeded westward." With the certain knowledge of at least one U-boat in the area, all guns were manned beginning two hours before sunset, an especially dangerous time, and "smoke pots [were] burned on rear ships of each column at dusk daily." Such precautions were vital because the enemy was stalking the convoy, finally attacking the port column about ten miles east of Algiers on 23 February. Because the *Brown* was on the starboard side of the convoy, Captain Carley was in no position to see what exactly was happening, but he could see "gun fire & destroyers speeding towards that direction."

As the convoy proceeded westward other ships joined it, including thirty from Algiers, so that after Oran, which it passed on the 24th, the convoy consisted of 102 ships. While off Oran, ships on the port side of the convoy sighted a submarine. Four or five ships spent about twenty minutes firing their guns in the general direction of the sighting, but there was no evidence of a hit. Apparently the U-boat commander decided not to risk an attack. Either he or another U-boat captain may have stuck with the convoy, however, because the next morning the escorts responded to a possible contact by dropping depth charges off the starboard side of the convoy.

On 25 February, when the convoy was about 120 miles east of Gibraltar, Capt. L. F. Welch, USN, in the British ship *Athelchief* in position 71 took over as convoy commodore from the British commodore. At 3:00 that afternoon the seventeen columns of the convoy started to maneuver to form into four columns to pass through the Strait of Gibraltar, and exactly twenty-four hours later again formed into a broad front of seventeen columns. Along the way ships had joined and left the convoy so that on leaving Gibraltar it numbered ninety-seven ships. The American escort, headed by the USS *Edison*, relieved the British escort on the 26th.[120] Consisting of fourteen destroyers, the American escort was, in Captain Carley's opinion, "a most welcome sight after 5 months in the Mediterranean," perhaps by implication another hint of anti-British feeling because the British at this time were responsible for Mediterranean escorts.

During much of the crossing the convoy encountered heavy seas, and only three days were "fine & clear." Otherwise nothing much happened, and on 11 and 12 March the convoy commodore, Captain Welch, shifted the positions of ships within the convoy preparatory to their steaming to different destinations. There was no contact with the enemy noted by Captain Carley and Lieutenant Zinn, and they were probably unaware that near Bermuda on 13 March the convoy changed course "to avoid U-Boat."[121] Three days later, thirty-one ships in columns one through four left for Hampton Roads, and the rest, now numbering sixty-six ships including the *Brown*, reformed and then headed for New York. The next day, 17 March, the convoy first formed into four columns and then into two as it approached New York,[122] arriving "off New York" late that night. The first ship was "in Ambrose" at 1:47 A.M. on the 18th, the last almost eight hours later at 9:27 A.M. The *Brown* had covered the 4,768 miles of the voyage in twenty-five days, nine hours, and thirty minutes at an average speed of 7.82 knots. Captain Carley's concluding remark about the voyage in his "Secret Log"—"Convoy very well handled throughout voyage"—again expresses his satisfaction with the American way of doing things.

4

Voyage 4

The Mediterranean Theater and the
Invasion of Southern France

THE *John W. Brown* was moored at Pier 12 in Brooklyn about a half mile south of the Brooklyn Bridge on Wednesday, 22 March 1944, when the new commanding officer of the Armed Guard unit, Ens. Joe B. Humphreys, communications officer Ens. John H. McClenahan, and twenty-six enlisted men boarded the *Brown* at 11:00 P.M. to relieve Lieutenant Zinn and his crew.[1] Originally scheduled to arrive on the 23rd, the new men had to rush aboard at this late hour on the 22nd because the *Brown* had received orders to move the next morning. Not expecting their replacements until morning, Lieutenant Zinn and his men were still packing. It was 3:00 A.M. by the time they left so that Ensign Humphreys and his men could settle in and get some sleep. To make matters worse, their first impression of the *Brown* was decidedly unfavorable: after her long voyage she was "filthy dirty" and "the officers and gun crews quarters were almost unbearable." Discovering the next morning that no meals were being served on board, what must have been a sleepy and grumpy gun crew shuffled ashore for an early breakfast so that they could get back before the 9:00 sailing time.

The *Brown* left Pier 12 as scheduled, rounded the southern tip of Manhattan, and steamed up the Hudson River to Blair Shipyard in Yonkers, New York, arriving shortly before noon. After lunch ashore, some of the men were given liberty, others cleaned their quarters, and a man was assigned to stand watch on each gun. The Armed Guard crew soon discovered that with shipyard workers aboard day and night there was little chance of getting any sleep. With the constant banging of the workers resounding through the ship and the inconvenience of not having the galley open, Ensign Humphreys decided that he should try to move his men ashore. He and Ensign McClenahan investigated and found that the Yonkers YMCA could provide "suitable quarters" for the men for fifty cents each a night, including "linen, soap, showers, and use of all recreational equipment." Quickly getting the approval of the captain, the purser, a personnel official from States Marine, and the port director, Humphreys soon had his crew on their way to the Yonkers YMCA. The two ensigns took rooms at the Henry Hudson Hotel. Although housed ashore, five men were aboard the ship at all times standing watch. Crew members not on watch had to attend musters on the ship at 9:00 A.M. each morning and then spend the day working on the guns and their quarters.

In view of the work to be done at Blair, it is no wonder that the workmen were noisy. When accommodations for troops had been installed on the *Brown* at the Bethlehem Hoboken Yard in June 1943, not all the work was up to specifications. Thus one set of jobs at Blair involved correcting deficiencies in the companionway openings, overboard discharges for the troop quarters, and the reinforcement of hatch corners.[2] Further changes in the troop areas resulted in quarters for thirty-three officers and twenty-two hospital patients in number 3 'tween deck and five hundred troops in number 2.[3] The frame and plates that had buckled when the *Zebulon Pike* rode over the *Brown*'s anchor cable the previous December were renewed and repaired at this time.[4] Another job involved the construction of additional quarters for Navy personnel on the bridge and boat decks so that if necessary the ship could house a total of three officers and forty enlisted men. One of the reasons for the increased space for the Navy was that two additional 3"/50s were installed on the *Brown*'s stern.

Even though the shipyard workers had not completed all the repairs and alterations, on 31 March the *Brown* moved back to Pier 12 in Brooklyn. The next day the Navy delivered cots, life jackets, and other supplies to the ship, and Navy ordnance chief petty officers came aboard to adjust the sights on the new 3"/50s and to service and repair the 5"/51. Although the *Brown* was not to leave New York for another week and a half, her fourth voyage officially began at Pier 12 Brooklyn at midnight Sunday, 2 April, and the new chief mate, Herbert W. Ritter, made his first entry in the "Deck Log." As part of the transition, Joseph W. Melendy, chief mate on the third voyage, was "officially relieved of all duties and detached from the vessel." This Sunday turned out to be a very busy one on the *Brown*. Shipyard workers had worked through the night and were still aboard at 6:00 A.M. when the *Brown* shifted to Pier 3, Bush Terminal, Brooklyn. On opening numbers 1 and 2 holds for loading, the crew found that the bottom of lower hold 1 was covered with water, and 2 had some oil in it. Chief Mate Ritter and Chief Engineer George E. Moore surveyed the holds and discovered that leaking from the tops of the deep tanks had caused an accumulation of water ranging from twelve inches at the forward end to eighteen at the after end of number 1 hold. Number 2 hold had about three-quarters of an inch of fuel oil across the after end. Shipyard workers from Blair pumped number 1 dry, tightened the bolts on the deep tanks, and cleaned up the oil in number 2. The deep tanks were tested the next morning and found tight. Two other gangs worked all day Sunday in numbers 4 and 5 holds building bins to hold high-explosive cargo.

Despite an early-spring snow, stevedores spent Monday, 3 April, loading ammunition in holds 4 and 5, thereby provoking an exchange of forms between the Army Transportation Corps and the Coast Guard because Pier 3 was "not a designated loading pier" for explosives. The Army requested a waiver because "shifting this vessel to an explosive anchorage or berth would result in missing a convoy," but the Coast Guard refused, whereupon the Army played its ace, a form issued under the authority of the secretary of war stating that "military urgency outweighs the marine hazard involved." With the obligatory paperwork thus completed by the Army, the Coast Guard granted the waiver.[5] Also on 3 April a "hot loop" phone was installed in the wheelhouse to connect the *Brown* to New York's Aircraft Warning Center, and Ensign Humphreys assigned men to cover it at all times.

On Tuesday, 4 April, stevedores began loading numbers 1 and 2 holds. On Wednesday the temperature was an unseasonably low thirty-six degrees, and less than two hours after starting work at 8:00 A.M. the stevedores had to close the hatches because of a heavy snowfall. The snow was still falling at 4:00 P.M. and the temperature had dropped to thirty-two degrees, but by 7:00 P.M. the stevedores were able to resume work on number 2 and continue through the night. Ensign Humphreys spent Wednesday checking supplies received the day before and preparing a report of missing items to send to the supply department. Meanwhile his "crew worked on the guns which were found in very bad condition. The previous crew had not taken good care of them." Wednesday, 5 April, was also the day that the new master, Capt. George N. Brown, joined the ship.

Except for the thirty-degree temperature, Thursday, 6 April, was a more typical day, with a new shift of stevedores working on all five holds. From then until Sunday morning, shifts of stevedores worked around the clock. On Friday at noon a U.S. shipping commissioner came aboard to sign on the forty-one officers and men in the crew. On the same day eight more men joined the Armed Guard crew, bringing the total of enlisted men to thirty-four. There were also discipline problems for Ensign Humphreys to face, as one man was found sleeping on duty and two others were not at their assigned posts. Humphreys ordered all three to forfeit their next liberties.

On Saturday, 8 April, Captain Brown received sailing orders for the *Brown* from the water division of the Army Service Forces. These orders provide an example of the meticulous planning that lay behind the movement of merchant ships during World War II:

> 1. Under the terms of charter, your cargo and supplies being properly stowed, and when in all respects ready for sea, you will comply with the following announced sailing orders: Vessel, SS "JOHN W. BROWN". Sailing hours and date: Your vessel is to be prepared to leave Pier 3, Bush Terminal at 0001 (12:01 A.M.) on 10th April 1944 and proceed to Hampton Roads. The actual hour of undocking will be given to you by the Navy Port Director, 17 Battery Place, N.Y.C., on whom you will call on 9th April 1944.
>
> 2. Upon arrival at Hampton Roads, Va., request pilots to take your vessel to anchorage "F" in Lynnhaven Sound. You are to attend a conference meeting at the office of the Navy Port Director, Navy Operating Base, Norfolk, Va., at 1400 (2:00 P.M.) on 12th April 1944 and obtain routing instructions for a voyage to a Mediterranean Port. You are to be prepared to leave Hampton Roads at 0001 (12:01 A.M.) on 13th April 1944. Actual port of discharge will be given you by the Convoy Commodore prior to your arrival.
>
> 3. Shore leave for your officers and crew in New York expires at 1200 (Noon) on 9th April 1944. No shore leave is to be extended while your vessel lies at anchorage in Hampton Roads, Va.[6]

Meanwhile, as loading continued on Saturday, 8 April, a conflict arose between Ensign Humphreys and Lieutenant Donovan, the Army cargo security officer assigned to the *Brown* for this voyage, as each tried to meet differing responsibilities. Notified by the port director that twenty-seven tons of ammunition for the *Brown*'s guns were being delivered, Ensign Humphreys conferred with Lieutenant Donovan about how to bring it aboard. Lieutenant Donovan, who had authority over the loading process, refused Ensign Humphreys the use of the *Brown*'s winches to load the ammunition on the grounds that all were needed for cargo. Because the *Brown*'s sailing orders stipulated that she be ready to sail at 12:01 A.M. on the 10th, Ensign Humphreys had to figure out some way to load the ammunition despite Lieutenant Donovan's refusal of help. By luck, the ammunition barge arrived at noon just as the longshoremen stopped for lunch, thereby freeing up the winches. The Armed Guard immediately took over number 5 winch to load ammunition into the after magazine. At 1:00 the longshoremen returned to work but could not resume loading number 5 hold because Ensign Humphreys was still using the winch. When Lieutenant Donovan found out what was happening, he ordered the loading of ammunition stopped so that the longshoremen could start work. Ensign Humphreys could do nothing but wait for another opportunity, which came forty minutes later when the longshoremen stopped work on number 4. The ammunition barge was moved to the port side, and the Armed Guard crew used number 4 winch to load the ammunition. At 7:00 P.M., when the last of the ammunition was finally aboard and stowed, the Armed Guard was granted liberty, except for one man who had been too drunk to help load the ammunition. Instead of liberty he got twelve hours of extra duty. This eventful Saturday also saw Radioman Third Class Michael Bugel report aboard, increasing the enlisted Navy personnel to thirty-five.

After working through the night, the civilian longshoremen stopped loading for the day at 6:00 A.M. on 9 April, Easter Sunday, but at 10:00 Army longshoremen came aboard to load mail into the number 1 'tween deck, and at 1:00 P.M. they began loading cargo into all five holds. Although the sailing orders had specified that shore leave for the crew was to expire at noon, Captain Brown restricted the ship at 11:00 A.M. That his authority in this matter applied only to the Merchant Marine officers and men is made clear by Ensign Humphreys's restricting the Navy enlisted men at 8:00 A.M. and allowing the officers—himself and Ensign McClenahan—to stay ashore until 4:00 P.M. Actually the two ensigns did not use their extra time ashore for recreation but instead went with Captain Brown to the port director's office. While there Ensign Humphreys checked on three of his men who had been given four-day leaves on the 6th and had been wired to return to the ship immediately. Two of them were back by midafternoon, and the third wired that he would return at 7:00 the next morning. That evening carpenters came aboard to begin shoring the cargo. Loading continued through the night, and as each hold was filled, the carpenters secured the cargo. The last of the cargo was aboard by 7:00 A.M. on Monday, and by 7:30, seven and a half hours later than the deadline set in the sailing orders, the shoring was done, the carpenters ashore, and the "crew [busy] securing [the] ship for sea." Since the member of the Armed Guard crew who said he would return at 7:00 did not show up, his gear was turned over to the Coast Guard unit on the pier with instructions to call the Armed Guard Center to have it picked up. At 8:38 A.M. the routine tests of the wheel, whistle, and engine room telegraph showed that all were in "good working order." The *John W. Brown* was ready to begin Voyage 4.

The *Brown* was part of the New York section of convoy UGS-39, bound for Hampton Roads to link up with the main body of the convoy. The New York section consisted of one French, five British, and thirteen American ships escorted by four destroyer escorts commanded by Lt. Comdr. H. E. Purdy, USNR, in the *Wingfield*. The convoy commodore was Comdr. L. P. Wenzell, USN, in the British-flag Liberty ship *Samdart*,[7] making her maiden foreign voyage after having been launched a month earlier at Savannah, Georgia.[8] The departure schedule for the *Brown* again illustrates the kind of detailed planning that went into the convoy system:

Cast off. Weighing Anchor	Estimated Time	0915
Underway	Estimated Time	0935
Narrows: Ft. Wadsworth abeam	Time	1000
Estimated speed to Gate	Knots	7.0
Gate abeam	Time	1015
Speed to Gedney Sea Buoy	Knots	7.5
Buoy No. 9 abeam	Time	1045
Speed while dropping pilot	Knots	4.0

Gedney Buoy abeam (after dropping pilot assume speed 9.0 knots)	Time 1135
Time reaching station—slow to 6.0 Knots	[Time] 1227
Increase speed on signal to 9.0 Knots	[Time] 1300
Buoy "G" abeam	Time 1239
Point "XRAY" abeam	Time 1341
Point "YOKE" abeam	Time 1425
Rendezvous "ZED" abeam	Time 1513

From the information given in the "Deck Log," it seems that the *Brown* was unable to keep precisely to the schedule. The "Deck Log" notes that shortly after 9:00 A.M. the pilot boarded; at 9:22 two tugs came alongside to assist; and within twenty minutes, about five minutes behind schedule, the *Brown* was "in stream off dock, tugs cast off." At 10:20 the "sub gate" was abeam, at 11:30 the pilot left, and at 11:31, when abeam Gedney Buoy at the end of Ambrose Channel, the *Brown* officially took departure. By this time she had made up for the lost time and was in fact four minutes ahead of schedule. Because the ships for their safety had "to get well closed up in convoy formation as soon as possible after passing rendezvous Point 'ZED,'" it was important that each ship keep close to schedule. At 3:30 P.M., some six hours after casting off, the nineteen ships formed into a convoy consisting of six columns with four ships in column four and three ships in each of the other five columns. The *Brown*, in position 53, was the third and last ship in column five.

Although the Office of the Port Director, Third Naval District, had warned on 9 April, the day before the convoy left New York, that "enemy mine fields have been laid in U.S. Coastal waters [and that] enemy activity may be expected along the entire route,"[9] nothing out of the routine occurred during the voyage south off the coasts of New Jersey, Delaware, Maryland, and Virginia. Until dark on the 10th and "from first light to destination" on the 11th, a blimp and two planes joined the four destroyer escorts to guard the convoy.[10]

To get a sense of his men in order to place them most effectively at permanent gun stations, Ensign Humphreys used part of the time on Tuesday, 11 April, for a "personal conference" during which he questioned each man about his age, family background, civilian occupation, gunnery experience, and date of service. Late in the afternoon, as the *Brown* approached the Virginia capes, a pilot came aboard, and shortly afterwards the *Brown* anchored at Lynnhaven anchorage just west of Cape Henry. On the way to the anchorage the *Brown* had come through some fog, and now at anchor with the temperature in the low fifties she was pelted by heavy rain during a thunder and lightning storm. In his last "Log" entry for the day, Humphreys recorded that two men had violated the regulations prohibiting drinking alcohol aboard ship; he punished them with twelve hours' extra duty. Humphreys seems to have had more trouble with discipline than Lieutenants Calvert and Zinn, but it is not clear whether the problems stemmed from less effective leadership, poorer quality of crew, more detailed reporting in the "Log," or simply that there were more men in his crew to get into trouble.

The *Brown* spent the next morning maneuvering while having her compass adjusted, and just before noon a Navy motor launch picked up Captain Brown, "Sparks," and the two ensigns to take them to a convoy conference at Little Creek. Among other points made at the conference, the masters were told to burn navigation lights during the sortie (the departure formation), to fall into two columns at Buoy 2CB, and then to proceed to the rendezvous point to form the convoy. Captain Massenberg, president of the Virginia Pilots Association, explained that about thirty-five pilots would be available for the first thirty-five ships in the sortie and that as soon as the pilots were dropped, they would be rushed back to the other ships waiting to leave.[11] Because the *Brown* was to be among the first thirty-five ships, a pilot came aboard that evening and spent the night on the ship. At 5:22 the next morning the crew "commenced heaving up"; at 6:01, one minute behind schedule, the *Brown* passed Cape Henry; and at 6:25 the pilot left. Convoy UGS-39, when formed up, consisted of ninety ships, and as number 62 the *Brown* was the second ship in the sixth column. Next to her in position 72 on the starboard side was the Navy oiler *Cossatot*.[12] The positions astern of the *Cossatot* were left empty so that she could easily drop back to refuel escort ships. The escort, led by Commander Nickerson, USCG, in the Coast Guard cutter *Bibb*, was made up of twenty-seven destroyers, destroyer escorts, and minesweepers. The convoy commodore was L. F. Welch in the *Toltec*.[13]

On 14 April, the first full day at sea, one of the men in the Armed Guard unit complained to Ensign Humphreys that his right arm was red and swollen from a booster shot he had received at the Armed Guard Center just before sailing. Thus began a worrisome episode that lasted for about three weeks. Finding the next day that the seaman's arm was still red and badly swollen and was causing a great deal of pain, Humphreys signaled the commodore in the *Toltec* for advice. Told to contact a ship with a physician on board, he signaled the *James Ford Rhodes* and gave a brief summary of the situation, noting in particular that the sailor had had a typhoid injection in his right arm a week earlier and that the swollen red area was six inches in diameter. The sailor's temperature, pulse, and respiration, however, were all normal. Humphreys pointed out that he had treated the sailor with hot epsom salt compresses, aspirin, and sulfa, but since there was no obvious improvement, he needed professional medical advice. The *Rhodes* signaled back that the physician advised sixteen grains of sulfa and ten grains of aspirin every four hours, the continuation of hot compresses, and liquids by mouth. As a precaution, Humphreys assigned a member of the Armed Guard to stay with the sick man. The next morning the sailor's temperature was still normal, but the sulfa had been discontinued at midnight because it made him nauseous. He was, however, still taking aspirin. These details were reported to the physician on the *Rhodes,* who advised Humphreys to continue the treatment and report back to him in twenty-four hours.

For the next two days the sailor seemed to improve, but on the 19th he had a relapse, with his temperature spiking to 101 and his pulse rate to 100. Obviously worried, Ensign Humphreys met with Captain Brown and Harry Rauch, the purser, to discuss what to do next, and the three agreed that they should immediately signal for medical help. But nothing is easy at sea under the best conditions, and wartime exigencies add other layers of difficulty. Just as the *Brown* was about to signal the *Rhodes,* the commodore ordered practice evasive maneuvers. With everyone on the ships concentrating on changing courses correctly, it was only after a "great deal of effort" that the *Brown* was able to send a message describing the sailor's condition and requesting that he be put under a physician's direct care. The answer from the *Rhodes*—that he continue the previously prescribed treatment and report back in twenty-four hours—must have dismayed Humphreys, who by now was convinced that the problem was too much for him to handle. He replied that the patient could not tolerate sulfa and that the skin on his arm was too tender for hot compresses. The only response from the *Rhodes* was "Wait."

Shortly afterwards the commodore signaled for a case history and diagnosis. Ensign Humphreys replied with a complete account of what had been going on, concluding with his opinion that the man should be seen by a physician. At 4:00 P.M. the commodore told the *Brown* to drop astern for the night and that an escort would take over the case. The destroyer escort *Vance* then came up, and once again Humphreys signaled a full account of the problem. This time, it seemed, Humphreys's message was bringing results because the *Brown* was told to pull ahead and to get a motor lifeboat ready to transfer the sailor to the *Vance*. As the *Brown* prepared to comply, however, the order was suddenly rescinded, and Humphreys was told to stop the sulfa and hot compresses and to give codeine for pain. Since there was no codeine aboard the *Brown*, morphine had to be given instead. The message ended with an order for the *Brown* to resume her station for the night and a promise to contact her in the morning. As the *Brown* began to maneuver to take her place at station 62, the commodore countermanded the order and signaled her to spend the night at station 78 instead, the next to last of the seven empty stations astern of the *Cossatot*.

As soon as the dawn watch was over the next morning, Ensign Humphreys checked the patient and found that "his arm had burst during the night." Humphreys again conferred with Captain Brown and then signaled the *Vance* a description of the man's condition, tersely adding, "Excess pus. Appears to be deep infection. Need doctor." More than two hours passed before the *Vance* responded, and then only to ask that the message be repeated. After the *Brown* complied, it appeared that something was going to happen because the *Vance* signaled that she would come alongside, which she did at 10:30 A.M. Dr. James Todd, an assistant surgeon in the U.S. Public Health Service, was transferred to the *Brown* in a breeches buoy, not an easy task on the open seas, even though there was no wind to speak of and the sea was "slight" with a "low long swell." Once Dr. Todd was aboard, the *Brown* resumed her position in the convoy. Probably not relishing more trips than necessary in a breeches buoy, Dr. Todd, after examining the patient, decided to stay on the *Brown* overnight. In his report, which was inserted in Ensign Humphreys's "Log," Dr. Todd described how he gave the patient an intravenous anesthetic of 0.5 grams of sodium pentothal and then incised and drained the abscess, obtaining about 200 cc (almost 6 ounces) of pus. He packed the wound with sterile gauze, applied hot wet compresses, and, after the seaman regained consciousness, gave him morphine for pain. The next morning Dr. Todd removed the pack from the wound and put on a dry dressing. He had given sulfadiazine orally, but since the infection was confined to the arm and since the sailor's temperature had returned to normal after the pus had been drained, Dr. Todd discontinued medication. All that needed to be done was to change the dressing, but he "thought that the large abscess pocket will take considerable time to heal." At 4:30 that afternoon the *Vance* came alongside and retrieved Dr. Todd, again by breeches buoy. He was no doubt grateful that the sea was still smooth and the ship "rolling easily." From then on, Ensign Humphreys dressed the arm periodically, noting constant improvement. He last mentioned dressing it on 7 May, more than two weeks after the operation, observing that "it looks satisfactory."

There was of course much more than an infected arm that required attention during this period. There was always the possibility of attack by the enemy, emphasized on 15 April, the day after the sore arm was first reported, when "the convoy commodore gave an emergency turn [signal] followed by 'Enemy submarines in Vicinity.'" That same day, Ensign Humphreys again had to deal with a breach of discipline when he learned that two of his men had missed dawn lookout; his assigning them two hours of extra duty seems extraordinarily light punishment for such a serious offense, especially with the threat of U-boats in the area. No one at the time could know, however, that it was extremely unlikely that there was in fact a U-boat nearby, because on 22 March, a little more than three weeks earlier, Adm. Karl Donitz, reacting to recent heavy U-boat losses, had "cancelled all further operations against convoys. . . . Never again were [Allied] convoys seriously threatened. . . . [By the end of May 1944] there were precisely three U-boats left in the whole vast [Atlantic] ocean which had so long been their main battle ground."[14] Of course no one in UGS-39 had an inkling of these facts, which have come to light through postwar research.

Ensign Humphreys also held field day, a cleanup day, on the 15th and then inspected his men's quarters and lockers. Meanwhile, Captain Brown, accompanied by Chief Mate Ritter, Chief Engineer Moore, Steward Herbert Sutherland, and Army cargo security officer Lieutenant Donovan, inspected "quarters, staterooms, troop quarters, & holds." This inspection revealed several flaws in the shipyard work that had to be repaired immediately. Perhaps the worst was a hole about two inches in diameter in the starboard side of the ship just above the number 3 'tween deck line. Apparently, during the installation of troop accommodations in number 3 an overboard pipe had been removed but the hole had not been plugged before it was covered. The problem was not detected until the *Brown* was at sea and water was discovered in the 'tween deck area. As a temporary repair, a plug was driven into the hole. In the same place, shipyard workers had broken a return pipe from a steam line and had not fixed it. As a result, steam from the line caused "excessive sweating with possible damage to the new troop quarters." Further inspection revealed "numerous breaks" in steam and water pipe connections, all of which the crew were able to fix. The last defect was a hole about two and a half inches in diameter in the main deck on the port side just forward of number 2 hatch, caused when shipyard workers removed a pipe from the fire main. The crew pounded a wooden plug into the hole as a temporary repair. Other than these defects, which the crew was able to fix, Captain Brown's inspection turned up nothing worth noting in the "Deck Log."

A few days later, however, a further example of the sloppiness and indifference of some shipyard workers came to light when another leak was found on the starboard side of number 3 'tween deck. As before, the problem stemmed from a hole made by the removal of an overboard pipe, but different in that a plate had been welded over the hole. The weld, however, was not tight. To get to the hole to seal it with a cement patch, the crew had to remove a toilet in the medical corpsmen's quarters in the 'tween deck.

On Sunday, 16 April, Ensign Humphreys recorded in his "Log" an incident that illustrates the cooperative spirit that usually—although not always—marked the relationships between Merchant Marine and Navy crews on merchant ships during World War II: "A representative of the Merchant crew called at my quarters this afternoon and advised me that they had unanimously voted to offer their services to assist the Armed Guard in manning the guns. I could call on as many as needed." After accepting the offer, Humphreys consulted Chief Mate Ritter, and the two of them, after agreeing not to consider men on the 4:00 to 8:00 watch, selected fifteen to be assigned "gun positions and given instructions and drill." Ensign Humphreys found them "most cooperative." Ironically, this harmony was followed by discord at mealtime the same evening when the Armed Guard crew became "noisy and boisterous" in the passageway and in their amidship quarters. Captain Brown conveyed his annoyance in his suggestion to Ensign Humphreys that he speak to his men about their conduct. At muster the next morning Humphreys made clear that he would not tolerate rowdy behavior and in the future would punish it severely. He then informed Captain Brown of the "steps taken," which apparently were sufficient because rowdiness was never mentioned again.

On the afternoon of 20 April, Captain Brown, Chief Mate Ritter, Lieutenant Donovan, and Ensign Humphreys inspected the guns, magazines, and the quarters of the Armed Guard crew. Humphreys was no doubt happy to report that the other officers were "very much impressed and pleased by the conditions found," and, reflecting his poor opinion of Lieutenant Zinn and his crew on the previous voyage, he observed that "the guns are all in first class condition for the first time since we have come aboard." At dusk a few hours later the escorts patrolling ahead of the convoy dropped some depth charges, indicating that they thought they had located a submarine. They again dropped depth charges at 1:00 A.M. the next morning, but it is unlikely that any U-boats were nearby. Rain began later in the morning and continued through most of the day. Since they could not work topside, the Armed Guard crew got "the opportunity to catch up on much needed rest."

The men were fortunate to have had their rest the day before, because they were kept quite busy on the afternoon of the 22nd. At 1:00 Ensign Humphreys held a gun drill with the Merchant crew. Then, after receiving permission from the commodore to practice firing the guns, the *Brown* increased speed to pull ahead and to the port of the convoy. When a safe distance away, Humphreys and the three gunners mates test-fired the two new 3"/50s at zero degrees and at seventy-five degrees elevation. The gun crews then practiced with all the guns, firing 3 rounds from the 3"/50 on the bow, 5 rounds from each of the 3"/50s on the stern, 1 round from the 5"/51 aft, and 480 rounds from the eight 20-mm guns. The Navy gunners and the Merchant Marine volunteers divided the time firing the 20 mm's. Only one round was fired from the 5"/51 because it fired as soon as the breech was closed, possibly because of a short circuit in the wiring to the gun's electric primer. Although Humphreys noted that his crew were looking into the problem, they did nothing the following day, a Sunday and therefore "a day of rest." The escorts, however, not taking "a day of rest," dropped more depth charges when they thought once again that they had located a U-boat. On Monday the Armed Guard were back at work. Those working on the 5"/51 found they could fix the short circuit by replacing the case on the firing key with a new one, and to make certain that it operated properly, they tested it with a primer. Anticipating an increased threat from the sky as the convoy neared Gibraltar, others were busy setting up sky lookouts and replacing a large amount of antiship ammunition in the 3"/50 ready boxes with antiaircraft ammunition. On the level of human comforts, Humphreys met with the steward to complain about the way bed linen and matches were distributed to his men. Apparently he was persuasive, because the steward promised to supply matches "as long as they held out" and to issue two sheets to each man.

The preparations for air attacks came none too soon, for on the following afternoon the *Brown* experienced her first air alert on this trip when the commodore signaled that an unidentified plane was approaching. Ten minutes later, however, he let the convoy know that the plane was friendly. Another friendly plane, a Navy Liberator, flew by a half hour later, at about the same time that the *Brown's* crew were holding fire and boat drills. As on the day before, matters having to do with protecting the ship and saving lives were mixed with less portentous but nonetheless difficult problems, in this instance with the trouble a messman was having in serving thirty-four meals in one hour in the Armed Guard mess, which can seat only twelve men at a time. Obviously the men could not linger over their meals, but in violation of regulations some of the pressure was relieved by letting Armed Guard crew sit at empty places in the Merchant crew's mess.

At 6:45 A.M. on 29 April the lookouts on the *Brown* sighted land. A little less than three hours later the convoy was abeam Cape Spartel at the western end of the Strait of Gibraltar, and at noon it passed the Rock of Gibraltar and entered the Mediterranean Sea. On the 30th some ships left the convoy, the first of a series of groups of ships to join and leave the convoy as it passed various North African ports on its way east through the Mediterranean. The *Brown* was one of thirteen ships going to Naples via Augusta.

The signs of war were more evident in the Mediterranean than in the Atlantic: just before dark, what appeared to be a small bomb floated past the *Brown*, and unidentified planes circled the convoy. The crew could still hear the planes after nightfall, and Ensign Humphreys assumed that they were German reconnaissance planes.

There were two air alerts on 1 May and one on the 2nd, during which the *Brown* and the other ships laid down smoke screens. On the 3rd, in accordance with a new escort system, HMS *Dart* relieved the American escort at the entrance to the Bizerte swept channel.[15] Prior to UGS-36, which passed Gibraltar on 30 March 1944, U.S. escorts transferred UGS convoys to British escorts off Casablanca. With UGS-36 and thereafter, U.S. escorts took the convoys all the way to Bizerte.[16]

Because the main enemy threat was from the sky rather than from under the sea, at sunset on 3 May the *Brown's* barrage balloon was put up. At this time the Germans had a total of 125 planes stationed in southern France, consisting of Ju. (Junkers) 88 and He. (Heinkel) 111 bombers and He. 177 long-range bombers armed with radio-controlled glide bombs.[17] In contrast, there were only fifteen U-boats in the Mediterranean, and after an unsuccessful attempt to send more, the U-boat command decided not to try again. By the end of May, Allied attacks had reduced the fifteen U-boats to eleven, and by the end of September, to zero. The success of the Invasion of Southern France in August deprived the Germans of airfields close to the Mediterranean, thereby eliminating the threat by air. As a consequence, "the sea became so peaceful that, beginning with UGS-60, which passed Gibraltar 27 November 1944, convoys were dispersed at Point Europa and the ships proceeded independently to their terminal ports."[18]

But all this was in the future: the 125 German planes and 15 U-boats were still threats when the *John W. Brown* arrived in Augusta on 5 May, passed through the submarine gate at the entrance to the harbor, and moved to an anchorage. The trip from Hampton Roads had taken twenty-one days and seventeen hours, had covered 4,720 miles at an average speed of 9.2 knots, and had consumed 3,220 barrels of fuel, roughly 145 barrels a day. Captain Welch, the convoy commodore, reported on Convoy Form "D" that the convoy averaged 9.6 knots to Gibraltar and 8.0 knots from Gibraltar to Bizerte. He also singled out the *Brown* and the *Abel Stearns* in position 63 directly astern of the *Brown* as "poor station keepers." There is nothing more specific than that, but at the convoy conference before the trip the point had been made that although station keeping is "an old subject . . . masters have got to exercise a little pressure on their mates and make them understand what 500 yards is."[19] Apparently discipline on the bridge was sometimes lax.

The British authorities who came aboard at Augusta informed the *Brown*'s crew that the ship would remain there for two days. This layover provided an opportunity for the Merchant and Armed Guard crews to lower a lifeboat to practice rowing. Late in the morning of the 6th, Lieutenant Commander Reynolds, USNR, of the Armed Guard Inspection Service came aboard to inspect the guns and the Armed Guard crew's quarters. Ensign Humphreys does not record the results of the inspection, but he does note that Commander Reynolds stayed aboard for dinner. Another example of harmonious relations between the Merchant and Navy crews occurred after dinner when Bos'n Matts Oman, a fifty-nine-year-old native of Finland, taught the Armed Guard crew how to rig a lifeboat. Several men were given an opportunity to have the "actual experience," and "all were taught how to lower a life boat." To conclude the lessons for the day, the radio operator showed them how to use the lifeboat radios.

With Captain Brown at the conn, the *Brown* departed Augusta the next morning in convoy VN-38, made up of twenty-five ships.[20] The convoy enjoyed an uneventful trip until just before midnight, when, about forty miles southwest of Salerno, it had to make an emergency turn while the escorts dropped depth charges. A little over four hours later, at 4:15 A.M. on 8 May as the *Brown* passed about fifteen miles west of Salerno, Ensign Humphreys was awakened when more depth charges were dropped and a lookout saw a "large flash" to starboard. No one on the *Brown*, however, was in a position to know what exactly was going on. Upon arrival in Naples four and a half hours later, the *Brown* anchored until a pilot came aboard to take her into a berth. Humphreys set the port watch and then went ashore to report to the Navy liaison officer and the port security officer and to pick up mail at the Fleet Post Office.

Despite the added complications caused by nearby Mount Vesuvius's spectacular and destructive eruption in late March 1944, the worst in seventy-two years,[21] conditions in Naples had improved during the three months since the *Brown*'s visit in February. The city's wounds, however, were still in the early stages of healing: the salvage teams had accomplished much, but "the harbor and port [were still] an absolute mess with all manner of ships sunk all over the place, both inside the channel and out,"[22] and when the crew went ashore they found a city that Ruth Gruber, who was there in July 1944, likened to a "lunar landscape." She saw a suffering city

Between December 1943 and January 1946, the *Brown* was in and out of
Naples sixteen times. This view of the harbor shows Mt. Vesuvius
in the background. *National Archives*

whose buildings "hung like rags. Whole streets were ripped up.
Houses were sliced down the front, with staircases that led nowhere
and curtains flying insanely in the wind. . . . Life was on the street in
this ravaged city. . . . Most of the people were in rags, children were
barefoot, but some of the Neapolitan women looked as lovely as
Renaissance madonnas. Others had bleached their hair blond, and
their dark roots were showing . . . making Naples look like a city of
big-bosomed sexy women with two-colored hair and high platform
shoes."[23] Desperate for money to survive, many had become prostitutes and openly solicited the servicemen and merchant sailors
roaming the devastated streets of Naples; worse yet, "it was not uncommon to see young Italian children pimping for their mothers,

sisters, and aunts."[24] All it cost was a couple of packs of cigarettes, candy, or bars of soap that the woman could sell on the wide-ranging black market or trade for food, clothing, or whatever else she needed. And as several members of the *Brown*'s crew were to discover, many were infected with venereal diseases.

On 8 May, just a half hour after the *Brown* had tied up, Army stevedores came aboard to begin what turned out to be around-the-clock unloading operations, and by the 12th they had finished discharging numbers 3 and 4 holds. The work continued without interruption from the enemy until 3:55 A.M. on the 14th, when the mournful wailing of air raid sirens sounded across the city. The general alarm immediately sounded on the *Brown*, loading operations stopped, all lights were turned off, and the longshoremen and crew took cover. The Armed Guard, under orders "not to fire under any circumstances while laying along side the pier," did not man the

The *Brown* was tied up in Naples during this air raid
on 14 May 1944. *National Archives*

guns. The crew could hear planes overhead, several of which were caught in the beams of searchlights as the shore batteries banged away with "a terrific barrage" and tracer shells lit up the skies with intricate and colorful patterns. Some bombs were dropped, but none near the *Brown*. "All clear" came about fifty minutes after the first alert had sounded. Suddenly all was quiet, and the men returned to whatever they were doing when the sirens started up. By midnight the next day all cargo had been discharged, and Chief Mate Ritter had inspected the holds and found them in good order for loading.

An hour later loading began, and it continued with only short interruptions for changing shifts, meal breaks, and two air raid alarms until completed on 18 May. In all the *Brown* had loaded 3,322 tons of high explosives and gasoline to take to the Anzio beachhead. Five officers and 170 enlisted men of the 690th U.S. Army Port Company then boarded the ship, bringing their own food and cargo gear. Following a procedure developed to reduce casualties and to speed up unloading, these men were put aboard to discharge the cargo when the *Brown* reached Anzio, after which they would return to Naples on the *Brown* and then move on to their next assignment.[25] Less than two hours after they embarked, the *Brown* weighed anchor and, with Captain Brown at the conn, left Naples.

The *Brown* sailed to Anzio with another Liberty ship, three LSTs (landing ship, tank), and six escort vessels. The landing at Anzio, Operation Shingle, under the command of Maj. Gen. John Lucas, had taken place on 22 January, some four months earlier.[26] Completely surprised by the landings and without adequate forces in the area, which was north of their main defensive line, the Germans could not stop the Allied armies from capturing Anzio and the nearby town of Nettuno and from consolidating their positions on the beachhead. Instead of capitalizing on the enemy's weakness and surprise to push ahead, however, General Lucas elected to spend the next several days building up his troop strength and supplies at the beachhead. Field Marshal Albert Kesselring, the German commander in Italy, used this interval to bring up troops, equipment, and supplies so that when General Lucas attempted to break out from the beachhead, he was stopped by fierce German resistance. However one may judge General Lucas's decisions, he seems to have missed a marvelous opportunity: "At the time of the Anzio landings, apart from a few coastal batteries, there were only two German battalions in the neighbourhood . . . [and as Gen. Siegfried Westphal, Kesselring's chief of staff later wrote] 'the road to Rome . . . was open. No one could have stopped a bold advance-guard entering the Holy City.'"[27] For about six weeks after the landings, fierce fighting caused heavy casualties on both sides, but the Allied forces were not able to advance much beyond the areas they had taken on D-Day.

From about the middle of March until the middle of May the intensity of the action subsided a bit, but, as Ensign Humphreys's "Report" and "Log" and the "Deck Log" make clear, the Allied forces and the enemy were far from inactive. In his "Report," Humphreys records that on 19 May, the day the *Brown* arrived at the beachhead, there was "continuous shelling of enemy lines by our batteries on shore. Occasionally thru-out the day and night shells from the German long range guns would drop in the Harbor Area." To provide some cover, ships in the harbor, including the *Brown*, frequently burned smoke pots at dusk. Col. E. L. Venzke, one of the officers of the 690th Port Company on the *Brown*, recalls that the "Anzio Express [a 218-ton gun mounted on a railway car] shelled us daily but nothing hit closer than 1/2 mile. The cruiser PHILADELPHIA and 2 destroyers were active—shelling German positions about 8 miles north of us."[28] Actually the *Philadelphia* was not the only cruiser shelling the Germans. The British cruiser *Dido*, the American *Brooklyn*, and the French *Emile Bertin* were also engaged. Between 12 and 31 May these four cruisers fired a total of fifty-three hundred rounds at shore positions.[29]

The *Brown* arrived at the Anzio beachhead at 8:00 A.M. on 19 May, anchored about two miles offshore[30] at the place designated by the port control vessel, and almost immediately began discharging cargo from all five holds into barges and into small but versatile amphibious DUKWs (pronounced "ducks"; DUKW was the manufacturer's letter code for the vehicle). Shortly after anchoring, someone noticed that the ship was not swinging at anchor. Several soundings were taken, all but one showing sufficient depth. The one exception, taken abreast number 4 hold, showed twenty-three feet, but since the *Brown* was drawing twenty-five feet aft, obviously she was resting on the bottom. The crew attempted to shift her, but "because of her sluggishness in answering the helm, the position of other vessels and the conditions of the weather [rain, choppy seas, and a fresh breeze], it was deemed less dangerous to remain in the original position." Meanwhile, stevedores continued to unload the *Brown*, and by nightfall she had been lightened sufficiently to swing freely. The

Brown's "Deck Log" makes it sound as though a mistake had been made in assigning her an anchorage where she could run aground, and perhaps it was a mistake. It is also possible, however, that the assignment was deliberate. Rear Adm. Frank J. Lowry, the naval commander at Anzio, often ordered merchant ships to save time by running aground and then anchoring. Emptying the ships floated them off.[31] The negative side to the admiral's idea, however, was the possibility of bottom damage, which the *Brown* in fact incurred.

On Sunday, 21 May, while the Armed Guard crew enjoyed a "day of rest," the Army stevedores continued to discharge cargo. Shortly after noon the British *LCT 388,* while maneuvering alongside, rammed the *Brown* on the starboard side amidships and ripped a one-foot-square hole on the Plimsoll deep-load line.[32] Apparently no immediate action was necessary, or perhaps possible, for it wasn't until the *Brown* returned to Naples that the crew repaired the damage. The next morning the concussion from the violent blast of a bursting shell or depth charge close to the ship broke the gauge glasses on an oil storage tank. About two hundred gallons of oil leaked out before the crew could make repairs.

The port anchor alone could not hold the *Brown* against a rising surf on the night of 22–23 May, and at midnight the starboard anchor was also dropped. The sea was still so turbulent at 6:30 A.M. that an LCT (landing craft, tank) found it impossible to tie up to the *Brown.* Even after moving to deeper water where the surf was not so heavy, the *Brown* broke six hawsers while tying up barges alongside. Despite the conditions, however, the stevedores were able to finish unloading the ship. While the men on the *Brown* were thus engaged on the 23rd, what was happening ashore is barely hinted at in Ensign Humphreys's observation that throughout the day "shells continue to fall in the harbor area [and] shore batteries [are] apparently laying down a continuous barrage." From their position more than two miles offshore, the *Brown's* crew were obviously unaware of the extent of the firepower unleashed as the breakout from the Anzio beachhead, Operation Buffalo, got under way. Maj. Gen. Lucian K. Truscott, Jr., who had replaced General Lucas as commander of VI Corps at Anzio, describes how at the 5:45 A.M. H-Hour "there was a crash of thunder and bright lightning flashes against the sky . . . as more than a thousand guns, infantry cannon, mortars, tanks, and tank destroyers opened fire. . . . [T]he ground quivered and trembled."[33] The breakout from Anzio was coordinated with a massive attack from the south by the American Fifth and the British Eighth Armies against the German forces on the Gustav Line, which bisected Italy roughly halfway between Anzio and Naples. The objective was Rome, taken about two weeks later on 4 June after a drive "characterized by the same bloodletting and painfully slow advances that were the hallmark of the entire Italian campaign."[34]

As if completely oblivious to the battle raging ashore, in the harbor the port security vessel brought an Army physician to the *Brown* to attend to some members of the stevedore gang who were ill. Ensign Humphreys, meanwhile, was concerned with the slowness of the troops who unloaded the ship, blaming their inefficiency on the officers in charge, who "were in no hurry . . . [thereby taking] at least thirty-six hours longer to unload the ship than was necessary." Although the Allies were now on the offensive, the enemy was fighting back: shortly before 1:00 A.M. on 24 May, when the crew rushed to their stations at the sounding of the general alarm, they found the harbor aglow in the light from flares and could watch patrol boats fire their guns, apparently at a German torpedo boat that had attempted to get into the harbor. An hour and a half later the air raid alarm sounded and enemy planes roared in dropping bombs. The antiaircraft guns didn't let them get in close, so no damage was done as far as the men on the *Brown* could see. The raid lasted fifteen minutes. Although there were no more alerts during the day, patrol boats dropped depth charges close by the *Brown* throughout the morning, presumably against midget submarines. Meanwhile the crew was sweeping up the holds and stacking dunnage.

The *Brown* left Anzio during the evening of 24 May in a convoy consisting of two Liberty ships, eight LSTs, and four escorts and shortly afterwards ran into rain squalls that severely limited visibility. As if weather conditions didn't create a sufficient hazard, at 10:00 P.M. the blacked-out ships were ordered to make three forty-five-degree turns in succession. In complete darkness, without radar and with radio silence imposed, the crew had no idea what the other ships were doing. Worried about collision, they no doubt felt like Ensign Humphreys, who commented that "the dawn was welcome this morning after a night of wondering where the other ships in the convoy were." There were no collisions, however, and at daybreak, despite continuing rain and mist, the ships in the convoy were able to resume their stations. Humphreys in his "Report" praised Captain Brown for "an excellent job under the circumstances."

The *Brown* arrived at Naples late in the morning of the 25th and tied up to a berth at noon. The starboard watch of the Armed Guard crew were granted liberty, and part of the Merchant Marine crew spent two hours putting a cement patch on the hole in the *Brown*'s side caused by being rammed by the British LCT in Anzio. The Coast Guard inspector at Naples, after examining the temporary repair, issued a "Certificate of Seaworthiness."[35] Shortly before midnight there was an air raid alarm, and enemy planes came over and bombed the harbor. The sky blazed with "an intense barrage" from the shore batteries and reverberated with the sounds of firing and exploding bombs. After forty-five minutes, the enemy bombers left and the all clear sounded. The crew inspected the ship, and although they found flak on the deck, it had caused no damage.

Early the next morning, 26 May, an Army officer and thirty-two enlisted men boarded the *Brown* to guard 336 POWs, who started embarking shortly afterwards. Later in the day an Army barge came alongside to deliver rations for the POWs. On the 27th the *Brown* and thirty-four other ships left Naples in convoy NV-41.[36] The next morning the convoy commodore ordered the ships in the convoy to hold firing practice. The *Brown*'s crew took their turn between 9:00 and 9:20. The 5"/51, the three 3"/50s, and the eight 20 mm's were all fired, with the Navy gunners firing half a magazine on each 20-mm gun and the Merchant Marine loaders the other half. One benefit of the practice was that it revealed problems with two of the 20-mm guns: number 5 jammed after a few rounds, and number 6 "would not fire at all." The gun crews quickly discovered the causes of the malfunctions and made the necessary repairs. A little over three hours later, the *Brown* arrived at Augusta and went to an anchorage in the harbor, where she remained for two days until the afternoon of the 29th, when she departed for Bizerte in the Mediterranean section of convoy GUS-41.[37]

The *Brown* arrived at Bizerte on 31 May and discovered shortly after arrival that her orders had been changed en route and that she was supposed to have gone to Oran. The convoy commodore, however, had failed to inform Captain Brown of the change. Apparently the authorities decided to change their plans for the *Brown* rather than send her on to Oran, because shortly after noon on 2 June she shifted from a anchorage in Lake Bizerte to a pier where she debarked 278 prisoners, leaving 58 aboard to be discharged the following morning, 3 June. That afternoon she shifted back to an anchorage in

Lake Bizerte. When the ship was secure, a boat drill was held during which number 3 boat was launched and the Merchant and Armed Guard crews were instructed in using it. After the drill the boat was used to take a liberty party to Ferryville, located at the southwest corner of Lake Bizerte. The next day someone worked out a system to dispatch liberty boats to Ferryville at 8:00 A.M. and 1:00, 6:00, and 10:00 P.M. every day while the *Brown* was at anchor. Early in the morning on Tuesday, 6 June, a pilot boarded to take the *Brown* to a quay near the ferry crossing, and at 1:30 P.M. stevedores began loading cargo. On Thursday, 406 Army personnel, including a few nurses,[38] embarked, and on Friday the stevedores finished loading the total of 939 tons of cargo. She left the next morning, 10 June, for Augusta with ten other ships joining convoy KMS-52, which was passing by Bizerte on its way east to Port Said.[39]

While the *Brown* was thus engaged, the Allies on 6 June had launched Overlord, the dramatic and climactic Normandy invasion that made the eventual defeat of Germany inevitable. Among the vast armada needed to transport troops and equipment across the English Channel was the Liberty ship *Benjamin Hawkins,* which had been launched at Bethlehem-Fairfield Shipyard on 7 September 1942, the same day the *Brown* was launched there. Walter J. Botto, who would later serve as the *Brown*'s second mate on Voyages 9 through 12, had recently graduated from the U.S. Merchant Marine Academy at Kings Point, New York, had married immediately after graduation, and shortly thereafter had signed on as the *Hawkins*'s third mate. He recalls that the *Hawkins* went to the Omaha beachhead carrying replacements for the 82d Airborne Division and a small group of reconnaissance pilots and their aircraft. For the next several months the *Hawkins* shuttled between Plymouth, England, and the beachhead, taking troops and equipment over and returning with German prisoners.[40]

The *Brown* arrived in Augusta on Monday, 12 June, two days after leaving Bizerte. A Navy lieutenant from the Armed Guard Inspection Service boarded the ship shortly after her arrival to talk with Captain Brown and to inspect the guns and the Armed Guard crew's quarters and heads. The lieutenant found everything satisfactory and, at Ensign Humphreys's invitation, stayed for dinner. The *Brown* left Augusta for Naples the next morning with thirty-two other ships in convoy VN-46,[41] arrived without incident the following afternoon, Wednesday, 14 June, and dropped anchor in Naples Bay. On Friday a

pilot took the *Brown* to a berth where the troops debarked and stevedores began unloading. Sometime during the morning on Sunday the
Armed Guard had to endure another inspection, this time by an ensign. Ensign Humphreys's terse comment that he thought "Sunday
morning a poor time" suggests some irritation with this visit, and
there is no mention of an invitation to dinner.

After unloading was completed at 2:45 A.M. on Wednesday, 21
June, the *Brown* shifted to an anchorage in the bay. She was still at
anchor on Saturday morning, 24 June, when two barges came alongside to load sea rations, life rafts, and life preservers in preparation
for her next mission. That afternoon the *Brown* left in convoy for
Anzio, where she arrived early the next morning and where on Monday she loaded about a thousand French Colonials—twice the
number she had accommodations for—and a jeep, "the personal car"
of a major in the Free French Army. In all probability these troops
were part of Gen. Alphonse Juin's Corps Expéditionnaire Française,
which was being withdrawn from the Italian campaign for reassignment to Lt. Gen. Alexander M. Patch's Seventh Army in preparation
for Operation Anvil, the Invasion of Southern France, which was to
occur in a little over six weeks.[42] Vernon Joyce, a member of the
Brown's Armed Guard unit, remembers that among the French Colonials were a group of black Senegalese soldiers, "all standing well
over six feet tall and exhibiting facial and body scars that apparently
were [inflicted as] part of their tribal ritual. . . . [They] spoke no English and very little French and were armed with standard American
weapons plus knives. . . . [W]e learned that these knives were primarily ceremonial in nature and that their tribal custom dictated
that when the knives were drawn they could not be replaced in their
sheath until blood was drawn." The soldiers slept on the deck and on
the hatches, and Joyce recalls that "the men going from the midship
housing to watch on the bow and stern proceeded very carefully.
None of us wanted to encounter or awaken these rather formidable
individuals."[43] These "individuals" were probably the Senegalese
troops who would later spearhead the successful attack against the
town of La Valette preparatory to the attack on Toulon.[44]

On Monday evening the *Brown* left Anzio in company with the
Liberty ship *Andrew Moore* and two escorts, and within the first
hour at sea the officers "conducted abandon ship drill for the troops."
By 8:00 the next morning the *Brown* was tied up at a pier in Naples
where the French troops debarked. Early in the afternoon stevedores

started unloading 40 doughnut rafts, 643 life preservers, and the French major's jeep. By noon on Wednesday, "excess life rafts" had been removed from the *Brown.*

Given the complexity of administration during wartime, it is not surprising that at 4:45 the next morning, Thursday, 29 June, a barge with a gang of soldiers aboard came alongside with eighteen life rafts for the *Brown,* presumably not the same ones that had been unloaded the previous day. The sheer number of ships made errors inevitable: during June 1944, for example, 496 merchant ships passed through Naples.[45] A few hours after the delivery of the life rafts another barge delivered about six hundred cases of rations and two hundred life preservers. At 2:00 P.M. the *Brown* left Naples in convoy bound for Cagliari, Sardinia, where she arrived at 5:00 the next afternoon. As the *Brown* came alongside a pier, a strong breeze caught her and banged her up against a wooden fender, "causing a small dent in the plating on starboard side opposite #1 hold." Once the *Brown* was tied up, longshoremen came aboard to get numbers 1 and 3 holds ready for loading. When the Liberty ship *John Lawson* shortly afterwards tied up alongside the *Brown,* the longshoremen began transferring explosives from the *Lawson* into the *Brown*'s 1 and 3 holds. Loading continued through the night and next morning until completed early Saturday afternoon. Then, starting at 7:00 P.M. that evening and lasting slightly over two hours, Italian soldiers boarded the *Brown.* Told that 1,050 troops were to embark, Captain Brown earlier in the day had written to the port commandant in Cagliari to point out that "the S.S. John W. Brown is permitted to carry from the Port of Cagliari to the Port of Naples one thousand (1000) troops. Transportation of more than this number of troops will leave the Master of this vessel in a position where he may be subjected to a heavy fine." He then asked for "documented authorization" for the fifty extra men.[46] Apparently he received authorization because more than a thousand—actually 1,017—finally embarked. Vernon Joyce recalls that the Italian soldiers were equipped with World War I weapons and fieldpieces: "We were astounded when these Italian troops told us, in a most aggressive manner, that they had joined the Allied side . . . to fight the Germans. With the equipment those guys had they weren't going to fight very many people very long."

The *Brown* left Cagliari late the next morning and joined a convoy to Naples. She arrived in Naples the next afternoon, but it wasn't until the following morning, 4 July, that she was able to tie up at a pier to debark the Italian troops. These men had spent what must have been three uncomfortable nights aboard the *Brown*, for more than a thousand men had to make do with accommodations designed for about half that number. Since the temperature was mostly in the upper seventies and there was no rain, spending the entire time on deck might not have been a hardship except for the loss of sleep. After the troops had left and after stores had been loaded from a barge, the *Brown* shifted to an anchorage in Naples Bay.

Early the next afternoon the *Brown* again left Naples for Cagliari. While at sea Ensign Humphreys at muster stressed to his crew, as he had many times previously, that they must take precautions to prevent venereal diseases if they had sexual relations with the women they met ashore. He also reminded them of Army regulations concerning troop transports and of the areas of the ship that are off limits to the Armed Guard crew. The *Brown* reached Cagliari at 5:45 P.M. on 6 July and was berthed by a pilot. With the recent VD lecture fresh in their minds, the Armed Guard crew took liberty ashore. Five gangs of longshoremen boarded at 8:00 P.M. to begin loading ammunition. Work was interrupted just before midnight when an air raid alarm forced everyone to take cover, but at 12:40 on Friday morning the all clear sounded and work on all five holds resumed shortly afterwards. Working around the clock, the gangs finished loading 889 tons of ammunition by Saturday morning, 8 July, and immediately afterwards 144 Royal Air Force and 759 Italian troops embarked. The *Brown* then moved out to an anchorage in the bay until noon, when she joined a convoy for the trip back to Naples, arriving at an anchorage there on Sunday afternoon. The *Brown* had covered the 282 miles at an average speed of 10.65 knots. On Monday evening the ship tied up at a pier, and the Royal Air Force troops debarked immediately afterwards. The Italian troops, however, had to spend another night aboard the *Brown* before debarking the next morning. The *Brown* then shifted to an anchorage in the bay.

Apparently Ensign Humphreys's lecture on Army regulations had not registered with all the members of the Armed Guard. After the Italian troops had left, Lieutenant Donovan, the Army cargo security officer, discovered that the blades were missing from one of the electric fans in the troop quarters. In searching the ship, he finally found them on a fan in the Armed Guard quarters on the starboard side. One of the crew admitted that he had given an Italian soldier three packs of cigarettes to get the blades, which were needed to repair the fan. Lieutenant Donovan decided to make a big issue over what was, after all, a small matter: first he lectured "the entire fo'castle . . . on taking government property," and then decided that the conduct of the guilty sailor during the rest of the voyage would determine his punishment, if any. Since nothing further was ever said, apparently the incident was then forgotten, as it should have been.

Back at a berth on Wednesday, 12 July, the *Brown* discharged cargo until Friday morning, when she shifted to another berth, a move that Ensign Humphreys implicitly criticized, noting that "three more hours and all the cargo could have been unloaded. . . . [Here] it is necessary for a barge to come along side." Unloading the rest of the cargo into a barge didn't cause much of a delay, however, requiring only three and a quarter hours. The next afternoon the *Brown* moved to an anchorage in the bay until the next Wednesday morning, when she shifted to a berth. Shortly afterwards it was discovered that there had been a mix-up somewhere and that the *Brown* was not the ship that was supposed to be at the berth. Thus, less than two hours after tying up she had to move back to an anchorage in the bay.

On 21 July, Ensign Humphreys was surprised to receive a communication from the "Naval Officer in Charge" to practice antiaircraft firing at 6:00 that evening, an order that violated the prohibition against firing in the port area. Humphreys's comment in his "Log" that because of the *Brown*'s position in the anchorage he decided to limit firing to three rounds from each of the 3"/50s clearly shows that he had misgivings about following the order. That he was right to be wary was borne out the following Wednesday when he, Lieutenant Donovan, and several gunnery officers from other merchant ships reported as ordered to the port office to explain why they had fired their guns while anchored in Naples Bay. The following day a Navy lieutenant from the port office boarded the *Brown* to inspect the Armed Guard and also to get a report from Ensign Humphreys about the firing. Two days later another officer from the port office, this time a lieutenant commander, came aboard to gather information about the firing. On this occasion Humphreys showed him the signal log in which Ensign McClenahan had entered the communication ordering the practice firing. As far as Humphreys was concerned, the matter ended there. One wonders, however, if the Navy ever discovered who gave the order and why.

For the Merchant crew, the days were given over to such maintenance jobs as putting fresh drinking water in the lifeboats and rafts

The USS *Catoctin*, AGC-5, was Admiral H. Kent Hewitt's flagship for the Invasion of Southern France. *Naval Institute*

and overhauling the lifeboat equipment. The monotony of shipboard life at anchor was broken on Monday morning, 24 July, when King George VI of England visited Naples. In honor of the visit, the crew by 8:00 A.M. had dressed the *Brown*, that is, had strung a line of flags from the bow to the tops of the foremast, mainmast, and mizzen-mast and then to the stern. At 9:30, when the king toured the harbor, the Armed Guard mustered at their gun stations in dress whites. Adm. H. Kent Hewitt noted in his diary that at 10:45 he attended a ceremony for the king aboard HMS *Orion*, at 11:10 he received the king aboard his flagship, USS *Catoctin*, and at 1:00 he went to Caserta to a luncheon in the king's honor.[47] With the king's visit to the harbor over by noon, it was back to overhauling lifeboats for the Merchant crew on the *Brown*.

The next morning the *Brown* moved to a berth. After first discharging twelve life rafts onto the pier, stevedores prepared the hatches for loading and at 9:00 that night started putting cargo and ammunition into the ship. After seventy-eight hours of around-the-clock work, the gangs finished loading the total of 1,792 tons of cargo at 3:00 A.M. on Saturday, 30 July. That afternoon the *Brown* embarked 15 U.S. Army officers and 299 enlisted men, and a couple of hours later shifted to an anchorage in Naples Bay. Then, for what must have been an extremely boring two weeks for everyone, but especially for the troops, the *Brown* swung at anchor. The Merchant Marine crew kept occupied "overhauling cargo gear" and doing "various jobs about the vessel," obviously nothing urgent. Twice during this time Captain Brown, on orders from the Army Water Division, shifted anchorages, the first time to a position off Torre Annunziata on Castellammare Bay and the second off Torre del Greco. About the only other breaks in the routine consisted of an air raid alarm and taking aboard as passengers a Navy officer and ten Navy enlisted men, the crews of two LCMs (landing craft, mechanized) that had been loaded on top of number 2 hatch. Because the *Brown*'s food supplies were running low, the Navy passengers occasioned some correspondence between Captain Brown and the commanding officer of the Amphibious Boat Pool of the Eighth Fleet, who in a 2 August letter informed Captain Brown that the eleven Navy men were "to be subsisted on the same basis as other Navy personnel aboard"—in other words, not like the Army passengers but instead like the Armed Guard crew whose meals were the same as the Merchant Marine crew's. Captain Brown responded immediately, pointing out that he could not comply, as "this vessel has very depleted stores due to the length of the present voyage," but that he was able to "provide meals for subject Navy personnel at the general mess for passengers aboard this vessel." A form letter dated 3 August from the War Shipping Administration office in Naples also stated that the Navy passengers were to be fed "on the same basis as the Armed Guard Crew," but Captain Brown didn't receive this letter until 9 August and there are no documents indicating that he changed his decision.[48]

Meanwhile, the Navy Armed Guard crew attested to the effectiveness of Ensign Humphreys's VD lectures when the Army physician conducted a short-arm inspection (that is, looked at each man's penis) and saw no visual evidence of venereal disease. As the days passed, however, the entries in Humphreys's "Log" clearly reveal that the men on the *Brown* were preparing themselves for something potentially more dangerous than the women of Naples. On 2 August, Purser Harry Rauch gave an hour-long first aid class for the entire crew. The entry for the next day states that "A Revised and Complete plan [for] General Quarters was presented to the Merchant Of-

ficers and Crew. Eighteen Merchant seamen were assigned gun positions. An emergency squad was organized and a First Aid Squad announced. All are due to report at the sound of General Quarters." Actually one had only to look out over the Bay and Gulf of Naples to
realize that something big was soon to happen. Admiral Hewitt recorded that the gulf and ports on it were crowded with "the assault
ships, landing craft and escort vessels of three major assault forces
[U.S., British, and French], and those of the Sitka force [a group of
two thousand U.S. and Canadian commandos] as well." The gather-
ing included Admiral Hewitt's flagship *Catoctin*, Admiral David-
son's *Augusta* in support of the Sitka group, the French battleship
Lorraine, the British cruiser *Dido* and destroyer *Lookout*, the U.S.
destroyers *Somers* and *Gleaves*, and forty-eight merchant ships. A
total of more than five hundred vessels destined for southern France
filled the Gulf: "Records indicate that 307 landing craft and seventy
five assault transports, assault cargo ships and merchant vessels
were loaded in the Naples area, and that assigned to them were 165
escorts."[49]

The idea for an invasion of southern France was proposed by the
American joint chiefs of staff in August 1943 at the Quebec Conference, where President Roosevelt and British Prime Minister Winston
Churchill met to plan Overlord, the cross-channel Normandy invasion scheduled for spring 1944.[50] The joint chiefs argued that an invasion in the south of France at the same time as Overlord would prevent the Germans from sending reinforcements to Normandy from
their divisions in the south, a rationale that makes clear that from
the beginning the Invasion of Southern France was considered an ad-
junct to the Normandy Invasion. The British agreed to the idea at
this time, but it was not long before Churchill began arguing for
stepping up the Italian campaign instead, a position he persisted in
almost up to the very moment of the landings in southern France.
General Eisenhower did the early planning for the invasion, code-
named Anvil, and by Christmas 1943 had decided the size of the invasion force and that the attack would take place along the Riviera
beaches some fifteen to twenty miles east of Toulon. Upon Eisenhower's being named supreme commander for Overlord, Field Marshal Sir Maitland Wilson assumed overall command of the Mediterranean theater. Although most of the senior officers responsible for
sea, air, and land forces had been selected and were in place, there
were still many differences of opinion and arguments concerning the

appropriate size of the invasion, where exactly it should take place, and, indeed, whether it should take place at all. However, even though it was finally decided not to cancel Anvil, it had to be postponed, primarily because there were not enough landing craft to mount both Overlord and Anvil simultaneously. Despite the postponement, planning continued and determinations were made, including the decision to invade between Cavalaire-sur-Mer and Agay, which are about forty-five miles apart.

On 5 March 1944, Lt. Gen. Alexander M. Patch, Jr., who had been the Army commander in the Guadalcanal campaign in 1943, was named commander of Anvil under the overall command of Field Marshal Wilson. Admiral Hewitt headed the Navy operations, and Brig. Gen. Gordon P. Saville the Army Air Force. The final plan as it evolved over the ensuing months called for airborne troops, French commandos and marines, and the American and Canadian commandos in Sitka group to land at various points around the invasion beaches during the night of 14–15 August. Then, at 8:00 A.M. on the 15th, three American infantry divisions, the 3rd, 45th, and 36th, would invade over beaches code-named Alpha, Delta, and Camel. Two and one-third French divisions were to land the next day and additional French troops on subsequent days until a total of ten divisions were ashore, altogether about 250,000 men from the three American infantry divisions and seven French divisions. The French forces were to move west to take Toulon and Marseilles and then join with the American forces moving north up the Rhone valley toward Lyon and Vichy.

Discussions about the details of Anvil continued into late June, with Churchill still pressing for cancellation. Gen. George C. Marshall, the U.S. Army chief of staff, in countering Churchill's arguments, stressed the importance of Marseilles and Toulon as potential debarkation ports, especially since the channel ports in northern France could not handle the thirty to forty divisions getting ready to come over from the United States. After several final exchanges between Roosevelt and Churchill, the issue was resolved in favor of Anvil, now renamed Dragoon. Despite his attempts to derail Dragoon, which lasted up to a week before the 15 August D-Day, Churchill decided to watch the invasion, since he had planned to be in Italy at that time anyhow.

Although arguments about the contribution of the Invasion of Southern France continue to this day, it has been called "one of the

most painstakingly planned, carefully coordinated, and magnificent-
ly executed amphibious assaults of the war."[51] Of course the absence
of strong enemy resistance contributed to the smoothness of the operation. All the objectives of the invasion were met: the French
forces took Toulon on 27 August and Marseilles on the 28th. Allen T.
Wilt in summary comments that by the end of August, "Allied commanders could indeed be pleased with the results. Three hundred
and eighty miles of French Mediterranean coastline had been liberated and the major ports cleared of the enemy. American forces, with
substantial help from the Resistance, stood at Grenoble, 200 miles
inland by road from the coast, and at Livron, 100 miles up the Rhone.
The FFI [French Forces of the Interior] was in the final stages of taking over the area west of the river. In short, most of southern France
was now in Allied hands."[52]

But all this was still in the future on Saturday, 12 August, when
Captain Brown, Ensign Humphreys, Ensign McClenahan, and
"Sparks" went to a convoy conference aboard the *Perko*. The next afternoon the *Brown* departed Naples in convoy for southern France.
Ships had been leaving the area in convoys throughout the day, and
at 2:00 P.M., an hour before the *Brown*'s departure, convoy SF-1,
which included the *Catoctin*, left Naples. Accompanying Admiral
Hewitt aboard the *Catoctin* were Secretary of the Navy James For-
restal, Generals Patch and Truscott, and French Adm. Andre Lemon-
nier. As convoy SF-1 "moved out of the bay in column . . . it passed
by a British Admirals barge . . . bearing Mr. Winston Churchill. He
was recognized and cheered all down the line by troops and crews. In
turn he waved encouragement at us with his famous 'V' sign and
wished us well."[53] Convoy SM-2, made up of forty-eight merchant
transports, including the *John W. Brown*, plus "10 other vessels with
escorts, carrying follow up troops and supplies for the VIth Corps . . .
followed in the wake of SF-1 at 9 knots."[54] The *Brown* had heaved anchor at 2:36 P.M. and departed Naples at 3:00. At 4:30 the men on the
Brown got a chance to see Churchill, who by then had transferred
from the admiral's barge to a British destroyer. Vernon Joyce remembers that the destroyer, with Churchill standing on the flying
bridge, passed "close aboard" the *Brown*.[55] But passing close to
Churchill was not the only excitement for the men on the *Brown*
that day. As they were leaving Naples, Navy Signalman George Ott
got a glimpse of a tug and garbage barge suddenly appearing off the
starboard side on a collision course. He quickly warned Captain

Brown, who ordered the engine full astern and took evasive action, thereby missing a collision by less than fifty feet.[56] As a busy and exciting day came to a close, the Merchant Marine and Navy crews practiced for what might lie ahead in a general quarters drill that included the participation of the new first aid and emergency squads.

Besides Naples, ships converged on southern France via various routes from Brindisi and Taranto in Italy, from Palermo in Sicily, from Malta, and from Oran. The *Brown* in convoy SM-2 followed route 1 and by noon on 14 August was 169 miles out of Naples steaming for the Strait of Bonifacio, which separates Corsica and Sardinia. At 10:00 that night SM-2 was at the eastern end of the strait,[57] and by noon the following day she had covered an additional 209 miles and was approximately 50 miles west of Calvi on the northwest coast of Corsica and 48 miles from her destination. En route to southern France, Ensign Humphreys and the Armed Guard crew reviewed plans for defending the ship and, to reduce the likelihood of shooting at friendly aircraft, studied dispatches about the kinds of planes that would be providing air cover. During the evening of the day before D-Day, the troops on the ships in the convoy heard a message from General Patch read over loudspeakers: "Soldiers of the Seventh Army: We are embarking for a decisive campaign in Europe. Side by side, wearing the same uniform and using the same equipment, battle experienced French and American Soldiers are fighting with a single purpose and common aim—Destruction of Naziism and the German Army. The agonized people of Europe anxiously await our coming. We cannot and will not fail. We will not stop until the last vestige of German tyranny has been completely crushed. No greater honor could come to us than this opportunity to fight to the bitter end in order to restore all that is good and decent and righteous in mankind. We are an inspired Army. God be with us."[58]

The *John W. Brown* arrived at the Delta assault area in Bougnon Bay off Ste. Maxime at 6:00 P.M., H-Hour plus 10, on 15 August, probably passing close to the battleship *Nevada*, which was leaving the area at the time.[59] Having received no orders about what to do on arrival, the *Brown* spent the next fourteen hours executing "various maneuvers awaiting naval instructions." Although the landing forces met light resistance, the enemy's attempts to fight back forced the ships near the beachhead to take defensive measures. Thus on receiving orders at 8:45 P.M. to make smoke, the *Brown* dropped two smoke pots. Ten minutes later there was an air raid signal, and the crew rushed to general quarters. Navy ships to the *Brown*'s starboard began a barrage. Among them was the battleship *Texas*, which with the coming of darkness had moved further offshore and was "steaming on various courses" in the Delta night retirement area about thirty-five miles offshore, near where the *Brown* was also maneuvering. At 8:55 the *Texas* "observed enemy [air]craft approaching . . . from port quarter under fire from vessels in vicinity." The plane was in range of the *Texas*'s guns three minutes later, and she opened fire with her 3"/50s and 40 mm's. When the *Texas* ceased fire after three minutes she had expended 121 rounds of 3"/50 ammunition and 462 rounds of 40 mm.[60] Not far from the *Texas*, the *Brown* was steaming in the opposite direction when, as Ensign Humphreys described the action, "planes approached from the east off our starboard bow." Nearby ships set the sky ablaze with antiaircraft fire, which got so intense that most of the planes quickly climbed to get out of range, but two peeled off, one heading directly for the *Brown*. Ensign Humphreys ordered the 3"/50s to fire with four-second fuses as the plane swooped at a sixty-degree angle parallel to the *Brown*'s starboard side. In contrast to the 121 rounds fired by the *Texas*, the *Brown*'s three 3"/50s fired a total of 17 rounds, scoring "several near hits." The plane did not get in range of the 20 mm's, and the 5"/51 did not elevate sufficiently to fire at aircraft. As the plane passed beyond the *Brown*, other ships picked up the barrage, but Ensign Humphreys was unable to see whether any hits were scored. The all clear came at 9:25 P.M. The attack had lasted about half an hour.

The *Brown* continued at "various courses" throughout the night awaiting orders. At 6:30 A.M. on 16 August, D-Day plus 1, a Navy enlisted man whose leg had been injured was transferred from an LCT to the *Brown* for treatment by the Army physician on board. By the time the man left four hours later, the *Brown* had finally anchored and had been discharging cargo for two hours into LCTs and LCMs. At noon vehicles were being discharged from all five hatches and troops were debarking with their equipment. Captain Brown in the "Secret Log" identified the first group to debark as "artillery personnel." Unloading continued sporadically because there were often long delays while the men on the ship waited for landing craft to come alongside to take on cargo. There was no enemy action that concerned the *Brown* until an air alert at 8:50 P.M. called the crew to general quarters: three Ju. 88s "approached the ships in the Bay from the east, followed by heavy anti-aircraft fire." The planes came to-

Shuttling between the beachhead at southern France and the Liberty
ships at anchor, these DUKWs are being used to
unload cargo. *National Archives*

ward the *Brown* "broad on the Port Beam." One of the planes "peeled
off and was lost in the gun fire." Ensign Humphreys ordered the
3"/50s to fire, and the crews got off eighteen rounds, but with "unknown" results. After the all clear at 9:30 P.M., discharging cargo resumed and continued during the night and the next day whenever
landing craft were available and the men were not taking cover during the six air raid alerts on the 17th.

And so it continued for the next several days, although never
again were there as many as six air raid alerts in a single day. The
Germans, however, persisted: a few minutes past 9:00 P.M. on 18 August a Ju. 88 attacked the USS *Catoctin*, Admiral Hewitt's flagship,
with what were "probably small anti-personnel bombs . . . one of
which hit on the after well deck, killing 5 enlisted men and injuring
3 officers and 29 enlisted men and injuring 4 enlisted men from the
U.S.S. PT 208 which was close aboard to starboard."[61]

An air raid alert on the 19th illustrates how the tensions of combat and the need to react instantaneously can cause potentially fatal
mistakes. Although Ensign Humphreys recognized the incoming

planes as American P-38 Lightnings, the men at the newly established shore batteries assumed they were enemy planes and opened
fire. Following the lead of the shore batteries, several ships also
opened fire, and the planes quickly flew away to safety. The next
night there was a particularly heavy attack, during which a group of
enemy planes approached off the *Brown*'s port beam at about three
thousand feet altitude. One of them, a Ju. 88, when "dead astern" of
the *Brown* "banked . . . for a run directly over the ship." All the Navy
and merchant ships within range opened such intense fire that the
noise of the other ships' guns prevented the *Brown*'s 3"/50 gun crews
from hearing Ensign Humphreys's order to fire. Thus the 3"/50s remained silent, but the crews of three of the 20-mm guns got so ex-
cited that they opened fire even though not ordered to, and indeed,
too far away from the plane to hit it. Fortunately, the barrage from
the other ships persuaded the Ju. 88 to leave while it could. The enemy, however, didn't provide the only danger. Concentrating on aiming their guns at low-flying enemy planes, a few gunners on other
ships didn't notice that they were firing in the direction of friendly
ships, the *Brown* among them. Ensign Humphreys complained in his
"Log" that "gunfire from surrounding ships was going over our stern
too close for comfort."

During the early morning hours of 21 August, a report that German torpedo boats were in the area brought the crew to battle stations, but none came near the *Brown*. Later that morning the rest of
the troops disembarked onto an LCI (landing craft, infantry). At
about noon the *Brown*, now completely empty, weighed anchor to
leave the beachhead, but then had to drop it again when the orders to
leave were rescinded. About four and a half hours later she again
weighed anchor, proceeded to the assigned rendezvous, and at 6:00
P.M. departed the beachhead in a convoy bound for Naples. Less than
two hours later the *Brown*'s radio operators were alerted that an air
attack was imminent, and soon afterwards two Ju. 88s approached
off the port bow. When they got close enough, Ensign Humphreys ordered first the 3"/50s and then the 20 mm's to open fire, expending
five rounds of 3-inch and nine hundred rounds of 20-mm ammunition. The best he could report, however, was that "near misses were
observed." The next morning the men were again at battle stations
for a half hour after being warned by the escort vessels that a submarine was operating somewhere off the starboard bow. The escorts
dropped depth charges, but with no evidence of success.

No other enemy activity interrupted the *Brown*'s return to an anchorage in Naples on Wednesday, 23 August. After shifting to another anchorage the next morning, the men on the *Brown* settled down to several days of what the "Deck Log" described as "various jobs about the vessel." Captain Brown on the 24th wrote to Commander Kerrins of the U.S. Coast Guard in Naples that the *Brown*'s bottom was "very badly fouled. As a result of this condition it is extremely difficult to maintain convoy speed. During the past voyage it was necessary to run with the by-passes open for the entire voyage."[62] Opening the bypass valves on the main engine allowed more than the normal amount of steam to enter the low- and intermediate-pressure cylinders, thus giving a boost to the engine to make it go faster. Captain Brown also stated—incorrectly—that the *Brown*'s bottom had not been painted since September 1942, almost two years earlier. It had in fact been painted while the *Brown* was drydocked in New York in early June 1943.

Just before noon on Tuesday, 29 August, the *Brown* after six days at anchor went in to a berth, and three gangs of stevedores then came aboard to discharge flatted cargo onto barges, a job that wasn't completed until midnight on the 31st. Meanwhile, fuel and water barges had come alongside to deliver 1,989 barrels of oil and 450 tons of water. On Saturday, 2 September, the *Brown* began loading rations for prisoners from a barge into number 1 'tween deck. In the evening, life rafts from alongside number 4 hatch and Army cargo gear were unloaded onto a barge. Early Sunday afternoon, the *Brown* embarked 28 German POW officers, 472 enlisted POWs,[63] and 1 MP officer and 31 enlisted MPs to guard them. Even before all the POWs had embarked, a pilot had arrived, and soon after all the prisoners were aboard he took the *Brown* to an anchorage in the bay.

The next morning, 4 September, the *Brown* departed Naples in convoy NV-62, made up of seventeen ships bound for Augusta.[64] En route Captain Brown held a fire and boat drill during which the POWs were taught how to use life preservers and rafts. The *Brown* anchored at Augusta early the next afternoon. Later in the afternoon Lieutenant Commander Slater, USNR, of the Armed Guard Inspection Service boarded the ship to inspect the guns and the Armed Guard crew's quarters, all of which he found in "good condition." Two of the Armed Guard crew, however, did not share the "good condition" of the guns and quarters, reporting to Ensign Humphreys that they thought they had contracted gonorrhea in Naples during the week after their return from southern France. Both were given sulfathiazole and ordered to report daily on their condition. Both men later needed a second round of sulfa before the symptoms disappeared.

On Wednesday, 6 September, the *John W. Brown* began her homeward journey in convoy GUS-51. Departure was at 7:00 P.M., and within an hour the *Brown* had taken her place in the convoy. GUS-51 had begun in Alexandria three days earlier and during most of the run in the Mediterranean was escorted by British vessels. The U.S. Navy destroyer escort *Otter* joined the convoy on 8 September while it was steaming at 8.5 knots in a three-column front through the Tunisian War Channel to the east of Bizerte. The convoy changed course on leaving the channel that night and the next morning formed into a "normal broad front of 13 columns."[65] The convoy at full strength numbered about a hundred ships, with Capt. Schuyler F. Cumings, USNR, in the *Esek Hopkins* serving as convoy commodore and about a dozen U.S. Navy ships serving as escorts for the Atlantic crossing.[66] Except for engine trouble that caused the *Brown* to stop the engine for a half hour on the 9th, the trip through the Mediterranean went smoothly. During the morning of the 12th the convoy formed into four columns to pass through the Strait of Gibraltar.[67] About a hour before passing Isla de Tarifa Light halfway through the strait, the *Otter* left her station "to come along starboard side of SS JOHN W. BROWN to render medical assistance" to an MP who showed symptoms of appendicitis. Alongside at 2:34 P.M., the *Otter* transferred Pharmacist Mate Greely Cain to the *Brown* at 3:15. Cain took only a minute or two to decide that a physician was needed. The soldier was then transferred to the *Otter* by breeches buoy at 3:32, followed three minutes later by the pharmacist mate.[68]

Two hours later the convoy was abeam Cape Spartel, and at 6:15 P.M. it began forming into a fifteen-column broad front.[69] The *Brown* was assigned station 76. The seas were smooth, the sky partly cloudy, and the air temperature seventy-five as the convoy steamed out into the Atlantic. During each of the next three days the ships received warnings from Captain Cumings that enemy submarines were nearby, but none was sighted—in all probability because none was there. The rest of the voyage was quiet.

The records of convoy GUS-51 include some details about the *Brown*'s condition at this time. Her foul bottom was again discussed: in a naval message dated 22 September the escort commander reported that the *Brown* was among the ships that needed their bottoms cleaned in order to improve speed. Presumably she was one of the "10 merships with foul bottoms" that prevented the convoy from having a speed of advance greater than 9.3 knots. The *Brown* was also among the several ships needing boiler work, but she was the only ship reported as needing repairs to the circulating and air pumps.[70]

As the days passed, the routine of the trip was uninterrupted except that on 21 September the *Otter* came along the port side of the *Brown* to return the MP. The transfer took only a minute.[71] None of the logs mention whether the soldier in fact had appendicitis, but since he spent nine days aboard the *Otter* his condition must have been fairly serious. Sunday, 24 September, found the *Brown* confronting heavy weather: as described by Second Mate Jakamovics in the "Deck Log," the sky was "heavily overcast," rain fell steadily, and the rough seas' northeasterly swell caused the ship to roll and pitch "heavily." This rough weather continued for the next several days. On the 26th, when about 250 miles east-southeast of the Virginia capes, forty-one ships, including the *Brown*, and five escorts left the convoy. These ships comprised the Chesapeake section of GUS-51. The *Brown* was among the five ships directed to "Hampton Roads for discharge of POW thence Baltimore."[72] The following afternoon the *Brown* twice had to reduce speed to dead slow because of water in the fuel, but after the second incident, which lasted forty minutes, she was able to continue at normal speed.

The "Deck Log" gives 3:30 A.M. on 28 September as the *Brown*'s time of arrival in the United States. After stopping for a pilot the *Brown* increased speed to full ahead, passing Cape Henry Light at 4:55. She entered the submarine gate across Hampton Roads at about 6:30 and anchored at 6:52. The *Brown* had covered 4,547 miles in twenty-one days and fourteen and a half hours at an average speed of 8.81 knots. About two hours later a U.S. Army debarkation officer came on board for ten minutes, probably relaying instructions about debarking the POWs. In the afternoon a pilot came aboard along with a U.S. Public Health Service physician from the quarantine station at Fort Monroe, who checked the Merchant Marine and Navy crews and the passengers for quarantinable diseases. Finding none, he issued a "Certificate of Discharge from National Quarantine," with the proviso that the ship "be mechanically cleaned and deloused in P.O.W. compartments."[73] The pilot took the *Brown* to another anchorage, after which officials from customs and immigration came aboard to take declarations. The next morning a pilot took the *Brown* to Pier 6 in Newport News, where she debarked the prisoners.

Among the prisoners was an arrogant and vain German colonel who "considered himself far and away superior to anyone aboard the ship, including our captain." Acting more like a cruise passenger than a prisoner, on pleasant days during the crossing he sunned himself every morning and afternoon on number 2 hatch and was openly annoyed if crew members happened to disturb him in the course of their duties. On debarking he appeared at the top of the gangway "in full field officer's uniform, medals and all" and demanded that he be saluted as he left. American MP officers stationed at the bottom of the gangway acknowledged his demand and ordered a group of Armed Guard sailors loitering on the pier nearby to join them in saluting the colonel. Several of the sailors simply walked away to avoid saluting, but the one or two who remained saluted as ordered as the stiffly erect colonel strutted by on his way to the deinfestation plant.[74]

After all the POWs had debarked, the troop quarters and number 1 'tween deck were "mechanically cleaned and deloused" as required. The *Brown* then moved to an anchorage, where she stayed for almost two hours until a Hampton Roads pilot came aboard to take her past Old Point Comfort and the submarine gate to a position off buoy 2 to await a Baltimore pilot. By early evening the *Brown* had a pilot aboard and was steaming up the Chesapeake Bay at full ahead. Meanwhile, Purser Harry Rauch had prepared a requisition for slop chest items needed for the next voyage. Since Merchant Mariners, unlike members of the Armed Forces, had to buy their clothing, the slop chest stocked slippers, shoes, boots, socks, gloves, dungarees, blue work shirts, underwear, and the like. Purser Rauch also ordered 72 tubes of Palmolive brushless shaving cream, 72 tubes of Ipana toothpaste, 72 of Pepsodent toothpaste, 48 combs, 24 briar and 24 corncob pipes, 60 decks of poker cards, and 12 of pinochle. Completing the requisition were 1,000 packages of Wrigley's gum, 1,000 of Beech-Nut gum, 2,000 assorted candy bars, 50 cases of Coca Cola, 100,000 each of Camel, Lucky Strike, and Chesterfield cigarettes, 10,000 each of Philip Morris, Old Gold, and Kools, and assorted pipe tobaccos, cigarette papers, and pipe cleaners.[75]

Sometime during the evening, the Armed Guard received orders by radio to have all the service ammunition on deck by arrival in Baltimore. The Armed Guard crew worked in "continuous rain" until midnight and then again early the next morning in occasional light rain to remove the ammunition from the magazines. At 8:26 A.M. on Saturday, 30 September, the *Brown* passed abeam Sandy Point Light just north of the present Bay Bridge and at 10:10 was abeam Fort Carroll in the Patapsco River near the present Francis Scott Key Bridge. When she dropped anchor twenty minutes later, the vessel *Mammy* almost immediately came alongside to remove the service ammunition, a job that took about an hour. While this was going on a customs officer made a ten-minute visit to the ship. In the afternoon, the *Brown* with a pilot aboard and two tugs alongside was taken to Maryland Drydock. At 5:00 P.M. a night mate reported aboard. Thus began the routine in port.

A quiet Sunday on the *Brown* was followed by a busy Monday, 2 October. A half hour after Chief Mate Ritter relieved the night mate at 7:30 A.M., three tugs came alongside and, without using the *Brown*'s engine, shifted her into dry dock. By 9:20 the *Brown* was "on the blocks," and shortly afterwards a hull inspector came aboard to begin the annual inspection. The hull was also examined by a surveyor from the American Bureau of Shipping, who found that the grounding at Anzio six month earlier had caused some minor damage to the after end of the bottom. The necessary repairs were quickly made, allowing the surveyor to recommend "that the vessel be retained in her present class with this Bureau."[76] During the afternoon, yardmen painted the *Brown*'s bottom, using a total of 140 gallons of three different kinds of anticorrosive and antifouling paints from the Baltimore Copper Paint Company. At 3:00 P.M. a shipping commissioner came aboard to pay off the crew, but Chief Mate Ritter stayed aboard until the voyage officially ended about a week later. Early the next morning, 3 October, the dry dock was flooded, and less than an hour later the *Brown* was afloat. With a dry dock captain piloting and three tugs in attendance, the *Brown*, without using her engine, was moved to Pier 3, Pratt Street. A short time later shipyard workers came aboard to make repairs "from wheelhouse to engine room," thereby beginning a routine eighteen-hour workday that continued to the official end of the voyage.

On 5 October, Lt. (jg) James R. Argo boarded the *Brown* to relieve Ensign Humphreys of command of the Armed Guard unit,[77] and the following morning William Leggett, the new second mate, and Albert Petrulis, the new third mate, arrived. Meanwhile, as shipyard workers continued with repairs, stores for the deck, engine, and steward's departments were taken aboard, including coal for the galley's coal stove. On the 10th, with three tugs alongside and a tug captain aboard, the *Brown* was shifted to the Standard Oil dock in Canton, where she took on 10,144 barrels of oil, which when added to the 880 barrels already on board made a total of 11,024 barrels. With the "Night Mate & Gangway watchman on duty," Voyage 4 officially ended at midnight on 10 October 1944.

5

Voyages 5, 6, 7, and 8
The Last Year of War

BY the fall of 1944, the Allies were successfully on the offensive, and it was clear that they would win the war. Hanson W. Baldwin, writing on 1 October in the *New York Times,* summarized the world situation as "overwhelmingly and increasingly favorable to the United Nations; the Axis cause, barring secret weapons or political or psychological imponderables, is hopeless. But the German Army has not yet been finally beaten, and Japan is still protected by a citadel of distance. There is still a war to be won."[1] As it turned out, winning would take eight more months in Europe and eleven in the Pacific at a terrible cost of death and destruction. As for the *John W. Brown,* by the fall of 1944 U-boats were no longer a significant threat anywhere in the North Atlantic. Thirty-one merchant ships were sunk there in all of 1944, but only four during October, November, and December.[2] As a precaution, however, ships continued to cross the Atlantic in convoys.

When Voyage 4 ended at midnight on 10 October 1944 the *John W. Brown* was moored to the Standard Oil docks in Baltimore, where she had taken on fuel. On the morning of the 11th she shifted to an anchorage[3] where she remained until the following morning, when she again shifted, this time to Pennsylvania Railroad Pier 1, the same pier where she has been berthed since the volunteer organization Project Liberty Ship towed her to Baltimore in August 1988. Not much happened as she awaited orders to sail. On 12 October, M. S. Applestein of the U.S. Customs Service came aboard to place under seal the 330,000 cigarettes and forty-eight pounds of tobacco[4] that Purser Rauch had requisitioned at the end of Voyage 4. On the 18th the port director in Baltimore ordered three of the Armed Guard unit detached for "disciplinary action." All had been AWOL, and one had also missed muster because he was too drunk to attend. As the crew readied the *Brown* for sailing on the 19th, the port director detached another of the Armed Guard crew who was AWOL. When the sailor didn't show up before sailing time, his gear was left with the Coast Guard at Pier 1.

At 8:00 P.M. on 19 October the *Brown* left Pier 1 for an anchorage where she stayed only a short time before steaming down the Chesapeake Bay to Hampton Roads. Poor visibility and stormy weather— the aftermath of a hurricane that had raged through the Gulf of Mexico, across Florida, and then northward with winds of fifty to seventy miles per hour at the Virginia capes[5]—forced the *Brown* to anchor just inside Cape Henry at about 10:00 A.M. on the 20th, and it wasn't until 4:30 that afternoon that she got to an anchorage in Hampton Roads to await docking.[6] The following morning, the 21st, the *Brown* tied up at Newport News to load general Army cargo and almost eleven thousand bags of mail[7] and to embark 356 Army personnel consisting of about 30 Army Air Force fighter pilots and troops of the 758th Tank Battalion, one of the few black units to fight in the European theater of operations.[8] Fireman/Watertender George Spittel has vivid memories of the troops embarking at Newport News: "The authorities let only those wives of the troops and pilots who were mothers-to-be to come down to shipside to bid farewell to their men. It was a sad parting—one that I wished I would have never had to witness. Some had to be virtually pulled from the arms of their mates and escorted up the gangplank by MPs. Tears and sobs were too numerous and painful. The men once on board didn't take their eyes off their wives and when the Brown sounded her whistle and we slowly departed from the dock the tears and sobs were even louder. The men were glued to the rail hollering farewells to their dear ones left ashore. And those wives left on the edge of the dock sobbing and waving farewells simultaneously in return—a scene I'll not forget for as long as I live."[9]

The *Brown* sailed from Newport News at 7:00 A.M. on the 22nd and by noon was thirty-nine miles at sea. During the day Captain

Brown had to shuffle some crew members to fill vital positions, most notably promoting George Parurs from AB to acting chief mate. Parurs probably had a foreign license that was not valid in the United States and thus had to sail as an AB, but in this situation Captain Brown could use the foreign license as justification for a temporary promotion. In addition, he promoted Wilfred Olsson from second assistant engineer to acting first assistant and William A. Frost from third assistant to acting second assistant.[10] The *Brown* was one of the fifty-eight ships in the Norfolk section of convoy UGS-58, which was joined by the twenty-seven ships of the New York section off Cape Henry. The two sections met at 3:00 P.M., and by 6:00 the convoy had formed into thirteen columns steaming first at six knots and shortly afterwards at nine.[11] The convoy thus consisted of eighty-five ships, later increased to eighty-seven by two "joiners." Capt. G. F. Bunnell, USNR, in the *Robert T. Hill* served as convoy commodore. The *Brown*, in position 74, was the fourth ship in the seventh column, the commodore's column. The escort group, which also joined off Cape Henry, was made up of eleven vessels commanded by Capt. W. R. Headden, USN, on the destroyer *Selfridge*.[12] In addition, land-based aircraft accompanied the convoy while it was in range of the United States, Bermuda, and the Azores, and "part of the time" in the Mediterranean. The enemy did not appear, however, and only once during the crossing did Lieutenant Argo note in his "Log" that an escort dropped depth charges.

During the first half of the crossing the weather was often heavy, with frequent strong winds and on one occasion "boisterous" seas. On one particularly stormy day, as an Armed Guardsman struggled to fit a canvas cover onto his 20 mm in number 1 gun tub on the starboard bow, the gusting, slashing wind suddenly caught the cover and filled it like a sail. Before the startled sailor could let go, the ballooning cover had lifted him out of the tub and dropped him onto the main deck about ten feet below. Lucky enough to be blown onto the deck and not overboard where he probably would have been lost in the frigid raging seas, the sailor was doubly lucky in that he wasn't killed or even badly hurt when he was flung onto the steel deck. Indeed, the Army physician who examined him found only a small scratch on his back and a skinned left leg.

Nineteen forty-four was a presidential election year, with President Roosevelt running for a fourth term against Republican nominee Thomas E. Dewey. Apparently Lieutenant Argo was in charge of

The *Brown* frequently encountered rough seas like these. *James P. Farley*

voting for both the Merchant Marine and Navy crews, for on 30 October he put up notices in the mess rooms announcing that on 2 November the crew could go to the wheelhouse to vote. Meanwhile, the convoy continued its eastward progress and on 3 November spent an hour and three-quarters maneuvering into a twelve-column front from the thirteen-column front it had formed on leaving Hampton Roads.[13] Two days later, when the convoy was about three days out from the Strait of Gibraltar, the destroyer escort *Varian* continued preparations for arrival in the Mediterranean by going among the merchant ships to "hand deliver" routing instructions from the convoy commodore.[14] Meanwhile on the *Brown* on this pleasant Sunday morning, Lieutenant Argo at 10:00 conducted a short open-air church service on one of the hatches. After a brief opening prayer repeated in unison, the men sang "What a Friend We Have in Jesus." A responsive reading followed that in one section gave the only acknowledgment in the whole service that the men were part of a war effort: to Lieutenant Argo's prayer "We pray thee for our country:

Thou hast made her free that we may freely love and serve her. Guide and sustain thy servant the President and all in lawful authority. Defend the true welfare of our land and people, and the cause of all the United Nations," the men responded "Help us to be good soldiers of liberty and justice, we humbly beseech thee." To conclude the service the group sang "God Bless America" and recited the Lord's Prayer, and Lieutenant Argo pronounced the benediction.[15]

As on previous trips, more and more Portuguese fishing boats were seen as the convoy neared the Strait of Gibraltar, but on this trip they were even more hazardous than usual. On 6 November, the USS *Scroggins*, an escort, tried to divert one of them out of the path of the convoy, but the fishing boat moved just enough to avoid getting hit and then slipped between the merchant ships and the escorts on the starboard flank.[16] At about dawn the next morning there were still fishing vessels about as the convoy plunged through rough seas with visibility at five miles. The convoy was steaming at 9.5 knots on course 084 about three hundred miles southwest of the Strait of Gibraltar when escorts spotted the Portuguese fishing vessel *Alberto Segundo* a short distance off the convoy's starboard beam moving at about 11.0 knots on course 045, a speed and course that would take her into the convoy. At 5:50 A.M. the Navy escort *Weber* left her station to try to get between the *Segundo* and the convoy in order to direct her away.[17] The *Weber* increased speed to 15.0 knots and signaled the *Segundo* to stop, but she ignored the order. At 5:55 the *Weber* "passed 500 yards astern" of the *Segundo*, now on course 354 heading directly toward the convoy and still moving at 11.0 knots. After passing astern, the *Weber* immediately changed course to 000 to come along the starboard side of the *Segundo*. As she began to overtake the *Segundo*, the *Weber* illuminated her with spotlights and prepared to give instructions over a bullhorn. At that instant the *Segundo*, without warning, changed course to 040, putting her directly in the path of the *Weber*, still steaming at 15.0 knots. The *Weber* immediately went to full astern and sounded collision quarters, but with no way to avoid a collision, she plowed into the *Segundo* "just abaft" her starboard bow. The *Weber* sustained a four-foot hole in the stem above the waterline and flooding in the forward peak tanks, "but not of such character as to greatly reduce the military efficiency of the ship." The *Segundo*, however, was so severely damaged that her master and twenty-two-man crew had to abandon ship and come aboard the *Weber* over the lifelines. It was simply luck that no one was killed or injured. The *Weber*, now joined by the *Otter*, remained near the *Segundo* for an hour and a half until she finally rolled over on her port side and sank. The *Weber* and the *Otter* then left the area to overtake the convoy, which by this time was about fifteen miles away. There is no evidence in her extant logs that anyone in the *Brown* knew of the incident.

But the men in the *Brown* were aware that at 8:00 the next morning, 8 November, the "escort on our starboard beam dropped several depth charges." Later that morning the convoy formed a four-column front to pass through the strait.[18] While steaming through the strait that afternoon, the men on the ships got an unexpected break in the routine when two PBY Catalinas put on an air show of sorts. As described by Lieutenant Argo, the two planes "flew an elliptical course across the columns of the convoy. On several of these flights they were within 500 yards of this ship at an altitude of about 100 feet. On one occasion they flew within 50 yards of the fantail at an altitude of about 50 feet." Meanwhile, the *Weber* left the convoy temporarily to go into Rosia Bay, Gibraltar, to debark the survivors of the *Alberto Segundo*.[19] As the convoy came to the eastern end of the strait, the British minelaying submarine *Rorqual* joined it. At 6:00 P.M., with Point Europa abeam to port seven miles, the convoy left the Strait of Gibraltar and began steaming at eight knots; at 7:00 it formed an eleven-column front.[20]

Four days later, when the convoy was off the coast of Algeria near Bougie, Commodore C. H. G. Benson, RN, on the *Noranda Park* in position 101[21] relieved Captain Bunnell as convoy commodore. The U.S. Navy ocean escort, however, continued with the convoy. By this time thirty-five ships assigned to the first four columns had been detached, leaving fifty-two to continue east in the Mediterranean. Of these, thirty-one, including the *Brown*, were bound for Augusta. Most of the rest were headed for the Suez Canal on their way to the Persian Gulf or India. That afternoon the convoy formed into a three-column front in preparation for entering the Tunisian War Channel east of Bizerte. During the night the Bône section left the convoy, and shortly before dawn on November 12 the convoy entered the swept channel.[22] At 9:15 A.M. British escorts relieved the American escorts.[23]

While the convoy was thus engaged, on the *Brown* there were problems of a different nature to deal with. On the 11th the Army physician aboard the *Brown* was again called, this time to examine one of the Armed Guard crew for gonorrhea. Finding that the sailor was infected, the physician treated him with sulfa and with the "wonder drug" penicillin, which only recently had become available for general use by the Armed Forces. Penicillin, some said, made gonorrhea no worse than the common cold.

The seas were heavy and the wind strong on the 11th, and although the seas were moderating on the 12th, and both the winds and sea were moderate on the 13th, the weather conditions made visibility so poor that to reduce the risk of collisions Commodore Benson ordered the ships to burn their blue stern lights on all three nights. At no other time during the entire voyage were lights shown. In a letter to his wife written on the 13th, just before arrival in Augusta, George Spittel, after commenting on the "tough going the past three days," told her that "the food situation is pretty bad" but that at an Army PX on board "I can get anything at all—all kinds of candy, cakes, Coca-Cola, Lifesavers, chocolates, all kinds of juice, plenty of chewing gum, etc."[24] In thinking about those days many years later, however, Spittel changed his mind about the food and conceded that it "wasn't bad at all considering the times. We had a very good 2nd cook and baker and he made excellent puddings—rice, bread, etc., baked to perfection."[25]

On 14 November the *Brown* anchored at Augusta. In his "Report" of the voyage to the Chief of Naval Operations via the port officer in Naples, dated 17 November, Lieutenant Argo complained that "approximately 2 ½ days were wasted by routing this vessel to Naples Italy via Augusta, Sicily, instead of directly to Naples Italy." In the "First Endorsement" to Lieutenant Argo's "Report," Lt. Comdr. C. W. Williams, Jr., USNR, the port officer in Naples, supported the idea of going directly to Naples, commenting that "inasmuch as ships are now being sailed independently through the Mediterranean, it is felt that loss of turnabout together with the pilferage and sale of ships stores to bum boats resulting from routing of ships via Augusta, Sicily, as experienced by this ship and numerous others, should be eliminated if possible." Bumboats caused problems wherever American ships went. Vernon Joyce recalls that the people in the bumboats in Augusta and the Strait of Messina were brazen and persistent in bringing their boats alongside ships to barter for American goods, especially cigarettes. On one occasion some of the men on the *Brown* traded cigarettes for some very large, juicy-looking oranges that turned out to be mostly rind with hardly any fruit. Feeling cheated and wanting to get even, they lured a bumboat alongside and then doused its occupants with the fire hose. As the *Brown's* crew laughed and jeered, the bumboat scurried out of range as fast as it could.[26] Despite the real problems caused by bumboats, which also included theft and prostitution, Commander Williams's suggestion was turned down in the "Second Endorsement" to the "Report" with the observation that although it would be desirable if possible to bypass Augusta, the commander in chief Mediterranean "considers it very necessary that vessels proceeding to Italian ports stop at Augusta for orders, in the interests of safety to shipping and to avoid port congestion at such ports as Naples and Leghorn." Thus although Augusta was no longer needed as a station on the Mediterranean convoy route, the port continued to be used for traffic control for a while longer. In due course even this function became unnecessary, and in February 1945, on Voyage 6, the *Brown* sailed directly to Naples on a course that took her north of Sicily rather than south and east via Augusta and the Strait of Messina.

The *Brown* remained in Augusta until the morning of 16 November, when she weighed anchor and sailed "solo" for Naples. Late that morning Lieutenant Argo held gunnery practice during which the 20-mm gunners took turns using number 7 on the starboard side aft to fire a total of 120 rounds at a kite target. The *Brown* arrived in Naples on the 17th, having made the 246-mile trip in twenty-one hours and forty-five minutes at an average speed of 11.3 knots. As George Spittel told his wife, "We opened her all the way up as soon as we got out of the nets [at Augusta] and didn't touch the throttle once until we got into the harbor of Naples," where she anchored for a while before going into a pier to debark the Air Force pilots and to take on food and water.[27] During the day the Army physician examined the sailor with gonorrhea, finding him, after six days of treatment, "free of discharge" and therefore cured.

At about noon on Saturday, 18 November, the *Brown* shifted from the pier to an anchorage in the Gulf of Naples. "From where we are anchored here," George Spittel wrote to his wife, "I can see the 'Isle of Capri,' which is just about two miles South of here. To the west towering up into the sky just in back of Naples I can see Mt. Vesuvius. In the day time you can see it smoking if it isn't covered by clouds."[28] The *Brown* swung at anchor in the Gulf of Naples until the 23rd, when she weighed anchor and departed Naples in convoy VN-78,[29] consisting of nine ships and two escorts bound for Piom-

bino, a little over two hundred miles north of Naples. As cargo operations at Piombino had ended two months earlier,[30] apparently the
port was being used as a traffic control station for Leghorn in much
the same way that Augusta was used for Naples. The *Brown* arrived
there in the afternoon of 24 November and the next morning departed in convoy for Leghorn, some forty miles further north, where
she anchored five hours later.

Leghorn had been taken by the Allies on 19 July 1944, about four
months earlier. As with Naples, the Germans before leaving had
done as much as they could to slow the Allies: "The northern and
southern entrances to the harbor were blocked by sunken ships, the
harbor and town were heavily mined, and enemy shelling for a time
delayed clearance. Quay walls had been shattered by explosives,
alongside berths were inaccessible, and rail facilities were inoper-
able."[31] Salvage crews repaired the facilities so effectively and quickly, however, that the port was able to handle its first Liberty ship, the
Theodore Sedgwick, on 20 August, a month after the Allies took the
city. By the time of the *Brown*'s arrival on November 24, three
months after the *Sedgwick*'s, Leghorn, with "twelve berths ready for
Liberties and another almost completed, one for coasters and one for
colliers, two for tankers, and several hards [ramps] for landing craft,"
was handling all supplies for the Fifth Army.[32] After anchoring, the
Brown debarked the troops of the 758th Tank Battalion. For the next
eight days she discharged cargo at Leghorn and on 2 and 3 December
loaded thirty-five tons of mail and twenty-three tons of post office
equipment.[33] She completed both loading and discharging on 3 December, two days later than necessary in Lieutenant Argo's opinion,
because of "inefficient handling and unloading of cargo from No. 5
hold . . . by U.S. Army port battalion."

On 4 December the *Brown*, along with three other ships and two
escorts, departed Leghorn for Piombino in convoy NV-80[34] and anchored there after a run of about four and a half hours. The next
morning she left Piombino in convoy for Naples, where she arrived a
little over twenty-six hours later. At Naples the *Brown* loaded cigarettes for Oran and, interestingly, two boxes, weighing seven tons, of
"personal impedimenta"—furniture, according to Lieutenant Argo—
to be delivered to a Mr. Malon C. Taylor in New York City.[35] One
wonders why the *Brown*, working for the Army Transport Service,
was used to carry seven tons of a civilian's personal property during
wartime, unless of course the whole business was a cover for some-

thing secret. On 7 December, the third anniversary of Pearl Harbor, the *Brown* departed Naples bound for Oran. As there was no longer a threat from U-boats and enemy planes south of Naples—one of the benefits flowing from the Invasion of Southern France—the *Brown* sailed "solo" and was not required to zigzag. At night she burned her sidelights and masthead lights at full brilliancy. The *Brown* endured three full days of "strong head winds," "fresh gales," and "heavy seas" before anchoring in Oran on 11 December. She discharged the cigarettes on the 11th and spent the 12th awaiting a convoy.

On 13 December the *Brown* departed Oran for the United States in convoy GUS-61,[36] consisting of sixty-nine ships under the command of Capt. C. B. Platt, USN (Ret.), in the Norwegian motor ship *Salamis* and an escort of ten ships under Captain Carlin in the Coast Guard cutter *Campbell*. The convoy passed through the Strait of Gibraltar shortly before noon on the 14th. Christmas morning found it steaming across a smooth sea about a thousand miles out of New York. For an hour between 10:00 and 11:00 in the morning the Navy escort *Wyffels* left her station to pass between columns five and six of the convoy as her crew sang Christmas carols.[37] George Spittel remembers that the *Wyffels* "had a fully decked-out Santa Claus waving and wishing everyone a Merry Christmas over a loud-speaker system and playing Christmas music—I noticed numerous wet cheeks among many of the armed guard who clambered to the rail. Some of these fellas were barely eighteen." That evening the *Brown*'s Merchant Marine and Navy officers held a surprise Christmas party for the crew in number 3 'tween deck. The officers had decorated it with tinsel and lights and served cookies, cake, candy, and punch. Captain Brown, Lieutenant Argo, and Lieutenant Tompkins, the other gunnery officer, spoke, and everyone joined in singing "White Christmas" and "I'll Be Home for Christmas." The crew were in high spirits as they ate and sang and joked with one another, but George Spittel's festive mood suddenly changed after a time when he recalled talking to the pilots and soldiers in this same space a month earlier and realized that some of them would never be home for Christmas again. The same thoughts may have occurred to others, for suddenly the party was over and men who had been cheerful and happy an hour earlier quietly returned to their quarters to get some sleep before going on watch.[38]

Sometime later that night, Third Mate Albert Petrulis was on his 8:00 to midnight watch on the flying bridge keeping an eye out for other blacked-out ships in the darkness and making certain that the *Brown* stayed on station as the convoy steamed across a smooth sea. About halfway through the watch, as he walked over to the starboard wing of the bridge, he heard something thud off the canvas dodger around the railing. Then he heard another thud and a splattering sound. Glancing down and seeing a snowball on the deck, he quickly looked up just in time to glimpse Second Asst. Engineer William Frost ducking behind the stack with about a dozen snowballs cradled in his arm. Petrulis chased after Frost, who kept throwing snowballs as the two men dodged behind the stack and scampered around ventilators in the confined space of the flying bridge. When Frost had thrown them all, they laughed together as Frost explained that he had made the snowballs from ice scooped off the pipes in the refrigeration system. Suddenly they became aware that Captain Brown had quietly joined them on the flying bridge. The captain asked how the watch was going, and Petrulis hastily assured him that nothing out of the ordinary was happening. The captain nodded, walked over to a ventilator and looked in it, looked back at Petrulis, slowly nodded his head, and without a word walked to the ladder to the bridge deck and went below. Frost and Petrulis immediately dashed over to peer down the ventilator shaft and were stunned to see that a snowball lay splattered on Captain Brown's desk directly below. When the two officers sheepishly admitted what they were doing and apologized to Captain Brown, they found out that the incident was even worse than they thought. The captain had been stretched out in his bunk reading when Steward Frederic Clar came by with a platter of cold sliced turkey left over from Christmas dinner. The steward put the platter on the captain's desk directly under the ventilator shaft outlet. As the captain strolled from his bedroom to the office, stretching sleepily and looking forward to a bedtime treat, suddenly there was a swooshing sound in the ventilator and a snowball plopped onto his desk right next to the plate of turkey. Surprised and startled, he went up to the flying bridge to investigate. Luckily for the two officers, Captain Brown could see the humor in the episode and accepted their apologies.[39] No doubt he chuckled to himself over their embarrassment.

On 26 December, Captain Platt, the convoy commodore, received a naval message from the commander of the eastern sea frontier ordering him to have the ships in the convoy "burn dim navigation lights" west of 072 degrees west latitude, about 240 miles off the coast of Virginia. This was yet another indication that by this stage of the war the danger of collision in tightly packed convoys was greater than the danger from U-boats. Shortly before the convoy reached 072 degrees on the 28th, it encountered northwesterly gales and "mountainous seas." A naval message that day from Captain Carlin, the escort commander, reported that the "convoy [was] spread out in gale on account of difference in ballasting. Some Liberties not ballasted and hove to." According to Captain Platt, the gale cut the convoy's speed of advance to about four knots. In the midst of the storm the New York section of GUS-61, consisting of the *Brown* and twenty-seven other ships, left the rest of the convoy and headed northwest at 5.5 knots. The New York section—except for the *Hilary A. Herbert,* which came in six hours later—arrived at Ambrose at 3:15 in the afternoon of 29 December.[40] The *John W. Brown* arrived inside the nets at 4:30 and at her anchorage in New York harbor an hour later.

Sometime during the next several days the *Brown* shifted to the 30th Street Pier in Brooklyn, where she definitely was on 4 January 1945.[41] On Saturday, 30 December, the morning after arrival, Lieutenant Argo mustered the Armed Guard crew to instruct them in security precautions in port, including how to handle the .45-caliber pistol and what to do in case of fire alarms and air raid alerts. And because at least one man obviously needed to hear the lecture, he again went over in detail how to avoid venereal diseases. This was also the Saturday that "they stopped cooking" on the *Brown,* forcing the crew to go ashore for meals.[42] On New Year's Day, Ensign McClenahan and twenty-eight enlisted men were detached, and on the same day Lt. (jg) Edward H. O'Connor and twenty-eight enlisted men boarded the *Brown* to replace them. Lieutenant Argo, who had been promoted to full lieutenant at the end of Voyage 5, stayed aboard to continue as Armed Guard commander for the sixth voyage, as did Lieutenant Tompkins. The Navy unit thus totaled three officers and thirty-eight enlisted men, two of whom were signalmen and three, radiomen. The Merchant Marine crew were paid off during the afternoon of 2 January, but George Spittel could not leave until a new fireman came aboard to relieve him, expected perhaps the next day, perhaps not until the end of the week. When he wrote to his wife that afternoon, he and the engineers were the only personnel aboard,[43] although Captain Brown, Purser Harry E. Rauch, Steward Frederic Clar, and three crewmen would continue on the next voyage. Spittel was probably able to leave for home the next day, 3 January, because on that date William Ward signed coastwise articles as fireman.

Foreign articles for Voyage 6 were signed in New York during the morning of 9 January,[44] and later that same morning the *Brown* sailed independently for Lynnhaven Roads, where she dropped anchor exactly twenty-four hours later.[45] She remained at Lynnhaven Roads for about four hours before leaving for Charleston, South Carolina. At about 5:15 the following afternoon, 11 January, when approximately sixty miles east of Cape Fear, North Carolina, the Navy lookouts sighted a floating mine about 250 yards off the *Brown's* starboard side and reported it to Third Mate William Griffin, on watch on the bridge in relief of Chief Mate Herman Yost, who was at supper. Griffin, who had seen the mine at about the same time, did not sound the general alarm, nor did he tell Captain Brown and Lieutenant Argo about it until a half hour later when he went to the saloon for supper. Because the mine by then was at least five miles away and darkness had fallen, Captain Brown "did not deem it advisable to return and hunt for it." Apparently Third Mate Griffin, on his first trip as an officer, was not aware that drifting mines should always be destroyed. Lieutenant Argo reprimanded the Navy signalman on watch who failed to inform him of the mine and "strongly urged" Third Mate Griffin to ring the general alarm if he ever saw another one. When the *Brown* arrived in Charleston, Lieutenant Argo reported the incident to the port director, Capt. W. Ancrum, USN (Ret.), who in turn reported it to the Chief of Naval Operations with the obvious comment that "it seems evident that neither the Third Mate nor the Navy Signalman had ever been impressed with the importance of destroying the mine." And there the subject ended. One can only hope that the mine never caused hurt.

On 12 January the *Brown* arrived at Charleston, where she loaded jeeps and other military vehicles on deck and added beer and cigarettes to the general Army cargo that had been loaded in New York. A large group of MPs guarded this tempting cargo, and they put anything that fell out of the cargo nets into a small fenced area they set up nearby.[46] With a draft of 25'9" forward and 28'5" aft, the *Brown* was now fully loaded.[47] But before leaving, what would seem to be a long overdue alteration was made: as Lieutenant Argo explained, the "W.S.A. replaced glass covers over magazine flood valves [used to flood the magazines in case of fire] with hinged screen covers having a hasp attached so they could be locked. The old covers with the glass could not be opened except by breaking the glass. For this reason the flood valves had not been tested." Now having easy access to them, Lieutenant Argo tested the fore and aft valves and found them "O.K."

On 13 January, William Ward was discharged from his coastwise voyage, and on the 14th he signed on for a foreign voyage. Shortly after noon on the 17th the *Brown* "cast off" and at 2:30 took departure from Charleston. As she steamed "solo" back up the coast at 10.5 knots, the *Brown* passed one freighter and three LCIs that were also headed north. After a 445-mile trip, she arrived at the Hampton Roads pilot station at 8:50 a.m. on the 19th and at 10:00 "arrived inside nets at entrance to Chesapeake Bay." During the *Brown's* four days in the area, she went into Newport News to embark fifty-four Army passengers. Sometime on the 20th a few members of the crew found a way to help themselves to some of the beer in the cargo. As Lieutenant Argo recorded the incident in his "Log," on 21 January "the Cargo Security Officer discovered that the cargo had been broached in #2 and #4 holds. About 15 cases of beer had been removed. Coast Guard and F.B.I. came aboard to investigate. The investigation revealed that only one Navy man was involved. [He] . . . drank 2 bottles of beer the night of 20 Jan. 1945 in the Chief Cook's foc'sle. The investigation revealed that he did not know the beer given him came from the cargo. The offenses he was guilty of were drinking aboard ship and entering the merchant crews foc'sles which are out of bounds. For this he was severely reprimanded."

On 22 January there was a convoy conference, and the next morning the *Brown* started to head out of Hampton Roads. While she was still in the Chesapeake Bay, however, a filter in her hot well got clogged,[48] stopping the flow of water from the condenser to the boilers. The *Brown* had to anchor while the filter was cleaned, but despite the delay she was able to catch up to take her place in convoy UGS-70 at 10:30 the next morning, 24 January. Convoy UGS-70 consisted of fifty-four ships spread out in twelve columns, with the *Brown* assigned position 53, the third ship in the fifth column. Among the other ships was the *Arthur M. Huddell*, which would be tied up next to the *Brown* some forty years later when both vessels were in the reserve fleet in the James River in Virginia and which would become a rich source of parts, including a rudder, for the restoration of the *Brown*. The convoy commodore was Comdr. Frederick T. Stevenson, USNR, in the *John F. Myers* in position 71, and the five escorts were commanded by Comdr. F. C. B. McCune, USN, in the destroyer *Ericsson*.

By the time the *Brown* assumed station on 24 January, the convoy was encountering heavy seas and westerly winds of up to fifty-six miles per hour. This weather lasted six days. On the *Brown* on the 25th "heavy seas tore all but one of the five smoke floats off the racks on the port side. One went over the side, one ignited on deck and the other two were recovered and lashed on deck." The crew then lashed down all the other smoke floats. Meanwhile water poured into the aft magazine through the ventilator, covering the decks in the 5"/51 and 20-mm powder rooms with about four inches of water before the crew managed to close the ventilator. The men then had to get the water out and check the ammunition for wet-ness. Fortunately the water had not got into the 5"/51 powder can-isters and the boxes of 20-mm ammunition. In his "Brief Narrative" on "Convoy Form 'D,'" Commander Stevenson recorded that from the 24th through the 26th the convoy as a whole reported ten life-boats and four rafts lost overboard and sixteen lifeboats and one raft badly damaged. In addition, the seas crashing over the decks dam-aged the deck cargo on a number of ships.

As the USS *Ericsson* was patrolling about five thousand yards ahead of the convoy at 3:00 A.M. on 25 January, the seas surging against her port side made her suddenly lurch so "heavily" to star-board that her steering power failed, a small electrical fire broke out, and the gyro system stopped. One crewman was injured, suffering a broken nose, abrasions on his chest, and a sprained back. The steer-ing was quickly restored and the fire extinguished, but it took four hours to fix the gyro. Meanwhile, out on deck the seas had washed the motor whaleboat away, but worst of all they had also swept a crew member overboard.[49] A naval message on the 25th from the es-cort tersely reported that the *Ericsson* was at 35° 28' N, 66° 56' W, to the northwest of Bermuda when the sailor, Boatswains Mate First Class John J. Nealand, was lost and that the rear escort, the *Bangor*, was to conduct a search until 9:00 A.M. Realistically there was no chance of finding Nealand in the darkness, especially in tumultuous seas with the wind roaring at about forty knots. But the impossible happened. At 3:30 A.M., about half an hour after Nealand had gone over the side, men on the *John F. Myers* heard a cry for help above the noise of the wind and sea. They threw a lighted life ring over the starboard side "in hopes that the man get it and be seen by the Escort." At 5:35 A.M., two hours later, the *Bangor* sighted a "floating light" that turned out to be attached to an empty life ring, presumably the one thrown by the *Myers.* The *Bangor* continued searching and at 7:35, against all odds, sighted a man clinging to a life float. In such bad weather it took another half hour of maneuvering before the *Bangor* was able to get close enough to the float to bring the man aboard. Nealand had been in the water for more than four and a half hours and had been carried some 20 miles by the sea. Although not hurt, he was "suffering from shock and exposure." An attempt on 31 January to return Nealand to the *Ericsson* had to be aborted because of heavy winds, and it wasn't until 8 February, after the two ships had tied up in Mers el-Kébir, Algeria, that he finally rejoined his ship.

Problems of one sort or another continued as convoy UGS-70 made its way across the hostile winter seas of the Atlantic. While the storm still raged, the blacked-out convoy on 26 January had to make an emergency turn to port at about 8:00 in the evening "to avoid other traffic" and was not able to resume base course for almost an hour. But the possibility of collision could not always be anticipated and avoided. At about 10:40 P.M. on the 31st, with the convoy still battling heavy seas and a strong northwest breeze, the *Michael Anagnos,* a Greek freighter in station 82, suddenly veered hard to starboard and collided with the *British Patience,* a tanker in station 92, causing heavy damage to both. The masters of the two vessels sent Commander Stevenson, the convoy commodore, a number of messages that, although conflicting in some details, nevertheless make clear that the *Anagnos* went out of control because her steering mechanism failed and that the *British Patience* could not take "avoiding action" in time. The *Anagnos* was so badly damaged that she had to leave the convoy to put in at the Azores for emergency repairs, but the *British Patience,* despite extensive damage, was able to continue on with the convoy.[50]

Commander Stevenson's summary on "Convoy Form 'D'" gives an idea of the kinds of activities that were more typical during convoy operations: eleven merchant ships, but not the *Brown,* held gunnery practice, seven asked escorts for medical assistance, and twelve had breakdowns that caused them to leave the convoy temporarily while repairs were made. As the convoy approached the Strait of Gibraltar on 7 February, Commander Stevenson ordered a four-column front and a speed of 8.5 knots. Once in the Mediterranean, he dispersed the convoy.[51] The *Brown* then proceeded toward Naples independently.

On 9 February the *Brown*'s engineers had to cut out the port boiler "because of overheating of back support I beam and boiler casings." Speed was reduced to about 8.5 knots, three less than the 11.5 knots the *Brown* had made the previous day. It took thirty-six hours, until the night of 10 February, for the boiler to cool sufficiently for the engineers to examine it and discover that the back fire wall had broken down.[52] On the 9th Lieutenant Argo had held target practice, but he could not fire the 5"/51 because with only one boiler in operation "it was not deemed advisable to use steam to operate the air compressor for the gas ejection system." The number 4 20 mm was also out of action because it lacked double-loading stop plungers and springs. Replacements were not available in Naples or Leghorn, but during the return trip someone on the *Brown* improvised parts that worked. It wasn't until the *Brown* returned to New York that the Navy supplied new springs, but even in New York there were no stop plungers.

The *Brown* arrived at Naples during the evening of 11 February, and the troops debarked the next day. On the 13th and 14th the brickwork in the boiler was repaired and the port superheater valve was removed, overhauled, and reinstalled.[53] The 15th and 16th were spent waiting for a convoy. On the 17th at noon the *Brown*, five other ships, and two escorts departed Naples in convoy VN-106[54] bound for Leghorn via Piombino. The *Brown* anchored at Piombino during the afternoon of 18 February and left early the next morning for the short run to Leghorn. That night and also the next day there were air raid alerts in Leghorn, but Lieutenant Argo saw no bombing. Because the *Brown* was in port, the Armed Guard did not man the guns.

From the 20th through the 26th the *Brown* discharged cargo. On the 24th, during their free time, some of the Armed Guard crew got up a game of touch football near the docks. In the course of the game one of the men was hit on his nose so hard that his buddies had to take him to the 10th Port Dispensary. There he was told to go to the 33rd General Hospital on the 26th—two days hence—for an X ray. At the hospital a physician didn't need an X ray to know that the nose was not broken. He gave the man some medicine for pain and sent him back to the ship.

On 27 February at 10:30 A.M. the *Brown* left Leghorn in convoy NV-109,[55] consisting of two ships and one escort. She arrived at

Piombino in the afternoon and left the next morning in a convoy of four ships but no escorts. As there was more danger from each other than from the enemy this far south of Leghorn, the convoy commodore ordered the ships to burn dim running lights at night. On 1 March the *Brown* arrived at Naples, where she took on water and fuel before departing for Oran the next afternoon with an Army physician aboard as a passenger. She sailed independently and at 6:45 P.M. turned on her running lights "at full brilliancy in accordance with sailing orders." The *Brown* arrived at Oran on the 5th and moored at berth 6, Mers el-Kébir, some fifteen miles further east. She spent the 6th and 7th waiting for a convoy, having moved during one of these days to an anchorage. On the 8th she departed in convoy GUS-76 for the United States. Carrying one thousand tons of sand as ballast,[56] her draft forward was 10'0" and aft 21'8".[57]

Convoy GUS-76 was made up of thirty-three merchant ships, with Comdr. Ralph S. Parr, USN, in the *Timothy Bloodworth* serving as convoy commodore. The five vessels in the escort group were under the command of Capt. H. S. Berdine, USCG, in the cutter *Gulfport*. Except for the *Brown*, the ships in the convoy had an uneventful crossing. At 2:40 P.M. on 14 March, about five days after passing through the Strait of Gibraltar, the *Brown* had to drop out of the convoy because the port boiler was "overheating from temporary repair of brick work."[58] Steaming on only the starboard boiler, she could not keep up with the convoy. At 6:00 P.M. she altered course to head for straggler route, the route designated for ships that had to leave the convoy. This action caused Commander Parr to complain in his "Appendix to Report on Convoy GUS-76" that he was "unable to get him [Captain Brown] to answer blinker . . . [and that Captain Brown] dropped astern and swung over to southward toward straggler route when less than 5 miles astern apparently declaring himself a straggler regardless of authority." Appended to this report is a handwritten note in pencil that the matter would be investigated at New York and that on 25 March 1945, the day after the convoy arrived there, it was decided that "no action [would be] taken as master seemed cooperative and sincere." At 4:30 A.M. on 15 March, the morning after the breakdown, the *Brown* changed course to 270, due west. Lieutenant Argo recorded in his "Log" that the *Brown* had managed to average 8.3 knots since leaving the convoy. By 10:00 on the 16th, not quite two full days after the fire wall had fallen, the repairs had been completed and, as noted by Lieutenant Argo, "full speed was resumed. A speed of over 10 knots was attained but the captain did not order a zigzag course [as was prescribed for stragglers]. The condition of the fire wall was found to be such that it might fall at any time. The captain therefore deemed it advisable to make port on the shortest possible course."

For the next five days the *Brown* averaged about 10.2 knots. On 22 March, when somewhat northwest of Bermuda, she confronted "strong gales & heavy beam seas." That night when the *Brown* was notified that her destination was New York, Captain Brown altered course from 293 to 338 degrees. The weather continued so bad— "whole gale & rough seas" on the 23rd—that the *Brown* covered only 168 miles, an average of 7.0 knots, between noon on the 22nd and noon on the 23rd. During the next twenty-four hours she picked up a bit to average 8.4 knots. Although the records are not clear as to when, at some point the *Brown* overtook the New York section of GUS-76, but she probably did not go back to her station in the convoy. What is clear is that the first of the twelve ships arrived at 3:48 A.M. on 24 March and the last at 8:18 P.M.[59] and that the *Brown* beat the last one in by a little more than four hours, arriving at the pilot station at 4:00 in the afternoon and at an anchorage in New York harbor at 5:30. She docked early the next afternoon. The voyage officially ended on 27 March 1945.[60]

There are only scraps of information about what happened during the next four weeks. Lieutenant Argo in his "Log" reported that at about 2:00 in the afternoon on 28 March burning rags were discovered in the "merchant crew quarters . . . port side." The fire alarm was sounded, and by 2:30 the fire had been put out. Between 10:00 A.M. and 3:35 P.M. on the 29th workers fumigated the *Brown*. During the fumigation, one petty officer and one seaman from the Armed Guard unit stood watch on the pier. When the work was done, the crew resumed the usual routine of port watches. It was also during this time that not quite half of the Armed Guard unit rotated out and new men were attached. Lieutenant Argo and Lieutenant (jg) O'Connor remained aboard, but Lieutenant (jg) Tompkins was replaced as junior gunnery officer by Lt. (jg) Paul F. Bolduc. The final Navy complement numbered three officers and thirty-eight men.

The seventh voyage of the *John W. Brown* began on 5 April 1945 with a new master, Capt. Andrew Lihz, in command of the forty-four-man Merchant Marine crew.[61] Although articles were signed on the 6th,[62] the part of the "Deck Log" from Voyage 6 starting on 7 April continued to be maintained through 11 April by Acting Chief Mate Archie M. Tagg, who had been second mate on Voyage 6, and by Acting Second Mate William V. Griffin, who had been third mate. According to the "Log," these were busy days. Sometime after fumigation on 29 March the *Brown* shifted to an anchorage where she remained until the afternoon of 7 April, when a tug came alongside and a pilot came aboard to shift her again. With the help of three additional tugs, by late afternoon the *Brown* was moored alongside an unfinished Liberty ship at Pier 44, Atlantic Basin Iron Works, just north of the tip of Red Hook in Brooklyn. Starting at 7:00 the next morning, 8 April, and lasting through 6:00 A.M. on the 11th, day and night shifts of shipyard boiler workers were aboard to repair the boiler. On the 8th men came aboard to install a Sperry gyrocompass, and after working through the night of 10–11 April they finished the job and left at 7:00 A.M. on the 11th, the day the *Brown* was scheduled to leave the Atlantic Basin Iron Works. Archie Tagg probably left at this time also: after recording in the "Log" that the boiler workers had left the ship and that he had called the mates and crew, he concluded his entries at 7:00 A.M. with the departure of the men who installed the gyrocompass. From this point, the entry for 11 April is in the handwriting of "D.F.H.," Donald F. Hewett, the third mate for Voyage 7. At about 8:30 A.M. a pilot boarded the *Brown* and two tugs came alongside to take her to an anchorage where she stayed briefly before shifting first to another anchorage and then to a pier, probably Pier 13, Staten Island, where she was on 17 April when workers from Atlantic & Gulf Stevedores, Inc., caused some damage to the ship.[63]

Meanwhile, one of the Armed Guard crew was paying for an extended weekend fling ashore when Lieutenant Argo placed him on "indefinite restriction" for being AWOL for three days. To make matters worse, the sailor, a seaman first class, had the bad luck to be "seen ashore by Lt (jg) S. N. Tompkins, the then Junior Gunnery Officer, wearing a 1st class rating badge, and various battle stars and commendation ribbons" that he was not entitled to. Apparently the commanding officer of the Armed Guard Center felt that the infractions required heavier punishment than restriction, for he detached the sailor from the *Brown* "for disciplinary action."

On 12 April the Allied nations were stunned by the news that President Franklin D. Roosevelt had died suddenly of a cerebral hemorrhage at the "Little White House" in Warm Springs, Georgia. His body was taken to Washington for a funeral service in the East Room of the White House at 4:00 P.M. on Saturday, 14 April. The new president, Harry Truman, proclaimed the 14th a "day of mourning and prayer," and "at the hour of the service the entire nation paid tribute to Mr. Roosevelt. The armed forces, over the world, paused five minutes for silent prayer wherever they were not engaged in actual combat."[64] On the *Brown* that day, Lieutenant Argo "mustered all hands [at 4:00] on aft. gun deck, stood at attention, uncovered, and observed 5 minutes silent period in commemoration of the late President Roosevelt." Adm. Emory S. Land, War Shipping administrator and chairman of the Maritime Commission, ordered all American merchant ships to carry their flags at half mast for thirty days and stated that "the merchant fleet has lost its most understanding and greatest friend. Franklin Delano Roosevelt knew more about ships and the men who sail them—Navy and merchant—than any other man who has ever held high office in this country. His understanding and knowledge of ships made possible a building and operations program without which the war would have been lost."[65]

After having taken on a full load of general Army cargo and trucks plus one Army passenger,[66] the *Brown* by 20 April had shifted to an anchorage in the Narrows off Staten Island.[67] She departed New York on the 23rd in convoy HX-352 bound for the Solent, the channel between the south coast of England and the Isle of Wight. On leaving New York there were sixty-one ships in the convoy, with the *Brown* in position 45, the fifth ship in the fourth column. Since, however, no ships were in the first three columns of the fifteen-column convoy, the *Brown* was in fact on the port flank of the convoy.[68] The convoy commodore was Comdr. W. B. Mills on the *Waterland*, a Dutch vessel, and the escort was composed of four Canadian Navy ships commanded by Lt. Comdr. J. C. Pratt, RCNVR, in the *Oshawa*,[69] a 230-foot minesweeper.[70] In coastal waters a distance of six hundred yards was maintained between columns and four hundred yards between ships in column, and on the open seas the distance was increased to one thousand yards between columns and five hundred yards between ships.[71]

Although the war was now quickly winding down, four U-boats were operating off the East Coast of the United States in early 1945. The three anywhere close to HX-352's route, however, had been sunk before the convoy left New York, and the fourth was sunk off the Virginia capes on 30 April.[72] These kills, however, did not end the

U-boat threat. The U-boat command, in a final offensive thrust in late March, sent out seven more boats, "Gruppe Seewolf," to attack convoys. Through information derived from British intelligence's breaking the ciphers by which the U-boat command communicated with its boats, the Allies were able to track the U-boats' south-westerly movement. Guided by this information, the U.S. Navy's Operation Teardrop, comprised of two forces each with two escort carriers and a large number of destroyer escorts, deployed to inter-cept the U-boats. Between 15 and 24 April, Operation Teardrop sunk four of the seven, but not before U-546 had sunk the destroyer escort *Frederick C. Davis* on the 24th.[73] Thus there were still three U-boats lurking in the area when HX-352 passed through. When the escorts dropped several depth charges at 7:50 P.M. on the 23rd, a little over twelve and a half hours out of New York, they may have been react-ing to an actual contact.

Heading in a northeasterly direction, the convoy passed the Mari-time Provinces of Canada, where it was joined by seventeen ships as it passed Halifax, Nova Scotia, and by an additional two from Sydney, Nova Scotia. These nineteen ships filled in the three vacant columns on the port side of the convoy, which now numbered eighty ships. On 26 April, at about the same time that the ships from Sydney joined the convoy, the four escorts were relieved by four other Canadian Navy ships, with the senior officer in the *Portage,* a minesweeper like the *Oshawa.* Shortly before noon the next day the Canadian destroyer tender *Melville* and the frigate *St. John* aug-mented the escort group as the convoy proceeded at 9.5 knots. A lit-tle less than two hours later there was more evidence that the enemy had not quit when the *Melville* "sighted wreckage and [an unoccu-pied] ship lifeboat."[74] Because three U-boats were known to have es-caped Teardrop, the "convoy gun practice" and "convoy emergency practice" held on 27 April were more than just routine. By late after-noon on the 27th the convoy had run into dense fog that reduced vis-ibility to about three hundred feet. Because no one, including the en-emy, could see anything through the fog, Lieutenant Argo decided to cancel dusk general quarters. By dawn on the 28th the fog had wors-ened, reducing visibility to about two hundred feet, but—whether in response to the enemy or to avoid other traffic—Commander Mills, the convoy commodore, ordered "a series of emergency turns." Whatever the danger, the situation must have been serious for Com-mander Mills to risk collisions in such limited visibility. The fog continued throughout the day, prompting Lieutenant Argo to cancel both dawn and dusk general quarters. Lieutenant Argo was no doubt referring to this time when he noted in his "Report" that "a stern light was burned several nights when visibility was extremely low." By 29 April the fog had lifted, although the sky remained hazy.

Otherwise the voyage was uneventful. In Europe, however, events of the greatest significance were occurring almost daily: on 27 April U.S. troops moving east and Soviet troops moving west met at the Elbe River some fifty miles south of Berlin; on the 29th Adolph Hitler appointed Grand Adm. Karl Doenitz head of the German government; on the 30th Hitler killed himself; on 2 May the German army in Italy surrendered; and on the 7th Gen. Alfred Jodl unconditionally surrendered all German armed forces, effective the following day. The eighth of May 1945 was thus proclaimed V-E Day by the Allies. Going from matters of vast historic dimension to the level of human error, the only item Lieutenant Argo considered worth recording in his "Log" during the period occurred on 5 May when one of the Armed Guard crew, who must have been lying in his bunk smoking at the time, "burned his chin, neck and chest, when he spilled lighter fluid on himself, which ignited." Certain that the man had suffered first-degree burns, Lieutenant Argo first applied tannic acid jelly. Later on he dusted the burns with sulfa powder, coated them with petroleum jelly, and then bandaged them. Lieutenant Argo's treatment must have worked, for he does not mention the incident again.

Late in the evening of V-E Day the *Brown* anchored in the Downs, a roadstead in the Strait of Dover, instead of the Solent, her original destination. Early the next morning the *Brown* left the Downs and headed into the North Sea bound for Antwerp. As she "sailed along the coast of Belgium [that evening, the crew] . . . could see lights on in the towns and villages. It was a most welcome sight and made us all feel good and gave us a sense of pride and satisfaction to know that we all had contributed to the defeat of the enemy in Europe."[75] The next day, 10 May, as the *Brown* made her way up the narrow and winding Schelde River, she passed several young women sunbathing on a grassy bank on the port side, in a way symbolizing that after seven years of war, Europe was again at peace. When the crew sighted the women, they rushed to the port rail waving and shouting to get their attention. A signalman who had brought the ship's telescope to get a better look got so caught up in the hilarity and good-natured rowdiness that he accidentally dropped the scope over the

The *Brown* passed this sunken ship in May 1945 while steaming
in the North Sea off the coast of Belgium. *James P. Farley*

side.[76] With the crew in the mood for fun, the *Brown* arrived at Antwerp that evening, a couple of days too late to be a part of the most spontaneous and uninhibited victory celebrations, but still in time to share in the exhilaration and excitement of the first few days of peace.

A little over five months had passed since the first American ship, the *James B. Weaver,* had arrived at Antwerp on 28 November 1944. As the Germans had done little damage to the port, it was not long before large amounts of military cargo were passing through the excellent facilities that prior to the war had made Antwerp comparable as a port to New York and Hamburg. From January through May 1945 an average of 501,771 long tons of cargo were discharged in Antwerp each month: "By V-E Day the American section of Antwerp had become the leading cargo port operated by the [U.S. Army] Transportation Corps in the European theater."[77]

After the *Brown* discharged her cargo at Antwerp, German POWs assembled bunks in the 'tween decks for the Army troops who were scheduled to embark in Le Havre.[78] On 19 May the *Brown* left Antwerp—in convoy despite the war's end in Europe—and arrived at the Downs the next morning. That night she left the Downs in convoy to go to St. Helen's on the northeast coast of the Isle of Wight, where she anchored for several hours on the 21st before leaving in convoy for Le Havre. Arriving there on the morning of the 22nd, she embarked 351 American troops, 31 of whom were officers liberated from German prison camps.[79] Donald Hewett, the third mate on the *Brown* at the time, recalls that on "arriving in Le Havre we set up a loud speaker at the gangway and as the troops came aboard we played the record 'Roll Out the Barrel.' Some of the troops were a little older than you would expect. I remember one soldier coming up the gangway remarking 'we were left over from the last war and they're just picking us up.'"[80] After about two and a half days in Le Havre, the *Brown* left in convoy on 24 May and dropped anchor at the Solent the following morning.

After two and a half days at anchor, the *Brown* departed the Solent on the 27th in convoy ON-305, the last convoy she would sail in. Six British and Canadian escorts accompanied the seventy-nine merchant ships, twenty-eight of which—including the *Brown*—were bound for New York.[81] Lieutenant Argo noted in his "Log" that "running lights were burned at full brilliance, blackout regulations discontinued, and dawn and dusk G.Q. discontinued in compliance with convoy sailing orders." The war in Europe was really over! Except for a day near the end of the voyage when the convoy encountered a "rough head sea" and averaged only 5.4 knots, the seas were either smooth or moderate, enabling it to average 9.5 knots overall. Nothing much out of the ordinary happened during the crossing. An Army physician who had embarked at Le Havre examined the knee of a sailor who had slipped on the freshly oiled main deck. On 31 May a smoke float went over the side: "investigation revealed that soldier passenger accidentally tripped securing hook." On 5 June there was another injury to a member of the Armed Guard unit requiring the physician's attention, this time an ankle hurt while the sailor was playing catch on the main deck. On the 10th, when the *Brown* was one day out of New York, the physician's services were again required, this final time to hold a short-arm inspection for the Armed Guard crew. Lieutenant Argo recorded that the physician found "All hands O.K."

At 7:00 the next morning, 11 June, the *John W. Brown* arrived at Army Base, Brooklyn, to debark her passengers.[82] The voyage officially ended the next day when the crew signed off.[83] It wasn't quite over for Lieutenant Argo, however; on the 13th a Lieutenant Smith

Homeward-bound troops board the *Brown* at Le Havre in late
May 1945. *Project Liberty Ship Archives*

from the Armed Guard Center, in a handwritten note on a separate
sheet in Lieutenant Argo's "Log," wrote that "your ship was inspected as of this date—It is recommended that quarters & heads be
reinspected—With this exception the ship was satisfactory." There is
no evidence that Lieutenant Argo did anything about cleaning up the
quarters and heads or that anyone from the Armed Guard Center followed up with a reinspection. The war in Europe, after all, was over.

Knowing they would soon be dispersed, the Armed Guard crew organized a farewell party at a tavern in Brooklyn owned by a relative
of one of the men. Before going on liberty on the night of the party,
the men were warned to get back to the *Brown* early the next morning before she shifted to an anchorage. Needless to say, a few, including James Munroe, stayed so late at the party that when they finally
returned to the pier they found the *Brown* under way a short distance
offshore. Those who got back in time lined the bulwarks waving exaggerated good-byes and laughing derisively at the men standing

helplessly at the end of the pier. Luckily they were able to hail a passing tug whose understanding captain took them to the ship. A Jacob's ladder—a nonrigid rope ladder with narrow steps—was thrown over the side of the *Brown,* and the men had to time a step or jump from the moving tug to the swaying ladder on the moving ship. Despite their condition after a night of partying, they all made it, but by the time they had climbed to the top of the ladder they had bruised and scraped knees and knuckles as souvenirs.[84]

The slacking off of tension on the Atlantic Coast and the uncertainty stemming from the fact that the war against Japan in the Pacific was far from over caused considerable confusion as the armed forces adjusted to the new circumstances. This confusion was reflected in a small way with the Armed Guard aboard the *Brown.* Between 13 and 16 June all the Navy personnel were detached, and then on the 16th Lt. (jg) Edward H. O'Connor, Gunners Mate Third Class John E. Walls, Signalman Second Class Joseph D. Brewer, and Seaman First Class Michael J. Tarbillo were reassigned to the *Brown.* Two days later Lt. (jg) Frank P. Bykowski and seven enlisted men were attached, increasing the Navy complement to a total of two officers and ten enlisted men.

Along about this time articles for a coastwise voyage must have been signed, because on 20 June the *Brown* left New York for Philadelphia, where she arrived on the 21st[85] and tied up at Pier 98, just upriver from the present Walt Whitman Bridge, to load 175.29 tons of cargo for the Army Ordnance Department and 4,829.27 for the Quartermaster Corps.[86] The cargo underlined the fact that fighting in Europe had ended: instead of ammunition and weapons (except for a gun for a medium tank), the cargo consisted in part of cars, trucks, spare parts for jeeps, nonperishable food (that is, dehydrated eggs and potatoes, powdered milk, beans, canned luncheon meat, and the like), lubricating oil, and such miscellaneous items as field ranges, shoe polish, can openers, and typewriter paper. Foreign articles for Voyage 8 were signed in Philadelphia on 23 June.[87] On 2 July, Lieutenant Bykowski and the seven enlisted men who had joined the ship for the first time on 18 June were detached, leaving behind Lieutenant O'Connor and the three enlisted men who were reattached on 16 June. Later in the day on 2 July the *Brown* left Philadelphia for Antwerp.[88]

Germany's surrender brought an end to masters' "Secret Logs" and to "Logs" and "Reports" by Armed Guard commanders, thereby eliminating the researcher's three richest sources of information.

Captain Lihz did not keep complete records in the "Official Log-Book," and the "Deck Log," if it still exists, has not been found. The available records do not even give the date of arrival in Antwerp. During unloading at Antwerp, the *Brown*'s cargo holds suffered "extensive damage," but the records do not establish responsibility.[89] When the cargo had been completely discharged, bunks were set up in the forward 'tween decks and 419 troops from various units embarked.[90] Max Grossman, the chief radio operator on this voyage, recalls that the *Brown* also loaded "the remains of the propulsion unit from a German V-2,"[91] one of the rockets with which the Germans had terrorized Antwerp during the winter of 1944–45, killing 3,752 civilians and 731 Allied servicemen.[92] The propulsion unit was being taken to the United States for study by rocket scientists and technicians. The *Brown* left Antwerp on 28 July[93] and arrived on 11 August at Hudson River Pier 64 at the foot of West 24th Street in Manhattan to debark her 419 passengers.[94] The *Queen Elizabeth* arrived in New York on the same day carrying fifteen thousand troops. Voyage 8 officially ended when the crew signed off on 16 August,[95] the day after V-J Day.

On 14 August, two days before the official end of the voyage, however, the *Brown* steamed up the Hudson River to the J. K. Welding shipyard in Yonkers, New York, to have her troop-carrying capacity increased to 562 for bringing troops home from Europe. Begun on 17 August and completed on 12 September,[96] the changes added the 'tween deck of number 1 hold to the troop-carrying facilities. The work involved adding entrances to number 1 'tween deck from the main deck and from number 2 'tween deck; installing sanitary facilities, lights, and a ventilation system in number 1 'tween deck; and replacing one of the generators in the engine room.[97] Besides inspecting the changes made to accommodate more troops, American Bureau of Shipping surveyors also visited the *Brown* several times between 17 August and 4 September to make the annual survey and the annual boiler survey. This intensive inspection found the *Brown* "in a satisfactory condition and fit to retain her present class with this Bureau."[98] On 13 September the 5"/51, the three 3"/50s, and the eight 20 mm's were removed.[99] With the ship now completely disarmed, the four remaining Navy personnel left on the same day. World War II was over, and the *John W. Brown* was now ready to do her share to carry supplies to a ravaged Europe and to bring the troops back home.

6

Voyages 9, 10, 11, 12, and 13

The Peacetime Trips

T HE SS *John W. Brown*'s ninth voyage, her first since V-J Day, began on 7 September 1945.[1] Because she would bring troops back on the return trip from Europe, her crew was between fifteen and twenty men larger than usual on a Liberty ship. Instead of one radio operator she carried three, and the steward's department was increased by the addition of three cooks assigned to the troops, plus bakers, butchers, messmen for the Army officers, and so forth. The *Brown* left New York for Baltimore on 15 September and arrived the next day.[2]

Meanwhile in New York, Army Pfc. Charles T. Belzak had recently completed a two-week transport services course to prepare him for staff duties aboard troopships bringing GIs back to the States. On 20 September he was assigned to the *Brown*, which at the time was loading wheat at the Pennsylvania Grain Elevator in Baltimore. Private Belzak joined Army Lt. Frank H. Stoll, transport commander, Army Lt. Al DeAngela, transport services officer, and two other Army enlisted men to complete the transport staff on Voyage 9.[3] The Army staff had quarters in the amidship house, and the enlisted men ate in what had been the Armed Guard mess during the war.[4]

The *Brown* left Baltimore on 25 September[5] bound for Marseilles. During the crossing she ran into such bad weather that water leaked through the escape hatches into number 2 'tween deck. To make matters worse, the "heavy vibration of the ship" opened a leak in the flanges of a scupper pipe running from the 'tween deck to the kitchen line. Water from these sources leaked from the 'tween deck into number 2 lower hold, damaging about twenty tons of wheat. These lines were not repaired until the *Brown* returned to the United States.[6]

Troubles continued as the *Brown* neared Marseilles in soupy weather early in the morning of 13 October. At 5:54 A.M., with Captain Lihz and Second Mate Botto on the bridge and AB Nicholas Samothrakis at the wheel, the *Brown* suddenly "went on ground off Bouc entrance," some twenty-two miles west of Marseilles. Instead of heading east directly into Marseilles, the *Brown* was steaming north in the Gulf of Fos toward Port de Bouc in order to pass through the canal at the head of the gulf into Étang de Berre, a tidal lake. But just before getting to the canal, the *Brown* grounded on submerged rocks.[7] Captain Lihz tried various speeds ahead and astern to work the ship free, but she was stuck fast. Fortunately, an initial examination turned up no damage, and the bilges remained dry.[8] The *Brown* had been moving slowly and thus grounded so gently that Third Mate Mazzie, asleep in his room, didn't feel the slight jar as the *Brown* came to a stop, but instead was awakened by the beam from the lighthouse flashing into his porthole.[9] It took a day and a half—until the evening of 14 October—to refloat the *Brown*, and then only after about five hundred tons of wheat had been discharged from the forward holds, four hundred tons of water had been pumped overboard, and 3,723 barrels of fuel (156,366 gallons) had been pumped into a barge. A tug then assisted the *Brown* to an anchorage[10] off St. Victoret, a town near the east end of Étang de Berre about twelve miles from Marseilles. Two days later, on the 17th, she was able to enter Marseilles and tie up at a grain elevator to discharge the wheat.[11] This move gave the Army enlisted men an opportunity to take a three-day pass, which they spent on the beaches at the U.S. Riviera Personnel Center, a recreation area for enlisted personnel at Nice.[12] Meanwhile, Army divers inspected the *Brown*'s bottom, Lt. Joseph A. Enos of the Army Corps of Engineers reporting on 25 October that the divers found "nothing out of the ordinary. No dents, sprung frames or breaks of any kind."[13]

Although the visit to Marseilles brought problems with it, it brought joy to one of the crew members in the steward's department who had fled his native France before the German occupation. During the years of the war he had been unable to see his mother, who had remained behind. On learning that the *Brown* was headed for Marseilles, he wrote to her so that she could arrange to meet the ship. Walter Botto, the second mate on Voyage 9, remembers that "this elderly, frail woman came down to the ship and it was a rather tearful moment to see, and I kind of well up a little when I think about it . . . we provided for her aboard the ship, . . . [made] her comfortable and let her stay there for a day or so . . . it was a happy reunion for him."[14]

On 22 October the *Brown* embarked 645 troops, somewhat over capacity, and departed Marseilles that evening.[15] Although the forward 'tween deck areas used for troop quarters had been hosed down after the cargo had been discharged, a strong odor of fermenting wheat remained to make queasy stomachs even queasier.[16] However, a real attempt was made to keep the GIs comfortable and pleasantly occupied. Chief Radio Operator Max Grossman remembers that "we had an Army officer in charge of troop entertainment who had lots of musical transcriptions and the equipment to play them; we rigged speakers up on the forward masts and also tied the public address

Elated GIs embark at Marseilles in October 1945. *Charles T. Belzak*

Second Mate Walter Botto takes a bearing
in the Mediterranean. *Charles T. Belzak*

system . . . into the short wave radio on the shack to broadcast news to the troops."[17]

The officer in charge of entertainment was Al DeAngela, a magician from Philadelphia whose professional name was Al Dee.[18] One of DeAngela's tasks was to put out a daily paper for the troops. Since there really wasn't much shipboard news, he was constantly looking for material. Walter Botto recalls that one day "in mid ocean we were just killing time and off watch, shooting the breeze and they're looking for material to write and one thing and the other and I'm listening and it kind of went through my mind" to write a humorous piece about "mail buoys."[19] The rough draft, typed for Botto on the radio shack typewriter by Charles "Marty" Schneider, the third radio operator on Voyage 9, begins:

> In confirmation of the many doubts which have arisen from time to time we wish to inform you that it will be possible to post your letters enroute on the high seas via the global sea postal system which is not yet a hun-

dred years old. Set up originally . . . in 1846, it has served the marine industry and Navy well and without praise.

Its objective was to make possible the posting and receiving of written correspondence & business matters prior to the advent of Marconi.

The nautical postal system reached the threshold of fame during our golden era of shipping when our sleek, trim clipper ships were astounding the globe with their record crossings. The slower and heavier sailing vessels would post copies of their partial payrolls, completed manifests, and other documentary matter in these buoys which are anchored every 500 miles along the steamship lanes for the clippers to pick up and deliver for them as often as a week before their eventual arrival into port enabling greater terminal efficiency. . . .

In use today only along low-powered steamship lanes over extremely long great circle tracks, it has been combined with air-mail postage. Letters are mailed at sea in buoys of the vessel's respective nation of registry . . . and left for the patrol to link delivery at the nearest port. From there they are forwarded via routine air mail channels.

Then follows a long description of the buoys used by various nations, the postage rates, special stamps, and the like. The account ends with the hope that

the war has not hampered these buoys. Some have been destroyed by depth charges and others by enemy hostilities while there have been unconfirmed reports of their being booby-trapped by the Axis. However, keep a lookout for the buoy with the big "yoke" flag, and have your letters in to the special service office properly marked in the usual stamp corner with air mail attached if you are not a merchant seaman.

This information was condensed from the March issue of Sea Lore magazine.

Supplementary information can be obtained at the reception desk of the liars club lounge, upper deck starboard side aft.

W. J. Botto
Historian de Mer[20]

Even though the last sentence gave away the joke, some of the GIs turned in letters to the troop commander's office. Carried away by the notion that so many men had believed the article, Botto and his accomplices decided to embellish it by actually coming across a mail buoy. To one end of a long broomstick they attached a cigar box and to the other a flashlight that turns on when inverted. After dark one night "we dropped this thing over the side . . . from the main deck where the midships house was, and someone would sight the buoy and we'd haul the thing up and they'd see us hauling this light up,

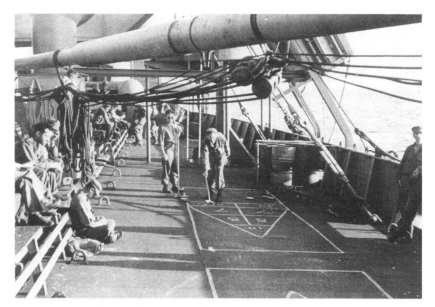

GIs relax on deck during the voyage home. *Charles T. Belzak*

and we pretended to put the mail . . . in it and drop it back over the side and sail on." Shortly afterwards it finally occurred to them that the letters were important to the GIs and to their families and friends, but Walter Botto doesn't remember how they admitted to the troops that it was all a joke: "I let the Army officer handle that part. I just provided the mischief."[21]

The *Brown* arrived off Staten Island shortly before 7:00 A.M. on 14 November, and as she made her way to Pier 15 to debark the troops[22] she was escorted by welcoming fireboats. A vocalist on one of the boats sang popular songs over the public-address system, and as the *Brown* edged alongside Pier 15 the troops were greeted by a military band.[23]

When the crew signed off on 16 November,[24] it marked the end of Matts Oman's service as bos'n on the *John W. Brown*. He had signed on for her maiden voyage in September 1942 and had sailed on all her subsequent voyages, and now at sixty years of age he signed off for the last time. Vernon Joyce, who was in the Armed Guard unit on Voyages 4 and 5, "greatly admired" Oman, "who was of Finnish birth and had some thirty-five or forty years at sea prior to my meeting him on the *Brown*. This man was certainly an expert seaman, quite friendly, something of a mentor to me. In order to learn more about seamanship, deck rigging, and so forth, I occasionally was allowed to work with the Merchant crew under the guidance of the Bos'n, and I am deeply indebted to him for some of the things he taught me that have stood me in good stead through the many years I spent in the United States Navy and Naval Reserve."[25]

Matts Oman was replaced as bos'n by Nicholas C. Samothrakis, who had sailed as AB on Voyages 6 through 9. Since Samothrakis continued as bos'n through the *Brown*'s thirteenth and final trip, he was aboard for a total of eight voyages over a period of a little less than two years. The man who made the most trips on the *Brown*, twelve, and served the longest, about three and a half years, was James E. Carter. He first joined the ship as an AB on Voyage 2, signed on as maintenance man on Voyage 3, and as carpenter on Voyages 4 through 13. Another with long service was Frederic Clar, steward on Voyages 5 through 13, a total of nine trips over slightly more than two years.

Shortly after arriving in New York the *Brown* went to the Bethlehem Steel 56th Street Yard in Brooklyn. Sometime between 16 and 23 November a radar set was installed at a cost of $4,950.[26] The *Brown* also spent time in dry dock while at the 56th Street Yard. On 19 November, the day before she was undocked, an American Bureau of Shipping surveyor examined her bottom to determine whether the grounding off Bouc a month earlier had caused damage. Having a better view than Lieutenant Enos and his divers, the surveyor found dents in several plates and distortion along a section of the bilge keel on the port side. Since there was no leakage, his recommendations for repairs "were not carried out at this time as the damages do not impair the seaworthiness of the vessel and may be dealt with at the owners convenience."[27]

On 20 November, the same day the *Brown* left the dry dock, the crew signed articles for the tenth voyage.[28] The new master, who would remain on the *Brown* through the rest of her seagoing career, was Capt. Alfred W. Hudnall. Sixty-four years old when he became master of the *Brown*, Captain Hudnall grew up in Northumberland County, Virginia, which is bordered by the Potomac River to the north and the Chesapeake Bay to the east. Starting at sea at age twelve, he worked his way up and during World War I was master of a troop transport. Among his World War II voyages were several to Murmansk.[29]

As with Voyage 9, the presence of troops on the return voyage necessitated a larger than usual Merchant Marine crew. Lieutenant DeAngela left the Army Transport Services staff, but Lieutenant Stoll continued, as did Private Belzak. The Army staff for Voyage 10 now numbered one officer and seven enlisted men. Three of the additional enlisted men, U.S. Army corporals, operated the newly installed radar equipment, which was still classified as secret under the Wartime Security Act.[30]

At 8:15 A.M. on 26 November the *Brown* left Brooklyn and sailed up the Hudson River to Albany, arriving at 8:00 that evening. She loaded 257,000 bushels of wheat at Albany and headed back down the Hudson at 7:00 A.M. on the 29th. Arriving back in New York City a little less than twelve hours later, she dropped anchor off the Statue of Liberty, took on fuel and water from barges, and left New York for Naples shortly before daybreak on 1 December.[31]

The "Night Order Book" for this voyage has survived, and from it one can get some idea of the *Brown*'s itinerary and of some of the routines at sea. Captain Hudnall pasted his "Standing Night Orders" inside the front cover of the book:

1. Keep a good lookout at all times.
2. Check course frequently on gyrocompass and magnetic compasses.
3. Observe the rules of the road.
4. Give passing vessels a wide berth.
5. Should the weather become hazardous call me.
6. Check all navigation lights during each watch.
7. During heavy seas, have the standby man check the gear, gangway, and weather side of vessel for security. Batten midship house exits on weather side.
8. Continue all courses as indicated through the night.
9. During radio watches notify operator when fog sets in.
10. If ever in doubt, call me immediately.[32]

Captain Hudnall usually wrote a comment in the "Remarks" column of the "Night Order Book": on 2 December, for example, "Continue course thru the night unless sea diminishes. If it does, call me for course change." Captain Hudnall signed his name to his orders each night, and the three mates also signed to show that they had read them.

After steaming southeast on 1 and 2 December, the *Brown* shifted on Monday, 3 December, to course 090, due east, and stayed on courses between 080 and 090 degrees through 15 December. After making course adjustments to pass through the Strait of Gibraltar, she steamed east in the Mediterranean Sea—slowed, however, by boiler problems that weren't finally fixed until a day before arrival in the Gulf of Naples.[33] On the 18th Captain Hudnall stated in the "Night Order Book" that "when light is abeam on Southern tip of Sardinia distance 10 miles off change course to make a landfall on South end of Capri." The *Brown,* however, still had at least twenty-four hours steaming time before reaching Capri, and Captain Hudnall's remarks for the next night again refer to making for the south end of the island. He then added that "if light is visible before daylight shape course to pass five miles to the right of it. Have [Army] radar boys check for bearings at four A.M. and frequently after unless a positive fix is secured." The instruction to pass five miles to the right—that is, to the south—of Capri pointed the *Brown* toward Salerno rather than Naples. However, her first port was neither Salerno nor Naples but rather Castellammare di Stabia in the eastern corner of the Gulf of Naples, some fifteen miles southeast of Naples. The fact that she didn't go immediately to Castellammare di Stabia but instead anchored near Capri in the Gulf of Naples on 20 December may explain her route around the southern side of Capri:[34] after passing to the right of Capri, she turned north to pass through Bocca Piccola (little mouth) between Capri and the mainland to her anchorage in the Gulf of Naples.

On the 22nd the *Brown* left the anchorage near Capri and went into Castellammare di Stabia, where she discharged about half the cargo of wheat. On Christmas Day 1945 she sailed from Castellammare di Stabia to Salerno, where she discharged the remainder of the wheat.[35] Meanwhile, Charles Belzak had been promoted to technician fifth grade (T/5), equivalent to corporal. Not having much to do until the troops came aboard, he and some others in his unit used their free time to visit the ruins at Pompeii on the day after Christmas. A few days later they took a boat to Capri, toured the island, and then treated themselves to a bit of luxury by spending the night at the Hotel Morgano-Tiberia Plazzo.[36] On New Year's Day 1946 the *Brown* went from Salerno to Naples to take on ballast and probably fuel and water.[37] For the last time during the voyage, Belzak and the other Army men were able to go ashore. On 3 January they climbed four thousand feet to the top of Mount Vesuvius, still smoking from its eruption ten months earlier, and that evening they went to a performance of Verdi's *La Traviata* at the San Carlo Opera House in Naples. The next day the *Brown* left Naples for Marseilles, arriving on the 6th.[38]

After embarking 565 officers and men of the 100th Infantry Division, the *Brown* sailed for home on 7 January. The Transport Staff recruited GI volunteers to organize activities to help the troops pass the time. One group put out the newsletter "Ship Stuff," a copy of which, the "Souvenir Edition," survives. An article titled "Impressions on Going Home" gives what was probably a typical reaction to the *Brown:* "What a tub: boy, is this going to be a slow trip. . . . She didn't look like much from the outside; but it's pretty nice inside. Hell, she may not be as fast as the Queen Mary but we sure have more room. . . . With all those games, books, and stuff this shouldn't be a bad trip at all. I think I'll go to that movie tonight. . . . What a night; if only I had a babe."[39] "Ship Stuff" also enumerates the range of facilities and activities available to the troops: a library, a radio broadcast room, movies on the after deck, tours of the ship, and on the next to last night out a variety show put on by thirteen soldiers and one Merchant seaman. The show included magic tricks, jokes, hillbilly music, and vocalists. Earlier in the voyage there had been a beauty contest to name Miss, Mrs., and Baby *John W. Brown*. The men competed by submitting photographs, and the winners, determined by vote, were announced at the variety show. A birthday party for the twenty-two men who had birthdays during the voyage followed the show. After singing "Happy Birthday," everyone was treated to cake, ice cream, and Pepsi-Cola.[40]

After the *Brown*'s departure from Marseilles on 7 January, Captain Hudnall's comments in the "Night Order Book" make clear that he expected to be off Cabrera Island, south of Mallorca, during the night of 8 January and at the east end of the Strait of Gibraltar by the following morning. However, the boiler broke down again at 11:00 A.M. on the 9th, forcing a reduction of speed to seven knots. By the morning of the 11th the engineers had repaired it and the *Brown* was once again steaming at full ahead.[41] Despite the reduced speed, the *Brown* had made it to the Atlantic Ocean side of the strait by the 10th and had set a course of 270, due west, which she held for the next nine days. Then, after two nights at 280, bad weather forced the *Brown* on 22 January to change to 260: Captain Hudnall ordered the mates to hold this course "thru the night unless wind and sea moderate or the wind shifts to the West or N. West. In that event as soon as the . . . [southerly] sea diminishes so we can do so with reasonable comfort change course to 280." A writer in "Ship Stuff" no doubt spoke for many others when he lamented, "I don't feel so hot." However, unlike some others he was able to boast that "I haven't fed the fish yet," and continued, "Some guys say to stay on deck all the time; others say to stay in your bunk all the time. It doesn't make a d— what I do; I still feel lousy inside. I wish this tub would stop rolling and tossing like that." The next morning he again observed that "this is some storm. I didn't sleep a wink last night; I spent all my time trying to stay in my sack. How would you like to have your bunk in the mess hall? I saw one guy get it. He was lying in his sack when she rolled really bad, one of the Joe's eating couldn't hold his tray and it went right into this guy's bunk. Breakfast in bed and he didn't like it."[42] Back on course 280 on the 23rd and 24th, the *Brown* arrived in New York in the morning of 26 January, having covered approximately 5,050 miles at an average speed of 9.2 knots.[43] At 2:00 P.M. she tied up at Pier 84 on the Hudson River to debark the troops. Lieutenant Stoll, Corporal Belzak, and the rest of the Army men left on 4 February.[44] With their departure the *Brown*'s service as a troop transport ended. Over the years she had carried about 1,100 men to Europe, about 1,000 POWs from Europe to the United States, and almost 2,000 troops home from Europe at war's end. In addition, while in the Mediterranean she had shuttled over 5,100 troops and 336 POWs between Italian and North African ports. Altogether a little over 9,500 men and a few nurses sailed as passengers on the *John W. Brown*.

The *Brown* remained in New York for the next three weeks. The "Deck Log" for Voyage 11 has survived and gives a clear picture of a peacetime trip. Kept by Chief Mate John Kvamme, Second Mate Walter Botto, and Third Mate Peter Mazzie, the "Log" records that Voyage 11 began at one minute past midnight on Saturday, 16 February 1946.[45] At 6:00 A.M. on an "almost cloudy" morning with the temperature at sixteen degrees, the crew started the gyrocompass and began getting the *Brown* ready to leave New York. At about 8:30 she left the pier and two hours later increased speed to full ahead and headed south along the New Jersey coast en route to Baltimore. As she left New York, the crew was busy "securing for sea, squaring deck, dumping garbage & washing down."

During the afternoon the *Brown* passed a quarter of a mile abeam the Barnegat Light Ship off Long Beach Island, New Jersey, and one and a quarter miles off the Brigantine sea buoy near Atlantic City. At 10:00 P.M. off Cape May a pilot came aboard to take her up the Delaware Bay and Delaware River to the Chesapeake and Delaware Canal. The *Brown* arrived at the canal at about 2:00 A.M. on 17 February and dropped anchor for almost four hours until a pilot arrived to guide her through the canal. After the canal pilot left at 8:44, a bay pilot came aboard for the trip to an anchorage in Baltimore. Second Mate Walter Botto, at the bottom of the page for 17 February, appended a "Voyage Summary" of the New York to Baltimore run:

Ambrose L/V to C. May
   120 mi   11h 16m   Sp. 10.6 Kts
C. May to C & D Canal
   54 mi   4h 27m   Sp. 12 Kts
        Detention at Canal 3h 39m
Canal Passage
   14 mi   2h 25m   Sp. 5.9 K
Canal to Baltimore
   42 mi   4h 12m   Sp. 10 K

While the *Brown* lay at anchor "awaiting dockage," stevedores came aboard to open the hatches, remove dunnage, and prepare the gear, booms, and holds for taking on a cargo of coal. The next morning, 18 February, the *Brown* tied up at the Curtis Bay coal pier, where in nine and a half hours she loaded 7,501.18 tons of coal. The voyage had been chartered by Dansk Kulimport Organisation to take the coal to "one safe port in Denmark."[46] Meanwhile she also took on water, and then after taking on fuel at the Socony Oil Dock during the early morning hours of 19 February, she shifted to an anchorage.

According to Captain Hudnall's "Official Log-Book," 19 February was the "date of commencement" of Voyage 11.[47] Since no troops were to be transported, only thirty-seven men signed articles, compared with sixty for Voyage 9 and sixty-one for Voyage 10. The crew spent most of the 20th cleaning, battening down hatches, and completing other chores in preparation for getting under way. At 8:15 P.M. the gyrocompass was started and set, and an hour later a pilot came aboard accompanied by a technician to calibrate the direction finder. The calibration process, which requires that a ship be under way, took longer than usual because a hot bearing forced the *Brown* to reduce speed for nearly an hour and a half. It was almost 1:00 A.M. when the technician finished so that the *Brown* could return to her anchorage. The technician went ashore, but the pilot stayed aboard because the *Brown* was scheduled to leave Baltimore shortly. She then headed south on a calm Chesapeake Bay with the temperature in the low thirties. After dropping the pilot, who by then had been aboard for about sixteen hours, the *Brown* took departure from the Virginia capes at 2:20 P.M. on 21 February. At 3:00 P.M. she passed a half mile abeam of the farewell buoy and at 11:30 P.M. changed course to 090 degrees to head due east toward her destination, Copenhagen.

On the third day out, 24 February, after having covered between eight and nine hundred miles, the *Brown* hit some of the notoriously bad weather that the North Atlantic is famous for, especially during the winter. At 8:00 P.M. the weather was "overcast & cloudy with heavy rain squalls, vessel rolling and laboring heavily. Shipping heavy seas on main decks." At midnight the *Brown*'s course was changed to 070 degrees "to ease vessel from rolling too heavily," but she was still "taking seas on fore deck." At about daybreak the heavy beam seas washing over the deck swept the number 1 life raft and the pudding booms (buffers between the boats and the side of the ship) for numbers 1 and 3 lifeboats over the side. Course was altered to 050 degrees to put the seas on the quarter rather than on the beam, but the *Brown* was still "rolling & laboring heavily" and "shipping heavy seas on deck" when Chief Mate Kvamme ended his watch at 8:00 A.M. During the morning the crew secured the lifeboats, rafts, and other gear on deck and made sure the hatches were tight. The numbers 1 and 3 lifeboats had to be lashed to the deck because the heavy seas crashing over the boat deck had washed them off the deck chocks. The scheduled fire and boat drill was canceled "due to excessively bad weather." During the afternoon the wind increased to force 8–9 (between 39 and 47 knots), causing another course change, this time to 020 degrees. Although the 30–40-foot seas continued to cause the *Brown* to roll and pitch heavily, the wind decreased to force 6 (22 to 27 knots) during the evening, allowing a course change to 060 degrees at 10:00 P.M. As the wind continued to abate during the early morning hours of 26 February, the *Brown* was able to resume course 090. Although she had gone through extremely heavy weather, the *Brown* had averaged 10.5 knots during the twenty-four hours ending at noon on the 26th. She continued to roll heavily at times during the day, but the weather improved so much that at midnight when he went off watch Third Mate Mazzie could report winds at force 3 (7 to 10 knots), a moderate sea and swell, and the *Brown* as a consequence "rolling moderately."

The 26th found the crew "employed washing bulk-heads & overhead in crew's alley ways, securing gear on deck," and working on a variety of other jobs. James Carter, the carpenter, spent the day building shelves in the engine room. Late in the afternoon the *Brown* had to stop the main engine because of trouble with the feed pump, the pump that supplies water to the boilers, but apparently the problem was minor, for an hour later she returned to full ahead. For the next few days the weather didn't cause problems, but on 3 March the *Brown* once again confronted the frenzy of "winter on the North Atlantic." The wind had begun picking up at dawn and at 8:00 A.M. was at force 8. At 1:00 P.M. course was changed from 065 to 100 "due to high seas breaking over decks & excessive rolling." The northwest winds reached a high of force 12 (above 65 knots), the top of the Beaufort scale, at 6:00 P.M. The wind and the mountainous seas forced the *Brown* to heave to at gyro course 345, about north-north-west, with the engine turning 50 rpm. At 10:30 P.M. course was changed to 360 degrees, due north. The wind stayed at force 10 (48 to 55 knots) during the early morning hours of 4 March. During the midnight to 4:00 watch Second Mate Botto recorded that "periodic inspections of deck [were] made as well as circumstances permitted. #4 boat found to be working loose from gripes. Present conditions prevent having it secured. Taking heavy seas over bulwarks, port & stbd sides & breaking over bow." Even though the wind again reached force 12 at 5:00 A.M., the "Bos'n and carpenter turned to securing life-boats, inspecting hatches & trimming ventilators."

Since the *Brown* had been hove to for eighteen of the past twenty-four hours, she covered only 130 miles at an average speed of 5.4 knots between noon on 3 March and noon on 4 March. During the afternoon of the 4th the seas "stove in" the "forward railing on boat deck, port side." To make an already difficult situation even more difficult, the feed pump acted up again, forcing the engineers to stop the engine at 3:45 P.M. They had it fixed in twenty-five minutes, and since the winds had decreased considerably by then, the *Brown* was able to steam at full speed. The wind picked up again during the night, and as the *Brown* plowed on during the early morning hours of 5 March heavy seas washing over the boat deck tore the port side life jacket box loose from its lashings. By the afternoon of the 5th, however, the winds and seas had moderated and the crew was "employed removing water from after ammunition locker, cleaning lockers, and checking on hatch-tarpaulins." By the end of the day the *Brown* was "rolling easily." The worst of the weather was over for this trip.

On Thursday, 7 March, when about thirty-three hundred miles out from New York, the *Brown* crossed meridian 12° W. For the Merchant Marine crew this meant a war bonus added to their base salaries, because even though the war in Europe had been over for ten months, the unions successfully argued that unrecovered mines still threatened ships. At this time the *Brown* was steaming to the northeast and was about two hundred miles off the coast of Scotland. That night she passed about ten miles off St. Kilda Island, which lies about fifty miles west of the Outer Hebrides. The next morning she was off the Butt of Lewis lighthouse on the northern tip of the Outer Hebrides and at 1:30 P.M. off Dunnet Head lighthouse at the western end of Pentland Firth. Since there were still magnetic mines from the war years in the area, the degaussing system was turned on at this time. Although Pentland Firth is a "narrow rock-strewn tidal channel" considered "one of the most perilous, unmanageable raceways of navigable water known to deep-sea sailormen,"[48] the *Brown* passed through with no trouble. That evening she arrived at Kirkwall in the Bay of Firth in the Orkney Islands to receive instructions on how to proceed through the swept channel in the North Sea to avoid minefields left over from the war.[49]

Ordered by the shore signal station to anchor about two miles off Helliar Holm, the *Brown* at 5:49 P.M. stopped the engine and dropped the port anchor forty-five fathoms in water fourteen fathoms deep. The engine was then ordered to half astern, but "before anchor could be brought up and secured, strong current [3.5 knots] caught vessel causing chain to run all out and break at a defective link." About 125 fathoms of chain were lost. Since the *Brown* was maneuvering in "narrow quarters," she quickly dropped the starboard anchor and had it brought up and secured just nine minutes after losing the port anchor. Shore officials and a routing officer came aboard immediately to instruct the *Brown*'s deck officers on the route to follow across the North Sea.

Just a half hour later the *Brown* was again proceeding to sea. As a further precaution against mines, the degaussing was kept on for the rest of the trip. By 8:00 P.M. she was turning 66 rpm steaming south-

east in the North Sea. After passing about thirteen miles off Kin-
nairds Head shortly before 3:00 A.M. on 9 March, the *Brown* then
proceeded south along the east coast of Scotland at eleven knots until 8:30 A.M., when she changed course to 096 degrees gyro to head in
an easterly direction. At 8:00, when Third Mate Mazzie relieved
Chief Mate Kvamme, the *Brown* was enclosed in dense fog. Shortly
after the 8:30 course change the fog suddenly lifted enough for Mazzie to realize that the barely visible sun was at his back, not in front
of him where it should have been if the *Brown* were headed east. The
Brown was in fact steaming west toward the coast of Scotland. Thoroughly alarmed, Mazzie immediately checked the gyro against the
magnetic compass and found that the gyro "must have gone hay-
wire." He called Captain Hudnall, Chief Mate Kvamme, and Second
Mate Botto, who all came running to the bridge, and Captain Hudnall took over. While all this was happening, a ship closer to shore
began sounding "U"—dot, dot, dash' in Morse code—to warn the
Brown that she was heading into danger. The *Brown* got back onto
course without a mishap, but from then on in his seagoing career
Peter Mazzie made it a practice to check the gyro against the magnetic compass frequently during his watch and always at a change in
course.[50]

At noon on 9 March the *Brown* crossed the Greenwich meridian
at latitude 56° 43' N. A half hour later she sighted a buoy, and for the
rest of the day she continued to pass a series of buoys that led her in
a generally northeasterly direction toward the southern end of Norway. Steaming through "hail squalls & light snow flurries" in moderately rough seas, the *Brown* by early afternoon on the 10th was
about a mile and a half off Rvingers lighthouse at the southernmost
tip of Norway. Ice squalls and snow flurries during the afternoon and
evening caused poor visibility, but finally at about 11:00 P.M. the
Brown arrived at the pilot station at the Skaw at the northernmost
tip of Denmark. After a pilot came on board, the ship steamed at full
ahead south-southeast in the Kattegat, the body of water separating
Denmark and Sweden. At 7:30 A.M. she passed the Anholt lightship
about halfway down the Kattegat, and at a few minutes after noon
the Kattegat pilot was replaced by an Ore Sund pilot, who took her
the rest of the way to a pier in Copenhagen. The trip had covered
4,256 miles over a period of seventeen days, one hour, and forty minutes at an average speed of ten knots.

Starting early the next morning, 12 March, stevedores spent two days discharging coal into barges. On the 14th the *Brown* shifted to the Danish Coal Company pier for a day to unload some more and then to another coal pier where stevedores worked around the clock for four days discharging the coal. The crew meanwhile worked about the ship cleaning, chipping, painting, and doing various odd jobs. One morning was spent painting the stack, which now in peacetime carried the emblem of States Marine Corporation.

Completely discharged on 19 March, the *Brown* shifted to an anchorage where she took on sand ballast from barges. Afterwards stevedores trimmed the ballast, closed the hatches, and dropped the booms. Altogether 1,860 tons of sand had been loaded in all holds except number 1:

number 2 lower hold—380 tons   'tween deck—300 tons
number 3 lower hold—500 tons
number 4 lower hold—345 tons
number 5 lower hold—185 tons   'tween deck—150 tons

Meanwhile the crew had spent the morning cleaning the decks, checking the lifeboats, and taking care of the baggage of the passengers who would come aboard later. Between 12:20 and 2:15 P.M. three radio repairmen were aboard to install a generator for the transmitter, and at 4:20 the passengers, one woman and nine men, came aboard. They were all licensed civilian airplane pilots who, under a U.S. government contract, had flown planes across the Atlantic for delivery in Denmark.[51] During conversations while at sea on the way home they told the *Brown*'s deck officers that Pan-American Airlines was looking for Merchant Marine officers to serve as navigators on airliners, but when Second Mate Walter Botto later checked into this opportunity, he found that Pan-American had all the navigators it needed.[52]

The *Brown* left Copenhagen early in the morning of 21 March. As she proceeded north in the Kattegat, the crew secured the ship for sea. At 8:50 that night she arrived at the entrance to the Kattegat, dropped the pilot, and a minute later took departure at full ahead. By noon the next day she had passed the southern end of Norway and was steaming west at 10.7 knots. At 4:00 A.M. on the 23rd she crossed the Greenwich meridian as she headed for Pentland Firth. Since there was no need to stop at Kirkwall on the westbound trip, the *Brown* passed through the firth and reached its western end at

10:51 A.M. During the twenty-four hours that ended at noon on 23 March the *Brown* had traveled 325 miles at an average speed of 13.0 knots, two knots above her rated speed. Sailing in a southeasterly direction, at 5:00 A.M. on 24 March she passed St. Kilda Island. There was now nothing but open ocean between the *Brown* and the United States.

Although the weather was not nearly as bad as on the outbound voyage, the *Brown* did have some days of rough seas that caused her to vibrate and to pitch and roll heavily at times. To get more stability, number 3 deep tank was filled with seawater as ballast. A week later, as the *Brown* approached the coast of the United States, the water ballast was pumped out. At 6:00 P.M. on 5 April the *Brown* passed six miles off the Chesapeake lightship, and at 7:15 she arrived at the Cape Henry pilot station. The *Brown* had covered the 3,857 miles between Copenhagen and Cape Henry in fifteen days, three hours, and twenty-four minutes at an average speed of 11.8 knots. As no pilot was available, Captain Hudnall decided to go on without one. A native of the Chesapeake Bay area with over fifty years at sea, Captain Hudnall obviously felt that he had the knowledge of the bay and the experience to take the conn himself. Averaging 12.5 knots at full ahead, he then steamed the *Brown* up the bay to Baltimore. At 5:40 A.M. on the morning of 6 April she passed Sandy Point just north of the present Bay Bridge and at 7:22 dropped anchor to await orders at the junction of the Curtis Bay and Fort McHenry channels in the Patapsco River. Later in the morning a physician from the U.S. Public Health Service came aboard to examine the passengers and crew, and early that afternoon she shifted to Pier 3, Locust Point, the Baltimore and Ohio Railroad Pier on the north side. One can assume that the passengers debarked at this time. Not much happened during the next few days before the official end of the voyage: on 7 April, U.S. Customs officials came aboard to seal the bonded stores that are always locked in port, specifically the cigarettes in the slop chest and the ship's liquor supply; early in the morning on the 8th the crew was "standing by to shift ship," but as nothing further is noted in the log, apparently the *Brown* remained at Pier 3; during the afternoon of the 8th exterminators worked aboard the ship; and on 10 April 1946 Voyage 11 officially ended.[53]

Although articles for Voyage 12 were not opened until 10 June 1946,[54] Captain Hudnall, the three deck officers, and twenty other crew members remained aboard. On 12 April shipyard workers from

Bethlehem Steel came aboard to start repairs and to make alterations in the crew's quarters. The workers were aboard for a total of eight days, working from 7:30 A.M. to 3:30 P.M., and for five of the days also from 5:00 P.M. until midnight. Except for an occasional comment that the workers removed the life rafts, took the gangway to the shop for repairs, and did some painting, the log does not say how many were involved and what exactly they did. The port anchor and chain lost at Kirkwall were replaced on 17 April, and Second Mate Walter Botto, on duty at the time, noted in the log that the carpenter and an AB painted anchor shots, that is, marked the chain with paint at fifteen-fathom (ninety-foot) intervals as it was taken aboard.

Not much happened on board the *Brown* after the shipyard workers left. On most days the crew did "various odd jobs" around the ship. On 23 April the carpenter and an AB did some painting in the officer's staterooms, and on the 24th the crew chipped and painted the hatch coamings. On the 25th the *Brown* spent about an hour shifting from Pier 3 to an anchorage.

The next four weeks passed with the crew doing routine odd jobs, chipping and red-leading hatch coamings, painting lifeboats, painting the boat deck, and the like. During this time Carpenter James Carter spent a day and a half installing shelves in the purser's stateroom. Just after midnight on 3 May the *Thomas Stone*, anchored much too close to the *Brown*, "swung into us on the aft part of boat deck by the stanchion (davit) on port side causing it to spring slightly." To prevent a recurrence, at 10:30 A.M. the *Brown* shifted enough to be clear of the *Stone*. The next afternoon Bos'n Samothrakis slipped while picking up a half-filled barrel of kerosene and immediately felt a pain in his side. Third Mate Peter Mazzie, the mate on duty, advised the bos'n to see a doctor, but the bos'n stubbornly insisted on continuing with his duties. Four days passed before the persistent pain convinced him to go the Marine Hospital, where a physician found that he had a hernia and recommended that he "be hospitalized or given light duty." The second alternative was chosen, and apparently the bos'n had no further problems because he sailed not only on Voyage 12 but on Voyage 13 as well.

While this was going on, not much happened to break the routine of shipboard life at anchor until 10 May, when the *Brown* shifted to Western Maryland Pier 5, Canton. A shore gang came aboard to get the holds ready to discharge the ballast, and after the *Brown* shifted the following morning to the next pier—number 6, which had an overhead crane—the crane was used to remove part of the ballast. The *Brown* then shifted back to Pier 5 "to finish taking ballast out with own gear." The stevedores finished discharging ballast on the 12th but refused to close the hatches. After the *Brown* shifted to an anchorage the next morning, the crew did the jobs that the stevedores had refused to do the previous evening, "putting beams on & closing hatches."

Not much happened during the next eight days covered by the log. On 15 May, a typical day, the crew was "employed chipping, scaling, and red-leading bulwarks on fore deck." On the 17th a launch brought food stores out to the *Brown,* and an Esso barge delivered fifteen hundred barrels of fuel oil. During the afternoon of the 18th the *Brown* was buffeted by the high winds and squalls that sometimes sweep across the Chesapeake Bay area without warning, causing "garbage [to be] strewn all over decks during windy blow" and making more work for the crew after the squalls passed a few hours later. Three days later another sudden squall came up with so much force that the *Brown* "swung rapidly about." Like many such storms on the Chesapeake, this one didn't last long, and the day ended "partly cloudy & clear." On the 23rd a water boat came alongside to deliver fresh water, and a garbage boat picked up her accumulation of garbage. The last entry for this day—"routine inspections made about ship—all O.K."—is also the last entry in the "Deck Log" for Voyage 11.

Captain Hudnall, Chief Mate Kvamme, Second Mate Botto, and Third Mate Mazzie stayed on the *Brown* for Voyage 12, which began on 10 June 1946.[55] Sometime between 23 May, the date of the last entry in the "Deck Log" for Voyage 11, and 18 June, the date the *Brown* left Baltimore for Hamburg, she had taken on a load of wheat that gave her a 26'06" draft forward and 30'2" aft. Other than the "Official Log-Book," the only document concerning this voyage is Captain Hudnall's "Night Order Book," which gives little information other than the courses he wanted to maintain. On 2 July, the last night for which there is a comment on the outbound trip, Captain Hudnall ordered the mate on watch, normally Third Mate Mazzie on the 8:00 to midnight, to "continue course until midnight unless light on Casquets is made before." This entry shows that the *Brown* at the time was in the western end of the English Channel. As she was in this area during the night of 2 July, she probably arrived at Hamburg sometime on 4 or 5 July to discharge the wheat. Walter Botto took advantage of the few days in Hamburg to buy a Plath sextant, considered the world's finest, and one of the cuckoo clocks for which Germany is famous.[56] On 9 July the *Brown* left Hamburg for New York.[57] On the 12th she passed Beachy Head at the southwestern end of the Strait of Dover.[58] The "Night Order Book" for 12 July and the following eight days called for a course of 257 degrees. On the 21st course was altered slightly, and again on the next day with the comment that the mate on watch should "keep a good lookout for trawlers. . . . And if light ship at Nantucket is not sighted by 3 A.M. call me." This reference locates the *Brown* off the coast of Massachusetts and getting close to home. She arrived in New York the next day, 23 July 1946.[59]

Captain Hudnall continued as master for Voyage 13, but all the deck officers and all but one of the engine officers changed. Articles for the thirteenth voyage were signed on 8 August 1946.[60] On the 9th the *Brown* sailed light from New York to Galveston, Texas, arriving on the 17th.[61] Between 27 August and 3 September, while the *Brown* was tied up at Pier 39, American Bureau of Shipping surveyor Robert P. Massey inspected the ship and conducted the annual load line and boiler surveys. His report, dated 3 September, illustrates the thoroughness of the bureau's inspections:

1. The steering arrangements, water tight doors in bulkheads, air and sounding pipes were examined and all found in satisfactory condition.
2. The ventilator coamings, hatch coamings, hatch covers, tarpaulins, battens, machinery casing, guard rails, bulwarks, freeing ports, protection for access to crews quarters were examined and all found satisfactory.
3. No alteration has been made in the hull, superstructure or means of closing openings in the superstructure which would affect the position of load line markings.
4. A general inspection of main and auxiliary machinery was made, anchor windlass and steering machinery tried out and all proved satisfactory.
5. The International Load Line Certificate #I-3174 was endorsed on September 3, 1946.
6. The two (2) water tube boilers, superheaters and main steam pipes were hydrostatically tested and boilers examined internally and externally together with superheaters and all found satisfactory.
7. All boilers mountings and safety valves were opened up for examination internally and all found satisfactory. All valves were overhauled by grinding in and repacking valve stems.

8. The safety valves were floated under steam pressure to their allowed working pressure by the U.S.C.G.

The annual boiler survey is now complete.

The above examination having been satisfactorily completed the vessel is considered eligible to retain her present class in the American Bureau of Shipping.[62]

Two days after the survey, at noon on 5 September, the Seafarers International Union and the Sailors Union of the Pacific, AFL, went on strike to protest the Wage Stabilization Board's refusal to approve wage increases that the unions had won in negotiations with shipowners.[63] At the beginning of the war the unions had negotiated for war-risk bonuses rather than increases in base pay, but with the war over and most of the bonuses eliminated, the unions were now seeking higher base pay. The issue was a complicated one because in June 1946 the National Maritime Union, CIO—which represented the *Brown*'s crew—had won a pay raise of $17.50 monthly for seamen. The AFL unions, however, were able to get $27.50. The Wage Stabilization Board, a federal government agency, ruled that the AFL unions could not receive more than the $17.50 that the CIO union had won. Hence the strike by the AFL unions. The National Maritime Union and the sixty-five thousand longshoremen on the Atlantic and Gulf Coasts honored AFL picket lines, thereby closing down the shipping industry in the United States. The *New York Times* on 7 September called the strike "the greatest in the country's maritime history in scope and effectiveness" and noted on 11 September that it had tied up 1,219 ships on the Atlantic, Pacific, and Gulf Coasts. The situation by this time had been further complicated by the announcement by Joseph Curran, president of the National Maritime Union, that the NMU would demand the same increases if the AFL unions got more than the $17.50 that the CIO unions had won. On 13 September the NMU, "in the absence of specific assurances that it, too, would be protected in its demand for parity of maritime wage rates . . . [announced] that it had gone on strike and considered its contracts void." Thus at noon on 13 September all but four of the *Brown*'s unlicensed crew left the ship on strike. Three firemen/watertenders and the carpenter stayed behind "as security watch and to keep the plant going," but at noon the next day these four men went out on strike also,[64] putting the responsibility for the ship wholly in the hands of the officers. The issues were finally resolved by arbitration a week later. Since the arbitration award gave the NMU wage parity with other unions, Joseph Curran on 21 September called off the strike, stating that the settlement was "the greatest victory achieved for seamen in our history." Thus between 11:00 A.M. and noon on the 21st the "unlicensed crew returned to . . . [the *Brown*] and resumed their regular duties."[65] Three days later the *Brown* made the short trip across Galveston Bay and up the San Jacinto River and Houston Ship Canal to Houston to take on a full load of grain. She left Houston on the 28th bound for Hull, England.

The *Brown* arrived at Hull on 22 October,[66] discharged the grain during the week following, and left for London on the 29th. There is no record of the date of arrival, but it was probably on the 30th. At London the *Brown*, for her final voyage home, loaded a cargo that contrasted sharply with the cargo she had carried on her maiden voyage just four years earlier. Instead of tanks, jeeps, P-40s, machine guns, ammunition, and other materials associated with death and destruction, her last cargo contained such items associated with pleasure and creative activity as ice skates, artists' colors, books for the librarian at Tufts College, musical instruments, tobacco, antiques, eau de cologne, wine, gin, and rum. There were also many cases of personal effects, trunks, and such miscellaneous items as woolens, linens, and dressed leather—the list is fourteen pages long. Thirteen cases of rockets and distress signals were stowed on deck, and Chief Steward Frederic Clar took responsibility for the one hundred crates of canned herring needing refrigeration. Except for the perfume and six cases of nitrates stowed in number 1 'tween deck and a very few items in numbers 2 and 5 lower holds, the cargo was placed in number 3 lower hold.[67] The cargo also included sixty-four bales of raw rabbit skins being shipped to a fur company in New York.[68] The *Brown* departed London on 1 November and arrived in New York on the 15th.[69] Her seagoing career as a cargo ship was over.

To appreciate the *John W. Brown*'s achievement during World War II, one must see it in relation to the total U.S. maritime effort. Attempting to visualize this effort, one author observed that in 1943 alone, "with the overseas movement of military goods and of men not yet at its peak, nearly forty-seven million tons of cargo were moved by sea, not including fuel oil and gasoline. This is the equivalent of a million freight-car loads, or ten thousand freight trains of a hundred cars each. Coupled car to car, they would make five solid trains stretching abreast from the Atlantic Ocean to the Pacific."[70] By V-J Day the U.S. Merchant Marine had carried a total of

268,252,000 tons of cargo, 203,522,000 tons of it dry cargo and 64,730,000 tons gasoline and oil. It had also carried more than seven million troops.[71] The five trains stretching from coast to coast to carry the dry cargo in 1943 would increase to about twenty-two to accommodate the dry cargoes of 1941–45. Just how vital these supplies were to the war effort is underlined by the estimate that between seven and eight tons of equipment per soldier were required in Europe, and about twice that in the Pacific.[72] Nothing makes clearer the crucial importance of controlling the seas in World War II so that the merchant ships could get through. The outcome of the war in Europe quite literally depended on the outcome of the Battle of the Atlantic.

The cost of transporting the needed cargoes and personnel was high. Of the approximately 6,000 American flag ships involved, the enemy sank 624, slightly over 10 percent, and of the 290,000 civilian Merchant Mariners who manned these ships, some 6,100 were killed. Only the U.S. Marine Corps had a higher percentage of fatalities.[73]

Although escaping some close calls, the *John W. Brown* got through the war undamaged by enemy action and was therefore able to fulfill her missions in supplying troops and equipment to the European theater during her eight wartime voyages. Steaming a total of about one hundred thousand miles, she carried approximately 52,525 tons of cargo and more than a thousand troops from the United States to the war zones. It would require eleven freight trains of a hundred cars each to carry that much cargo. While steaming between various Mediterranean ports, she moved about 15,585 tons of cargo, more than 5,100 troops, and 336 POWs. Inbound, the *Brown* up to mid-August 1945 transported to the United States about 8,645 tons of cargo, about 1,000 POWs, and 770 homeward-bound GIs.

In her five postwar voyages the *Brown* steamed about thirty-nine thousand miles, carrying to a war-ravaged Europe more than 37,500 tons of cargoes necessary for survival. On two of her return trips she brought more than twelve hundred GIs home. Altogether, between 1942 and 1946 the *John W. Brown* steamed about 139,000 miles, carrying about 114,260 tons of cargo. Without fanfare, she had done everything asked of her.

Afterword

L ESS than two weeks after the *John W. Brown* arrived in New York in November 1946, the War Shipping Administration transferred her to the Board of Education of New York City for use as a vocational high school. She remained in this service until 1982, a span of thirty-six years.

Meanwhile, foreseeing that eventually New York would no longer want the *Brown*, the National Maritime Historical Society in 1978 sponsored a "Liberty Ship Seminar" on preserving the ship when her schoolship days ended. The present Project Liberty Ship organization that evolved from the seminar has the mission of maintaining the *Brown* as an operational museum ship and as a memorial to the men and women who built and served on Liberty ships during World War II.

In 1983 the *Brown* was towed to the Reserve Fleet in the James River near Williamsburg, Virginia, where she became the roost for hundreds of pigeons and began to deteriorate. The *Brown* was not forgotten, however, and in 1985 members of Project Liberty Ship successfully petitioned to have her named to the National Register of Historic Places.

The major problem to be solved if the Project was to retrieve the *Brown* from the Reserve Fleet was to find a suitable berth somewhere. Unsuccessful in the New York area, the Project in 1988

On her first Chesapeake Bay cruise after restoration, the *Brown* on 21 September 1991 carried about six hundred passengers.
Sherod M. Cooper III

looked to possibilities in Baltimore. When the Maryland Port Administration offered the use of Pier 1 on Clinton Street, the Project lost no time in towing the *Brown* to Baltimore. The ship has been berthed at Pier 1 since August 1988 while Project Liberty Ship volunteers have logged over three hundred thousand hours working on her.

By September 1991 restoration had progressed to the point that the *Brown* was able to steam with six hundred guests aboard for a six-hour cruise on the Chesapeake Bay. Since then she has visited several Chesapeake and Delaware Bay ports, including Norfolk, Philadelphia, Camden, New Jersey, and Wilmington, Delaware, and has made coastwise voyages to New York, Boston, Halifax, Nova Scotia, and Wilmington, North Carolina. The Project aspired to steam her across the Atlantic for the June 1994 fiftieth-anniversary commemoration of the Normandy Invasion, but time and money ran out before her hull could be restored sufficiently to allow her to cross the ocean safely. With a long history behind her, the SS *John W. Brown* is poised to steam into an even longer history ahead.

Notes

CHAPTER 1

1. Text of "Fireside Chat," *New York Times,* 30 December 1940.

2. Roskill, *The War at Sea,* 1:617–18, 2:486.

3. "The Liberty Ship," 152.

4. Records of the American Bureau of Shipping, "Hull Classification Report," SS *John W. Brown,* Report no. 251, 26 October 1942, 2.

5. Bourneuf, "Workhorse of the Fleet," 76.

6. Fuel consumption calculated from data in "Abstract Deck Log," Voyage 1.

7. "The Liberty Ship," 152.

8. "Specifications for the Construction of a Single Screw Cargo Vessel, Design EC2-S-C1," sec. 17, p. 1.

9. "The Liberty Ship," 152, and advertisement for "South Bend Galley Ranges" on p. 192 in the same issue.

10. [Berry], *Gunners Get Glory,* 169–70.

11. Account of James W. Munroe, seaman first class on the *Brown*'s Voyages 6 and 7, p. 3, Project Liberty Ship Archives (hereafter PLSA).

12. O'Flaherty, *Abandoned Convoy,* 16.

13. [Berry], *Gunners Get Glory,* 170.

14. Sawyer and Mitchell, *The Liberty Ships,* 14.

15. *The Bethlehem Liberty Fleet,* 11.

16. Records of the Maritime Administration, "Report of Progress as of September 30, 1942: Vessels Complete & Under Construction," Report no. 57, 1 October 1942.

17. See Lane, *Ships for Victory*, 55–66, for details about the expansion of the program.

18. *Production System, Bethlehem-Fairfield Shipyard*, 4.

19. *The Bethlehem Liberty Fleet*, 12.

20. Records of the Maritime Administration, telegram dated 7 September 1942 from J. M. McInnis to Adm. H. L. Vickery.

21. Crane, "Headaches Precede Champagne," [1].

22. Records of the American Bureau of Shipping, "Hull Classification Report," SS *John W. Brown*, Report no. 251, 26 October 1942, 1.

23. Records of the Maritime Administration, "Report of Progress . . . Vessels Complete & Under Construction," Report no. 55, 1 August 1942, and Report no. 56, 1 September 1942.

24. Records of the American Bureau of Shipping, data from files on the *John W. Brown*.

25. Records of the Maritime Administration, "Report of Progress . . . Vessels Complete & Under Construction," Report no. 55, 1 August 1942.

26. Industrial Union of Marine and Shipbuilding Workers of America Collection, Series 8, Subseries 1, Box 4, "Plans Under Way for Union to Sponsor Labor Day Launchings," *Shipyard Worker*, 10 July 1942, 1.

27. Industrial Union of Marine and Shipbuilding Workers of America Collection, Series 8, Subseries 1, Box 4, "IUMSWA Names 2 'Liberty Ships' for Labor Men," *Shipyard Worker*, 21 August 1942, 1–2.

28. Industrial Union of Marine and Shipbuilding Workers of America Collection, Series 8, Subseries 1, Box 4, "Lo 43 to Honor Labor Chiefs in Dual Launchings," *Shipyard Worker*, 4 September 1942, 1–2.

29. Records of the Maritime Administration, letter from Wade Skinner to commissioner of customs, 3 September 1942.

30. Letter from Bertha Gainsley, Brown's daughter, quoted in *Liberty Log*, Spring/Summer 1989, 6.

31. Industrial Union of Marine and Shipbuilding Workers of America Collection, Series 8, Subseries 1, Box 4, "John W. Brown, Labor Veteran, Killed Hunting," *Shipyard Worker*, 27 June 1941, 1.

32. Industrial Union of Marine and Shipbuilding Workers of America Collection, Series 5, Locals, Box 19, letter from John W. Brown to Philip Van Gelder, 24 September 1940.

33. Industrial Union of Marine and Shipbuilding Workers of America Collection, Series 1, Subseries 4, Box 1, letter from John W. Brown to Philip Van Gelder, 13 November 1940.

34. Industrial Union of Marine and Shipbuilding Workers of America Collection, Series 5, Locals, Box 19, "John W. Brown Dies from Gunshot Wound: Well Known Labor Leader Believed Victim of Accident at His Woolwich Home," *The Bath Daily*, 20 June 1941.

35. Crane, "Headaches Precede Champagne," [1].

36. *Baltimore Sun*, 24 September 1942.

37. *Baltimore Evening Sun*, 7 September 1942.

38. *Baltimore Sun,* 8 September 1942.

39. *Baltimore Evening Sun,* 7 September 1942.

40. Ibid.

41. *Program, Labor Day Ceremonies.*

42. *Baltimore Sun,* 8 September 1942.

43. Industrial Union of Marine and Shipbuilding Workers of America Collection, Series 1, Subseries 4, Box 5, "Text of Speech Delivered by John Green, National President, Industrial Union of Marine and Shipbuilding Workers of America, CIO, at the Bethlehem-Fairfield Shipyard, Baltimore, Maryland, Labor Day, September 7, 1942, Carried by Coast-to-Coast Hookup."

44. *Baltimore Evening Sun,* 8 September 1942.

45. *Program, Labor Day Ceremonies.*

46. *New York Times,* 6 September 1942.

47. "Outfitting: How Liberty Ships Get Equipment Explained," *Baltimore Sun,* 24 October 1943.

48. Ibid.; *Production System, Bethlehem-Fairfield Shipyard,* 17–18.

49. Records of the Maritime Administration, letter from J. F. Devlin to States Marine Corporation, 15 August 1942.

50. Nielsen, "The Maiden Voyage," and Nilsen, "Album."

51. Records of the American Bureau of Shipping, "Hull Classification Report," SS *John W. Brown,* Report no. 251, 26 October 1942, 2, 25.

52. Trials of SS *Santiagos Iglesias.*

53. John W. Hart, telephone interview by author, 3 December 1992.

54. Records of the Maritime Administration, U.S. Maritime Commission, "Certificate of Delivery of Vessel," 19 September 1942; WSA form certifying delivery, 19 September 1942; and WSA form filled out by States Marine Corporation, 17 April 1945.

55. "Abstract Deck Log," Voyage 1; Records of the American Bureau of Shipping, "Hull Classification Report," SS *John W. Brown,* Report no. 251, 26 October 1942, 25.

56. "Abstract Deck Log," Voyage 1.

57. Records of the War Shipping Administration, "Allocations," Entry: 3, Box 1.

58. Since the Merchant Marine did not normally use the twenty-four-hour military time system during World War II, I do not use it in this book.

59. Ralph Albers, interview by author, aboard SS *John W. Brown,* 12 June 1993.

60. Hearing before Subcommittee on Merchant Marine, attachment to statement of Ian A. Millar, 133.

61. George L. Spittel to author, 14 September 1991, PLSA.

62. Spittel, "Notes on the J. W. Brown Voyage #5."

63. Copy of "Crew List, United States Coast Guard," Voyage 13, PLSA.

64. "Arming of Merchant Ships," 140.

65. *General Instructions for Commanding Officers of Naval Armed Guards on Merchant Ships, 1943,* 32.

66. "Arming of Merchant Ships," 140.

67. Nameplate data, 5"/51 gun at the Navy Museum, Washington, D.C., and *Jane's Fighting Ships of World War II,* 254.

68. *Naval Ordnance and Gunnery,* 115.

69. Descriptive information mounted on 3"/50 on *John W. Brown.*

70. Vernon Joyce to author, 26 May 1993, PLSA.

71. *Naval Ordnance and Gunnery,* 166, 184.

72. *General Instructions for Commanding Officers of Naval Armed Guards on Merchant Ships, 1943,* 35.

73. "Historical Narrative of Port Director—New York," 503–4.

74. *General Instructions for Commanding Officers of Naval Armed Guards on Merchant Ships, 1943,* 28.

75. *General Instructions for Commanding Officers of Naval Armed Guards on Merchant Ships, 1944,* 26–27.

76. [Berry], *Gunners Get Glory,* 191.

77. Vernon Joyce to author, 26 May 1993, PLSA.

78. De La Pedraja, *The Rise and Decline of U.S. Merchant Shipping,* 145.

79. *On a True Course,* 57.

80. Figures from Lehman and Yarmon, *Opportunities in the Armed Forces,* 278–81, 402–3.

81. Hearing before Subcommittee on Merchant Marine, letter written in late 1943 or early 1944 from Telfair Knight, Assistant Deputy Administrator, War Shipping Administration, to Arren M. Atherton, National Commander, The American Legion, attached to statement of Ian A. Millar, 112.

82. Calculations based on figures in "War-Risk Bonuses for Seafaring Personnel," 11–14.

83. Hearing before Subcommittee on Merchant Marine, Telfair Knight letter, 112.

84. Ibid., 113.

CHAPTER 2

1. *Baltimore Sun,* 28 September 1942.

2. *Variety,* 30 September 1942, 42.

3. *Baltimore Sun,* 30 September 1942.

4. Unless otherwise noted, the information about the *John W. Brown* in this chapter comes from the "Abstract Deck Log," the "Deck Log" for Voyage 1, and the "Log" and "Reports" of Lt. (jg) Charles F. Calvert, Navy Armed Guard commander on Voyage 1.

5. Bloxsom, "Recollections," 33.

6. Ibid., 41.

7. Lieutenant Calvert was born in 1916 and joined the Navy on 1 November 1940 (*Register of Commissioned and Warrant Officers,* 183).

8. Lott, *Most Dangerous Sea,* 68–69.

9. Bloxsom, "Recollections," 35–36.

10. "Historical Narrative of Port Director—New York," 357.

11. See van der Vat, *The Atlantic Campaign,* 269–71.

12. Records of the War Shipping Administration, "Persian Gulf—Schwenk Reports, October 1942," Entry: RSA, Box 27.

13. Ibid.

14. "Historical Narrative of Port Director—New York," 364–65.

15. Unless otherwise noted, details about NG-314 are from Convoy Sailing Orders, Box 44.

16. Quoted in "History of Convoy and Routing," 24.

17. Count of names in the crew list of the "Official Log-Book," for Voyage 1, pp. 5–6.

18. "Historical Narrative of Port Director—New York," 537–38.

19. Ibid., 537.

20. Ibid., 418.

21. Ibid., 537.

22. Deck Log, USS *Simpson.*

23. Morison, *History of United States Naval Operations,* 1:264.

24. Ibid., 1:414.

25. Deck Log, USS *Simpson.*

26. Convoy and Routing Files, GZ-9, Box 42.

27. Nielsen, "The Maiden Voyage," 8.

28. Ibid., 8–9.

29. Kenneth Nielsen, interview by author, aboard SS *John W. Brown,* 8 September 1995.

30. Deck Log, USS *Borie.*

31. Ibid.

32. Deck Log, USS *Barry.*

33. Deck Logs, USS *Barry* and USS *Borie.*

34. Bloxsom, "Recollections," 37.

35. Nielsen, "The Maiden Voyage," 10.

36. Ralph Nilsen to author, 27 June 1989, PLSA.

37. Ralph Nilsen to author, 28 July 1989, PLSA.

38. Ibid.

39. *Newsweek,* 26 October 1942, 75.

40. Nielsen, "The Maiden Voyage," 12; Ralph Nilsen, videotaped interview by Brian Hope, 26 October 1989, PLSA.

41. Bloxsom, "Recollections," 38–39.

42. Sawyer and Mitchell, *The Liberty Ships,* 171.

43. Bloxsom, "Recollections," 39.

44. Ibid.

45. Gerald Griffin, Robert Bloxsom, and Jerome Mamo, videotaped interview by Brian Hope, 23 May 1990, PLSA.

46. Morison, *History of United States Naval Operations,* 1:411.

47. Reports of Navy Armed Guard Commanders, SS *Jonathan Elmer.*

48. Muggenthaler, *German Raiders of World War II,* 248–49, 253, 259 (map).

49. Bloxsom, "Recollections," 40–41.

50. Ibid., 42.

51. Records of the War Shipping Administration, "Mr. McPherson's Desk File," Entry: RSA, Box 74.

52. Records of the War Shipping Administration, "P.G. Monthly Reports by Seaholm on Persian Gulf Ports for Clearance," Entry: RSA, Box 67.

53. Records of the War Shipping Administration, "P.G.—Congestion in Persian Gulf Ports," Entry: RSA, Box 67.

54. Motter, *The Persian Corridor,* 6–7.

55. Ibid., 5, 481–83.

56. Records of the War Shipping Administration, "P.G. Monthly Reports by Seaholm on Persian Gulf Ports for Clearance," Entry: RSA, Box 67.

57. Motter, *The Persian Corridor,* 392.

58. Ibid., 312–13, and chart 6, 505.

59. Records of the War Shipping Administration, Eugene Seaholm to A. E. King, 26 October 1942, Entry: RSA, Box 67.

60. Records of the War Shipping Administration, "Persian Gulf," 4 February 1943 report of W. H. Lock, British Ministry of War Transport Representative for Iraq and Iran, Entry: 4, Box 3.

61. Records of the War Shipping Administration, "P.G. Monthly Reports by Seaholm on Persian Gulf Ports for Clearance," Entry: RSA, Box 67.

62. Ibid.

63. Bloxsom, "Recollections," 42.

64. "Official Log-Book," Voyage 1, p. 30.

65. Bloxsom, "Recollections," 42–43.

66. Records of the War Shipping Administration, "P.G. Monthly Reports by Seaholm on Persian Gulf Ports for Clearance," Entry: RSA, Box 67.

67. Ralph Nilsen to author, 27 June 1989, PLSA.

68. Records of the War Shipping Administration, "Outward Cables re Inbound Convoys and Routing—1943–1944," Entry: RSA, Box 71.

69. Records of the Maritime Administration, memo dated 13 April 1943 from F. M. Darr, Vice President, Isthmian Steamship Company, to A. E. King, Director, Division of Traffic-Ship Operations, War Shipping Administration.

70. Convoy and Routing Files, PA-29/PB-31, Box 118.

71. *United States Maritime Service Training Manual: Engineering Branch Training,* 69.

72. Bloxsom, "Recollections," 48.

73. Ralph Nilsen to author, 28 July 1989, PLSA.

74. Ralph Nilsen to author, 27 June 1989, PLSA.

75. Gerald Griffin, Robert Bloxsom, and Jerome Mamo, videotaped interview by Brian Hope, 23 May 1990, PLSA.

76. Convoy and Routing Files, CN-16, Box 15.

77. Ralph Nilsen to Michael Gillen, 26 June 1989, PLSA.

78. Nilsen, "Album."

79. Convoy and Routing Files, BT-11, Box 10.

80. *Jane's Fighting Ships of World War II,* 98–99.

81. World War II War Diaries, USS *Goff*, Box 897.

82. Convoy and Routing Files, BT-11, Box 10.

83. Ibid.; World War II War Diaries, USS *Goff*, Box 897.

84. Nielsen, "The Maiden Voyage," 14.

85. Morison, *History of United States Naval Operations*, 1:146.

86. Nielsen, "The Maiden Voyage," 13–14.

87. "Inward Foreign Manifest," PLSA.

88. Ralph Nilsen to author, 28 July 1989, PLSA.

89. Convoy and Routing Files, TAG-60, Box 137.

90. Morison, *History of United States Naval Operations*, 1:410.

91. Convoy and Routing Files, GN-60, Box 28.

92. Nielsen, "The Maiden Voyage," 5.

93. "Official Log-Book," noted on cover.

94. Records of the Maritime Administration, memo dated 26 November 1943 from R. W. Seabury, Assistant Deputy Administrator for Maintenance and Repair, to the Administrator, War Shipping Administration.

95. Clogher, "Cargo Security Officers," 133.

96. Records of the American Bureau of Shipping, Report no. D-6576, 3 June 1943.

97. Records of the American Bureau of Shipping, Report no. D-6577, 3 June 1943.

98. Wardlow, *The Transportation Corps*, 300.

99. Nesdale and Clogher, "Liberty Ships as Troop Transports," 122.

100. Charles, *Troopships of World War II*, 355, 359–60.

101. Records of the Maritime Administration, American Bureau of Shipping, "Inter-Office Correspondence, From: New York Office, To: All Coast Offices, Subject: Liberty Ships Troop Conversion," 19 October 1943, and memo dated 26 November 1943 from R. W. Seabury, Assistant Deputy Administrator for Maintenance and Repair, to the Administrator, War Shipping Administration.

102. "S.S. 'JOHN W. BROWN'—Voyage #2—Deck Department," carbon copy of orders from various vendors, PLSA.

103. Records of the Maritime Administration, copy of American Bureau of Shipping Certificate no. NY-9767-X, 11 June 1943.

CHAPTER 3

1. "Official Log-Book," Voyage 2, p. 3.

2. Warren Wagenseil, third mate on Voyage 3, telephone interview by author, 24 April 1994.

3. Unless otherwise noted, the information about the *John W. Brown* in this chapter comes from the "Secret Log for a United States Merchant Vessel" kept by the master, William E. Carley, and from the "Log" and "Reports" of Lt. (jg) Arley T. Zinn, Navy Armed Guard commander.

4. Convoy and Routing Files, UGS-11, Box 154.

5. Records of the War Shipping Administration, Records of Maxwell

Brandwen, "Army Loadings—Beginning April 29, 1943 thru June 13, 1943," Entry: 4, Box 1.

6. "Historical Narrative of Port Director—New York," 333–34.

7. Records of the Office of the Chief of Transportation, "Record of Vessel Performance, New York Port of Embarkation, Calendar Year Ended 31 December 1943," Box 253.

8. Records of the War Shipping Administration, Records of Maxwell Brandwen, "Army Loadings—Beginning June 14, 1943 thru July 31, 1943," Entry: 4, Box 1.

9. UGS Convoy Files, 1942–1945, UGS-11.

10. Convoy Sailing Orders, UGS-11, Box 101.

11. Convoy and Routing Files, UGS-11, Box 154.

12. "Official Log-Book," Voyage 2, pp. 22–24.

13. Clogher, "Cargo Security Officers," 135.

14. Carbon copy of rosters of U.S. Army and Royal Navy personnel, PLSA.

15. B. W. Arrance, interview by author, 18 June 1990.

16. "History of Harbor Entrance Control Post, Fort Story, Cape Henry, Virginia, 1941–1945," 62.

17. "First Draft Narrative," 515, 523.

18. Unless otherwise noted, the information about UGS-11 is from Convoy and Routing Files, Box 154.

19. "History of the Port Director's Office, Fifth Naval District," 91.

20. Records of the Office of the Chief of Transportation, "Special Article—I: Liberty Ships as Troop Carriers," Box 272.

21. UGS Convoy Files, 1942–1945, UGS-11.

22. Convoy and Routing Files, UGS-11, "Brief Narrative of the Voyage," Box 154.

23. Y'Blood, *Hunter-Killer,* 282–83.

24. Ibid., 34, 70, 280.

25. World War II War Diaries, USS *Core,* Box 759.

26. Convoy and Routing Files, UGS-11, "Brief Narrative of the Voyage," Box 154.

27. Typed and handwritten menus for 27 June through 6 July 1943, PLSA.

28. B. W. Arrance, interview by author, 18 June 1990.

29. World War II War Diaries, USS *Core,* Box 759.

30. World War II War Diaries, USS *Wyffels,* Box 1584.

31. Convoy and Routing Files, UGS-11, "Brief Narrative of the Voyage," Box 154.

32. Farrar, *A Ship's Log Book,* 169–70.

33. Convoy and Routing Files, UGS-11, "Brief Narrative of the Voyage," Box 154.

34. Richard Schiff to author, 14 January 1991, PLSA.

35. Convoy and Routing Files, UGS-11, "Brief Narrative of the Voyage," Box 154.

36. Convoy and Routing Files, Naval Message from CTF 62, 20 July 1943, Box 154.

37. Morison, *History of United States Naval Operations,* 10:116.

38. Convoy and Routing Files, UGS-11, "Brief Narrative of the Voyage," Box 154.

39. Deck Log, USS *Bogue.*

40. Richard Schiff, "Commentary," *Boca Raton News,* 21 May 1990.

41. Richard Schiff to Marilyn Shapiro (written at sea), 18 August 1943, photocopy, PLSA.

42. Convoy and Routing Files, UGS-11, "Brief Narrative of the Voyage," Box 154.

43. Y'Blood, *Hunter-Killer,* 70.

44. Ibid., 70–73, 76.

45. World War II War Diaries, USS *Hobby,* Box 946.

46. Convoy and Routing Files, UGS-11, "Brief Narrative of the Voyage," Box 154.

47. Ibid.

48. Convoy and Routing Files, KMS-20, Box 72.

49. Convoy and Routing Files, UGS-11, Convoy Form D, Box 154.

50. Records of the War Shipping Administration, Records of Lewis W. Douglas, "North Africa April 1943," Entry: Douglas, Box 12.

51. Statement by Third Mate Armstrong, typescript and two carbons, PLSA.

52. "Official Log-Book," Voyage 2, p. 31.

53. Records of the Office of the Chief of Transportation; the number of officers and enlisted men comes from Hampton Roads Port of Embarkation, Historical Report no. 5: "Personnel Debarked at Hampton Roads Port of Embarkation July, August, September [1943]," Box 270.

54. Records of the Office of the Chief of Transportation, letter dated 12 July 1943 from Col. R. M. Hicks, Transportation Corps, to Howell B. Smith, Acting Assistant to Director of Allocations and Assignments, War Shipping Administration, Box 47.

55. B. W. Arrance to Brian Hope, 21 June 1989, PLSA.

56. Richard Schiff to Brian Hope, 19 April 1990, PLSA.

57. Sawyer and Mitchell, *The Oceans, the Forts, and the Parks,* 13.

58. Convoy and Routing Files, GUS-11, Box 35.

59. "Official Log-Book," Voyage 2, p. 2.

60. Convoy and Routing Files, GUS-11, "Brief Narrative of the Voyage," Box 35.

61. World War II War Diaries, USCGC *Bibb,* Box 638.

62. Convoy and Routing Files, GUS-11, "Brief Narrative of the Voyage," Box 35.

63. Convoy and Routing Files, GUS-11, Box 35.

64. Convoy and Routing Files, GUS-11, "Brief Narrative of the Voyage," Box 35.

65. Richard Schiff, interview by author, 22 May 1990.

66. World War II War Diaries, USS *Bogue,* Box 648.

67. Ibid.

68. World War II War Diaries, USCGC *Bibb,* Box 638.

69. "History of Convoy and Routing," 43.

70. "Official Log-Book," Voyage 2, p. 27.

71. Convoy and Routing Files, GUS-11, "Brief Narrative of the Voyage," Box 35.

72. Ibid.

73. Records of the Office of the Chief of Transportation, Hampton Roads Port of Embarkation, Historical Report no. 5, Box 270.

74. "Official Log-Book," Voyage 3, p. 3.

75. Records of the American Bureau of Shipping, Report no. 5228, 11 September 1943.

76. UGS Convoy Files, 1942–1945, UGS-18.

77. Ditto copy of manifest, PLSA.

78. Records of the Office of the Chief of Transportation, Hampton Roads Port of Embarkation, Historical Report no. 5, Box 270.

79. An excellent account of operations can be found in D'Este, *World War II in the Mediterranean,* chapters 5–7.

80. UGS Convoy Files, 1942–1945, UGS-18.

81. Convoy and Routing Files, UGS-18, Convoy Form D, Box 155.

82. "Official Log-Book," Voyage 3, p. 19.

83. Convoy and Routing Files, "Brief Narrative [UGS-18]," Box 155.

84. "Events of Our Voyage."

85. *New York Times,* 19, 20 October 1943.

86. Baran, "Journal."

87. Convoy and Routing Files, Box 163.

88. "Official Log-Book," Voyage 3, p. 18.

89. Records of the Office of the Chief of Transportation, "U.S. Army Transportation and the Italian Campaign," 53–54, Box 142.

90. Ibid., 60.

91. Ibid., 65.

92. Convoy and Routing Files, NV-8, Box 90.

93. "Events of Our Voyage."

94. Convoy and Routing Files, MKS-31, Box 80.

95. "Mail Delivery to U.S. Army Transport Service Personnel," mimeographed memo dated 29 December 1942, PLSA.

96. Convoy and Routing Files, KMS-33, Box 72.

97. "Events of Our Voyage."

98. Schofield, *Eastward the Convoys,* 97.

99. Convoy and Routing Files, VN-11, Box 163.

100. "Events of Our Voyage."

101. Convoy and Routing Files, NV-11, Box 90.

102. Eliot, *Allied Escort Ships of World War II,* 290, 503.

103. See also the "Official Log-Book," Voyage 3, p. 18.

104. Baran, "Journal," 24 December 1943.

105. "Events of Our Voyage."

106. Ibid.
107. Records of the Maritime Administration, letter of 27 January 1944 from D. S. Brierley, Director, Foreign Repairs and Salvage, to States Marine Corporation.
108. See Records of the American Bureau of Shipping, Report no. E-795, 30 March 1944.
109. "Events of Our Voyage."
110. Convoy and Routing Files, NV-14, Box 90.
111. Convoy and Routing Files, MKS-36, Box 80.
112. "Events of Our Voyage."
113. "Official Log-Book," Voyage 3, p. 17.
114. Convoy and Routing Files, VN-19, Box 163.
115. Dorling, *Western Mediterranean*, 201.
116. "Events of Our Voyage."
117. "Official Log-Book," Voyage 3, p. 17.
118. Rohwer, *Axis Submarine Successes*, 255, 304.
119. Ibid., 255; Sawyer and Mitchell, *The Liberty Ships*, 99, 123.
120. World War II War Diaries, USS *Edison*, Box 823.
121. Convoy and Routing Files, GUS-31, Box 37.
122. World War II War Diaries, USS *Edison*, Box 823.

CHAPTER 4

1. Unless otherwise noted, the information about the *John W. Brown* in this chapter comes from the "Secret Log for a United States Merchant Vessel," kept by the master, George N. Brown; from the "Deck Log" for Voyage 4; and from the "Log" and "Reports" of Ens. Joe B. Humphreys, Navy Armed Guard commander.
2. Records of the American Bureau of Shipping, Report no. E-796, 30 March 1944.
3. Records of the Office of the Chief of Transportation, memo dated 16 August 1944 from William McCarthy, Atlantic District Port Steward, Box 637.
4. Records of the American Bureau of Shipping, Report no. E-795, 30 March 1944.
5. Documents dated 3, 4, 6, and 8 April 1944, PLSA.
6. Convoy Sailing Orders, file on UGS-39, Box 105.
7. Information on New York section from ibid.
8. Sawyer and Mitchell, *The Liberty Ships*, 165.
9. Convoy and Routing Files, UGS-39, Box 157.
10. UGS Convoy Files, 1942–1945, UGS-39.
11. Ibid.
12. Ibid.
13. Convoy and Routing Files, Box 157.
14. Roskill, *The War at Sea*, vol. 3, part 1: 258–59.
15. World War II War Diaries, USCGC *Bibb*, Box 638.
16. "History of Convoy and Routing," 41.

17. Roskill, *The War at Sea,* vol. 3, part 1: 310.

18. Morison, *History of United States Naval Operations,* 10:273; and Roskill, *The War at Sea,* vol. 3, part 1: 246–47, 327.

19. UGS Convoy Files, 1942–1945, UGS-39.

20. Convoy and Routing Files, VN-38, Box 163.

21. *New York Times,* 24 March 1944.

22. "Remembrances of Vernon Harold Joyce," 4.

23. Gruber, *Haven,* 57, 60–61.

24. "Remembrances of Vernon Harold Joyce," 5.

25. E. L. Venzke, "JOHN W. BROWN and the 'Anzio Express,'" *Liberty Log,* Spring 1985, 3.

26. For a full account, see chapters 4 and 5 in Linklater, *The Campaign in Italy.* This is the source of my information.

27. Strawson, *The Italian Campaign,* 144.

28. Venzke, "JOHN W. BROWN and the 'Anzio Express,'" 3.

29. Roskill, *The War at Sea,* vol. 3, part 1: 322.

30. Bykofsky and Larson, *The Transportation Corps,* 210.

31. Morison, *History of United States Naval Operations,* 9:356.

32. Carbon copy of Captain Brown's report and statement, dated 26 May 1944, PLSA.

33. Truscott, *Command Mission,* 371.

34. D'Este, *World War II in the Mediterranean,* 176.

35. Carbon copy of Captain Brown's report and statement, dated 26 May 1944, PLSA.

36. Convoy and Routing Files, NV-41, Box 90.

37. Convoy and Routing Files, GUS-41, Box 37.

38. "Remembrances of Vernon Harold Joyce," 7.

39. Convoy and Routing Files, KMS-52, Box 72.

40. Botto, transcription of interview, 8–9.

41. Convoy and Routing Files, VN-46, Box 163.

42. See D'Este, *World War II in the Mediterranean,* 180.

43. "Remembrances of Vernon Harold Joyce," 5–6, and Joyce, transcription of interview, 3.

44. Wilt, *French Riviera Campaign,* 125.

45. Roskill, *The War at Sea,* vol. 3, part 2: 75.

46. Carbon copy of memo from Captain Brown to the port commandant, Cagliari, Sardinia, 1 July 1944, PLSA.

47. Hewitt Papers, "Personal Diary of Vice Admiral H. K. Hewitt," Box 5.

48. Two letters dated 2 August 1944 and one form letter dated 3 August 1944, PLSA.

49. Hewitt Papers, "The Landing of the Seventh Army in Southern France. Operation Anvil-Dragoon," 33–34, Box 4.

50. Unless otherwise specified, all details and quotations in the following account of the Invasion of Southern France come from Wilt, *French Riviera Campaign.*

51. *Dictionary of American Naval Fighting Ships,* 55.

52. Wilt, *French Riviera Campaign,* 145–46.

53. Hewitt Papers, "The Landing of the Seventh Army in Southern France. Operation Anvil-Dragoon," 40, Box 4.

54. Ibid., 41.

55. Joyce, transcription of interview, 6.

56. George Ott to Brian Hope, 18 December 1988, PLSA.

57. "Invasion of Southern France," Report of Naval Commander, diagram VIII.

58. "Invasion of Southern France, 15–28 August 1944," Battle Studies, Box 1.

59. World War II War Diaries, USS *Nevada,* Box 1256.

60. World War II War Diaries, USS *Texas,* Box 1510.

61. World War II War Diaries, USS *Catoctin,* Box 702.

62. Carbon copy of letter from Captain Brown to Commander Kerrins, USCG, 24 August 1944, PLSA.

63. Convoy and Routing Files, GUS-51, Box 38.

64. Convoy and Routing Files, NV-62, Box 90.

65. World War II War Diaries, USS *Otter,* Box 1288.

66. Convoy and Routing Files, GUS-51, Box 38.

67. World War II War Diaries, USS *Otter,* Box 1288.

68. Deck Log, USS *Otter.*

69. Ibid.

70. Convoy and Routing Files, GUS-51, Box 38.

71. Deck Log, USS *Otter;* World War II War Diaries, USS *Otter,* Box 1288.

72. Convoy and Routing Files, GUS-51, Box 38.

73. "Certificate of Discharge from National Quarantine," 28 September 1944, PLSA.

74. "Remembrances of Vernon Harold Joyce," 11, and Joyce, transcription of interview, 9.

75. Carbon copy of "Slop Chest Requisition," 29 September 1944, PLSA.

76. Records of the American Bureau of Shipping, Report no. 13199, 10 October 1944.

77. "Log" of Lt. (jg) James R. Argo, Navy Armed Guard commander on Voyages 5, 6, and 7.

CHAPTER 5

1. Hanson W. Baldwin, "The Outlook in the War," *New York Times,* 1 October 1944, sec. 1, p. 12.

2. Terraine, *The U-Boat Wars,* 768.

3. Unless otherwise noted, the information about Voyage 5 of the *John W. Brown* in this chapter comes from the "Secret Log for a United States Merchant Vessel" kept by the master, George N. Brown, and from the "Log" and "Reports" of Lt. (jg) James R. Argo, Navy Armed Guard commander on Voyages 5, 6, and 7.

4. Carbon copy of customs form 3203, dated 12 October 1944 at Pier 1 Canton, PLSA.

5. *New York Times,* 19, 20 October 1944.

6. George L. Spittel to his wife, 20 October 1944, PLSA.

7. Convoy and Routing Files, UGS-58, Box 159.

8. Richard Price to author, 16 October, 13 November 1990, and George L. Spittel to his wife, 20 October, 13 November 1944, PLSA.

9. Spittel, "Notes on the J. W. Brown Voyage #5."

10. "Official Log-Book," Voyage 5, p. 8.

11. World War II War Diaries, USS *Otter,* Box 1288.

12. Convoy and Routing Files, UGS-58, Box 159.

13. World War II War Diaries, USS *Weber,* Box 1558.

14. World War II War Diaries, USS *Otter,* Box 1288.

15. Carbon copy of "Church Service," SS *John W. Brown,* 5 November 1944, PLSA.

16. World War II War Diaries, USS *Otter,* Box 1288.

17. Details about this incident are from Convoy and Routing Files, UGS-58, Box 159; from World War II War Diaries, USS *Weber,* Box 1558; and from the Deck Log, USS *Weber.*

18. World War II War Diaries, USS *Otter,* Box 1288.

19. World War II War Diaries, USS *Weber,* Box 1558.

20. World War II War Diaries, USS *Otter,* Box 1288.

21. World War II War Diaries, USS *Selfridge,* Box 1440.

22. World War II War Diaries, USS *Weber,* Box 1558.

23. World War II War Diaries, USS *Selfridge,* Box 1440.

24. George L. Spittel to his wife, 13 November 1944, PLSA.

25. Spittel, "Notes on the J. W. Brown Voyage #5."

26. "Remembrances of Vernon Harold Joyce," 3–4.

27. George L. Spittel to his wife, 19 November 1944, PLSA.

28. Ibid.

29. Convoy and Routing Files, VN-78, Box 163.

30. Bykofsky and Larson, *The Transportation Corps,* 212.

31. Ibid., 212–13.

32. Ibid., 213–14.

33. Records of the Maritime Administration, carbon copy of letter from J. L. Holmes to States Marine Corporation, 20 December 1944.

34. Convoy and Routing Files, NV-80, Box 90.

35. Convoy and Routing Files, GUS-61, Box 39.

36. Ibid.

37. World War II War Diaries, USS *Wyffels,* Box 1584; Deck Log, USS *Wyffels.*

38. Spittel, "Notes on the J. W. Brown Voyage #5."

39. Albert Petrulis, videotaped interview by Brian Hope, 9 September 1989, PLSA.

40. Convoy and Routing Files, GUS-61, Box 39.

41. Records of the Maritime Administration, copy of American Bureau of

Shipping Certificate no. NY-8954, 4 January 1945.

42. George L. Spittel to his wife, 2 January 1945, PLSA.

43. Ibid.

44. Records of the Maritime Administration, WSA form filled out by States Marine Corporation, 17 April 1945.

45. Unless otherwise noted, information about Voyage 6 comes from the "Secret Log for a United States Merchant Vessel," kept by the master, Capt. George N. Brown; from the "Log" and "Reports" of Lt. James R. Argo, Navy Armed Guard commander; and for 7–11 April 1945 from the "Deck Log."

46. James Farley, a signalman on Voyages 6 and 7, in a conversation with the author aboard the *Brown*, 8 March 1989.

47. "Official Log-Book," Voyage 6, p. 3.

48. Convoy and Routing Files, UGS-70, Box 160.

49. Details about this incident are from the following: Convoy and Routing Files, UGS-70, Box 160; World War II War Diaries, USS *Ericsson*, Box 843; Deck Log, USS *Ericsson*; World War II War Diaries, USS *Bangor*, Box 614; Deck Log, USS *Bangor*; and the "Log" of Lt. (jg) Merle D. Beauchamp, Navy Armed Guard commander in SS *John F. Myers*.

50. Convoy and Routing Files, UGS-70, Box 160.

51. Ibid.

52. "Official Log-Book," Voyage 6, p. 10.

53. Ibid.

54. Convoy and Routing Files, VN-106, Box 163.

55. Convoy and Routing Files, NV-109, Box 90.

56. Convoy and Routing Files, GUS-76, Box 41. The details that follow are from this file.

57. "Official Log-Book," Voyage 6, p. 3.

58. Ibid., p. 10.

59. Convoy and Routing Files, GUS-76, Box 41.

60. "Official Log-Book," Voyage 6, p. 3.

61. "Official Log-Book," Voyage 7, pp. 3, 5–6.

62. Records of the Maritime Administration, WSA form filled out by States Marine Corporation, 15 June 1945.

63. Records of the Maritime Administration, U.S. Maritime Commission "Closing Form," 11 March 1953.

64. *New York Times*, 14, 15 April 1945.

65. Ibid., 15 April 1945.

66. Convoy Sailing Orders, HX-352, Box 41.

67. See Records of the American Bureau of Shipping, Certificate no. NY-1265, in Record no. 6037, 20 April 1945.

68. Convoy Sailing Orders, HX-352, Box 41.

69. Convoy and Routing Files, HX-352, Box 63.

70. *Jane's Fighting Ships of World War II*, 91.

71. Convoy and Routing Files, HX-352, Box 63, and Convoy Sailing Orders, HX-352, Box 41.

72. Morison, *History of United States Naval Operations*, 10:342–44.

73. Lundeberg, "Operation *Teardrop* Revisited," 211–12, 217–25.

74. Convoy and Routing Files, HX-352, Box 63.

75. J. Richard Argo to author, 25 June 1992, PLSA.

76. Ibid.

77. Bykofsky and Larson, *The Transportation Corps*, 320–23.

78. Donald F. Hewett (third mate on Voyage 7) to author, 17 July 1989, PLSA.

79. *New York Herald Tribune*, 12 June 1945, and Argo's "Report."

80. Donald F. Hewett to author, 17 July 1989.

81. Convoy and Routing Files, ON-305, Box 113.

82. *New York Herald Tribune*, 12 June 1945.

83. Records of the Maritime Administration, WSA form filled out by States Marine Corporation, 15 June 1945.

84. Account of James W. Munroe, seaman first class on Voyages 6 and 7, p. 9, PLSA.

85. *New York Maritime Register*, 27 June 1945, 14.

86. U.S. Army "Transportation Corps Ocean Manifest" with "Recapitulation Sheet" for Voyage 8, PLSA. Details about the cargo come from this document.

87. Records of the Maritime Administration, WSA form filled out by States Marine Corporation, 22 August 1945.

88. "Official Log-Book," Voyage 8, p. 3.

89. Records of the Maritime Administration, letter from Edward A. Neiley, Assistant General Counsel, WSA, to C. Collar, Adjuster, WSA, 4 June 1946.

90. Max Grossman (chief radio operator on Voyage 8) to author, undated [late September 1990], PLSA; *New York Herald Tribune*, 11 August 1945.

91. Max Grossman to author, undated [late September 1990].

92. Gilbert, *The Second World War*, 621.

93. Reports of Navy Armed Guard Commanders, SS *John W. Brown*, "Maintenance Report" filed by Gunners Mate Third Class John E. Walls.

94. *New York Herald Tribune*, 12 August 1945.

95. Records of the Maritime Administration, WSA form filled out by States Marine Corporation, 22 August 1945.

96. Records of the Office of the Chief of Transportation, Boxes 46 and 47.

97. Records of the American Bureau of Shipping, Report no. F-2159, 14 September 1945.

98. Records of the American Bureau of Shipping, Report no. F-2035, 4 September 1945.

99. Bureau of Ships, General Correspondence, 1940–1945, Box 1317.

CHAPTER 6

1. "Official Log-Book," Voyage 9, p. 3.

2. *New York Maritime Register*, 26 September 1945, 24.

3. Belzak, "United States Army History," 3.

4. Charles T. Belzak, telephone interviews by author, 11, 19 June 1992.

5. Belzak, "United States Army History," 3; "Official Log-Book," Voyage 9, p. 3.

6. "Official Log-Book," Voyage 9, p. 14.

7. Belzak, "United States Army History," 4.

8. "Official Log-Book," Voyage 9, p. 13.

9. Peter Mazzie to author, 13 February 1989, PLSA.

10. "Official Log-Book," Voyage 9, p. 13.

11. Belzak, "United States Army History," 4.

12. Ibid.

13. "Official Log-Book," Voyage 9, p. 14.

14. Botto, transcription of interview, 13.

15. Belzak, "United States Army History," 4.

16. Belzak, telephone interviews by author, 11, 19 June 1992.

17. Max Grossman to author, undated [late September 1990], PLSA.

18. Walter Botto, supplementary interview by author, 26 April 1989.

19. Botto, transcription of interview, 10–11; Walter Botto, supplementary interview by author, 26 April 1989.

20. Botto, "Mail Buoys? Of Course!"

21. Botto, transcription of interview, 11–12.

22. *New York Herald Tribune,* 15 November 1945.

23. Botto, transcription of interview, 12–13.

24. Records of the Maritime Administration, WSA form filled out by States Marine Corporation, 7 December 1945.

25. "Remembrances of Vernon Harold Joyce," 12.

26. Records of the Maritime Administration, WSA radar installation form, 28 November 1945.

27. Records of the American Bureau of Shipping, Report no. F-3120, 19 November 1945.

28. Records of the Maritime Administration, WSA form filled out by States Marine Corporation, 14 February 1946.

29. "Ship Stuff," [11].

30. Ibid., 12.

31. Belzak, "United States Army History," 4.

32. "Night Order Book." Unless otherwise noted, this is the source of information about Voyage 9.

33. Belzak, "United States Army History," 4.

34. Ibid.

35. Ibid., 5.

36. Ibid., 4–5; Charles T. Belzak, telephone interviews by author, 11, 19 June 1992.

37. Belzak, "United States Army History," 5; Charles T. Belzak, telephone interviews by author, 11, 19 June 1992.

38. Belzak, "United States Army History," 5.

39. "Ship Stuff," [9].

40. Ibid., [7].

41. Belzak, "United States Army History," 5.

42. "Ship Stuff," [9].

43. Mickey O'Bott [Walter Botto], "Crows Nest," in "Ship Stuff," [7].

44. Belzak, "United States Army History," 5.

45. Unless otherwise noted, information about Voyage 11 comes from the "Deck Log."

46. Records of the Maritime Administration, letter from R. A. Molloy, Moore-McCormack Lines, to F. M. Darr, Director, Division of Traffic, WSA, 29 April 1946.

47. "Official Log-Book," Voyage 11, p. 3.

48. Schofield, *Eastward the Convoys*, 86–87.

49. Peter Mazzie to author, 12 September, and Walter Botto to author, 24 September 1991, PLSA.

50. Peter Mazzie to author, 12 September 1991, PLSA.

51. Walter Botto, supplementary interview by author, 26 April 1989.

52. Ibid., and letter to author, 24 September 1991.

53. "Official Log-Book," Voyage 11, p. 3.

54. Records of the Maritime Administration, WSA form filled out by States Marine Corporation, 29 June 1946.

55. "Official Log-Book," Voyage 12, p. 2.

56. Walter Botto to author, 24 September 1991, PLSA.

57. "Official Log-Book," Voyage 12, p. 3.

58. Convoy and Routing Files, Ship Movement Cards, Box 386.

59. Ibid.

60. Records of the Maritime Administration, WSA form filled out by States Marine Corporation, 12 September 1946.

61. *New York Maritime Register*, 28 August 1946, 36.

62. Records of the American Bureau of Shipping, Report no. 12,656, 3 September 1946.

63. The details about the strike are from the *New York Times*, 5, 6, 7, 8, 10, 11, 13, 21 September 1946.

64. "Official Log-Book," Voyage 13, p. 13.

65. Ibid.

66. *New York Maritime Register*, 20 November 1946, 36.

67. Carbon copy of the United States Lines form "Stowage of Special Cargo," 1 November 1946, PLSA.

68. Records of the Maritime Administration, "Correction on Manifest," 18 December 1946.

69. *New York Maritime Register*, 20 November 1946, 36.

70. Anderson, *The Merchant Marine and World Frontiers*, 115.

71. Levine and Platt, "The Contribution of U.S. Shipbuilding and the Merchant Marine," 204.

72. Ibid.

73. Valle, "United States Merchant Marine Fatalities," 259–60.

Works Cited

PRIMARY SOURCES

"Abstract Deck Log." Voyage 1. SS *John W. Brown*. Project Liberty Ship Archives.

"Arming of Merchant Ships and Naval Armed Guard Service." United States Naval Administrative Histories of World War II. Office of the Chief of Naval Operations. Typescript. n.d. Navy Department Library. Washington, D.C.

Baran, Paul. "Journal." Project Liberty Ship Archives.

Belzak, Charles T. "United States Army History." Photocopy of typescript. Project Liberty Ship Archives.

Bloxsom, Robert. "Recollections of My Time at Sea." n.d. Project Liberty Ship Archives.

Botto, Walter. "Mail Buoys? Of Course!" Photocopy of typescript. Project Liberty Ship Archives.

———. Transcription of interview by the author, 26 April 1989. Project Liberty Ship Archives.

Bureau of Ships. General Correspondence, 1940–1945. National Archives. RG 19.

Convoy and Routing Files. Tenth Fleet. National Archives. RG 38.

Convoy Sailing Orders. National Archives. RG 181.

Deck Logs. SS *John W. Brown*. Voyage 1, 17 December 1942–13 June 1943; Voyage 4; Voyage 6, 7 April 1945–11 April 1945; Voyage 11. Project Liberty Ship Archives.

Deck Logs. USS *Bangor*, USS *Barry*, USS *Bogue*, USS *Borie*, USS *Ericsson*,

USS *Otter,* USS *Simpson,* USS *Weber,* USS *Wyffels.* National Archives. RG 24.

"Events of Our Voyage." By [Charles E. Albert, radio operator on Voyage 3]. Typescript carbon. Project Liberty Ship Archives.

"First Draft Narrative." Prepared by the Historical Section, Fifth Naval District. Vol. 2. United States Naval Administration in World War II. Commandant, Fifth Naval District. Typescript, n.d. Navy Department Library. Washington, D.C.

Hearing before Subcommittee on Merchant Marine of Committee on Merchant Marine and Fisheries on H.R. 679. U.S. House of Representatives. 99th Congress, 2nd Session. 13 August 1987. Washington, D.C.: Government Printing Office, 1987.

Hewitt (Adm. H. Kent) Papers. Operational Archives. Naval Historical Center. Washington, D.C.

"Historical Narrative of Port Director—New York, Third Naval District, 15 October 1939 to 14 August 1945." Vol. 2. United States Naval Administration in World War II. Typescript, n.d. Navy Department Library. Washington, D.C.

"History of Convoy and Routing." United States Naval Administration in World War II. Headquarters of the Commander in Chief, United States Fleet, and Commander, Tenth Fleet. Typescript carbon, May 1945. Navy Department Library. Washington, D.C.

"History of Harbor Entrance Control Post, Fort Story, Cape Henry, Virginia, 1941–1945." Vol. 4, Supplement 23. United States Naval Administration in World War II. Commandant, Fifth Naval District. Typescript, n.d. Navy Department Library. Washington, D.C.

"History of the Port Director's Office, Fifth Naval District." Appendix Vol. 4, Supplement 20. United States Naval Administration in World War II. Commandant, Fifth Naval District. Typescript, n.d. Navy Department Library. Washington, D.C.

Industrial Union of Marine and Shipbuilding Workers of America Collection. Historical Manuscripts and Archives Department. University of Maryland College Park Libraries.

"Invasion of Southern France." Vol. 5. United States Naval Administration in World War II. Report of Naval Commander, Western Task Force, Vice Adm. H. K. Hewitt. 15 November 1944. Navy Department Library. Washington, D.C.

"Invasion of Southern France, 15–28 August 1944." Battle Studies, World War II. National Archives. RG 332.

Joyce, Vernon H. Transcription of interview by the author, 2 April 1989. Project Liberty Ship Archives.

Logs of Navy Armed Guard Commanders, SS *John F. Myers.* National Archives. RG 24. Box 413.

Logs of Navy Armed Guard Commanders, SS *John W. Brown.* National Archives. RG 24. Box 420.

Nielsen, Kenneth W. "The Maiden Voyage of the S.S. *John W. Brown*, 29 September 1942 to 27 May 1943." Typescript, 1 August 1989. Project Liberty Ship Archives.

"Night Order Book." SS *John W. Brown*, Voyages 10 and 12. Project Liberty Ship Archives.

Nilsen, Ralph. "Album." n.d. Project Liberty Ship Archives.

"Official Log-Book." SS *John W. Brown.* Voyage 1. National Archives, New York Branch. Log 95. Accession No. 026-52-B0075. Location No. 4-0753043.

———. Voyage 2. National Archives, Philadelphia Branch.

———. Voyage 3. National Archives, New York Branch. Log 840. Accession No. 026-52-D0075. Location No. 4-0753107.

———. Voyage 4. National Archives, Philadelphia Branch. Log 425.

———. Voyage 5. National Archives, New York Branch. Log 14. Accession No. 026-52-E0075. Location No. 4-0753172.

———. Voyage 6. National Archives, New York Branch. Log 1257. Accession No. 026-52-E0075. Location No. 4-0753194.

———. Voyage 7. National Archives, New York Branch. Log 2424. Accession No. 026-52-E0075. Location No. 4-0753214.

———. Voyage 8. National Archives, New York Branch. Log 3151. Accession No. 026-52-F0075. Location No. 4-0753234.

———. Voyage 9. National Archives, New York Branch. Log 4059. Accession No. 026-52-F0075. Location No. 4-0753251.

———. Voyage 10. National Archives, New York Branch. Log 364. Accession No. 026-52-G0075. Location No. 4-0753268.

———. Voyage 11. National Archives, Philadelphia Branch. Log 2571.

———. Voyage 12. National Archives, New York Branch. Log 2506. Accession No. 026-52-G0075. Location No. 4-0753312.

———. Voyage 13. National Archives, New York Branch. Log 3341. Accession No. 026-52-H0075. Location No. 4-0764079.

Program, Labor Day Ceremonies: In Recognition of Labor's Efforts in Building Ships for Victory. Baltimore: Bethlehem-Fairfield Shipyard, 7 September 1942.

Project Liberty Ship Archives. Miscellaneous Documents.

Records of the American Bureau of Shipping. SS *John W. Brown.* Paramus, N.J.

Records of the Maritime Administration. SS *John W. Brown.* USMC and WSA (1936–1950). Ship Files (901). Accession No. 51A-142. RG 178. Box 293.

Records of the Office of the Chief of Transportation. Historical Program Files, 1940–50. National Archives. RG 336.

Records of the War Shipping Administration. National Archives. RG 248.

"Remembrances of Vernon Harold Joyce Aboard S.S. *John W. Brown.*" Transcription of a tape recording by Vernon H. Joyce on 27 January 1989. Project Liberty Ship Archives.

Reports of Navy Armed Guard Commanders, SS *John W. Brown.* National Archives. RG 38. Box 379.

Reports of Navy Armed Guard Commanders, SS *Jonathan Elmer.* National Archives. RG 38. Box 381.

"Secret Log[s] for a United States Merchant Vessel." SS *John W. Brown.* National Archives. RG 181. Box 166.

"Ship Stuff." Newsletter for passengers on Voyage 10. Souvenir Edition, January 1946. Photocopy of original owned by Gabriel Augustine. King of Prussia, Pa. Project Liberty Ship Archives.

"Specifications for the Construction of a Single Screw Cargo Vessel, Design EC2-S-C1." United States Maritime Commission, February 1941. Mimeograph. Project Liberty Ship Archives.

Spittel, George L. "Notes on the J. W. Brown Voyage #5 to Naples 1944." [December 1989]. Typescript. Project Liberty Ship Archives.

Trials of SS *Santiagos Iglesias.* Records of the Maritime Administration. File No. MCE-961. Accession No. 51A-142. RG 178. Box 179.

UGS Convoy Files, 1942–1945. National Archives. RG 181.

United States Maritime Service Training Manual: Engineering Branch Training. War Shipping Administration, n.d.

World War II War Diaries. National Archives. RG 38.

SECONDARY SOURCES

Anderson, Robert Earle. *The Merchant Marine and World Frontiers.* New York: Cornell Maritime Press, 1945.

[Berry, Robert]. *Gunners Get Glory: Lt. Bob Berry's Story of the Navy's Armed Guard.* As told to Lloyd Wendt. New York: Bobbs-Merrill, 1943.

The Bethlehem Liberty Fleet. Baltimore: Bethlehem-Fairfield Shipyard, n.d.

Bourneuf, Gus. "Workhorse of the Fleet." Reproduction of unpublished typescript.

Bykofsky, Joseph, and Harold Larson. *The Transportation Corps: Operations Overseas. United States Army in World War II—The Technical Services.* Washington, D.C.: Office of the Chief of Military History, United States Army, 1957.

Charles, Roland W. *Troopships of World War II.* Washington, D.C.: Army Transportation Association, 1947.

Clogher, C. P. "Cargo Security Officers." In *The Road to Victory: A History of Hampton Roads Port of Embarkation in World War II,* vol. 1, ed. William Reginald Wheeler. Newport News, Va.: Yale University Press, 1946.

Crane, William B. "Headaches Precede Champagne." *The [Baltimore] Sunday Sun Magazine,* 11 October 1942, [1].

De La Pedraja, Rene. *The Rise and Decline of U.S. Merchant Shipping in the Twentieth Century.* New York: Twayne, 1992.

D'Este, Carlo. *World War II in the Mediterranean: 1942–1945.* Chapel Hill, N.C.: Algonquin Books of Chapel Hill, 1990.

Dictionary of American Naval Fighting Ships. Vol. 11. Washington, D.C.: Government Printing Office, 1963.

Dorling, "Taffrail" Taprell. *Western Mediterranean, 1942–1945.* London: Hodden and Stoughton, 1947.

Eliot, Peter. *Allied Escort Ships of World War II.* Annapolis: Naval Institute Press, 1977.

Farrar, Captain Frank F. *A Ship's Log Book,* ed. Dorothy B. Maxwell. St. Petersburg, Fla.: Great Outdoors, 1988.

General Instructions for Commanding Officers of Naval Armed Guards on Merchant Ships, 1943. 3rd ed. Washington, D.C.: Government Printing Office, 1943.

General Instructions for Commanding Officers of Naval Armed Guards on Merchant Ships, 1944. 4th ed. Washington, D.C.: Government Printing Office, 1944.

Gilbert, Martin. *The Second World War: A Complete History.* New York: Henry Holt, 1989.

Gruber, Ruth. *Haven: The Unknown Story of One Thousand World War II Refugees.* New York: Coward-McCann, 1983.

Jane's Fighting Ships of World War II. New York: Military Press, 1989.

Lane, Frederic C. *Ships for Victory: A History of Shipbuilding under the U.S. Maritime Commission in World War II.* Baltimore: Johns Hopkins Press, 1951.

Lehman, Maxwell, and Morton Yarmon. *Opportunities in the Armed Forces.* New York: Viking, 1942.

Levine, Daniel, and Sara Ann Platt. "The Contribution of U.S. Shipbuilding and the Merchant Marine to the Second World War." In *America's Maritime Legacy: A History of the U.S. Merchant Marine and Shipbuilding Industry since Colonial Times,* ed. Robert A. Kilmarx. Boulder, Colo.: Westview Press, 1979.

"The Liberty Ship." *Marine Engineering and Shipping Review* 47, no. 4 (April 1942): 146–65.

Linklater, Eric. *The Campaign in Italy.* London: Her Majesty's Stationery Office, 1951.

Lott, Arnold S. *Most Dangerous Sea: A History of Mine Warfare, and an Account of U.S. Navy Mine Operations in World War II and Korea.* Annapolis: U.S. Naval Institute, 1959.

Lundeberg, Philip K. "Operation *Teardrop* Revisited." In *To Die Gallantly: The Battle of the Atlantic,* ed. Timothy J. Runyan and Jan M. Copes. Boulder, Colo.: Westview Press, 1994.

Morison, Samuel Eliot. *History of United States Naval Operations in World War II.* Vol. 1: *The Battle of the Atlantic, September 1939–May 1943.* New York: Little, Brown, 1960.

———. Vol. 9: *Sicily—Salerno—Anzio, January 1943–June 1944,* Boston: Little, Brown, 1954.

―――. Vol. 10: *The Atlantic Battle Won, May 1943–May 1945.* Boston: Little, Brown, 1956.

Motter, T. H. Vail. *The Persian Corridor and Aid to Russia. United States Army in World War II—The Middle East Theater.* Washington, D.C.: Office of the Chief of Military History, Department of the Army, 1952.

Muggenthaler, August Karl. *German Raiders of World War II.* Englewood Cliffs, N.J.: Prentice-Hall, 1977.

Naval Ordnance and Gunnery. Rev. ed. Standards and Curriculum Division, Training, Bureau of Naval Personnel, 1946.

Nesdale, F. P., and C. P. Clogher. "Liberty Ships as Troop Transports." In *The Road to Victory: A History of Hampton Roads Port of Embarkation in World War II,* vol. 1, ed. William Reginald Wheeler. Newport News, Va.: Yale University Press, 1946.

O'Flaherty, "Ferocious." *Abandoned Convoy: The U.S. Merchant Marine in World War II.* New York: Exposition Press, 1970.

On a True Course: The Story of the National Maritime Union of America, AFL-CIO. Washington, D.C.: National Maritime Union of America, 1967.

Production System, Bethlehem-Fairfield Shipyard. New York: Bethlehem Steel Company, Shipbuilding Division, n.d. Reprinted from *Marine Engineering and Shipping Review* (October 1942).

Register of Commissioned and Warrant Officers of the United States Naval Reserve, 31 July 1944. Washington, D.C.: Government Printing Office, 1944.

Rohwer, Jurgen. *Axis Submarine Successes, 1939–1945.* Annapolis: Naval Institute Press, 1983.

Roskill, S. W. *The War at Sea, 1939–1945.* Vol. 1: *The Defensive.* London: Her Majesty's Stationery Office, 1954.

―――. Vol. 2: *The Period of Balance.* London: Her Majesty's Stationery Office, 1956.

―――. Vol. 3: *The Offensive.* Part 1: *1st June 1943–31st May 1944.* London: Her Majesty's Stationery Office, 1960.

―――. Vol. 3: *The Offensive.* Part 2: *1st June 1944–14th August 1945.* London: Her Majesty's Stationery Office, 1961.

Sawyer, L. A., and W. H. Mitchell. *The Liberty Ships: The History of the "Emergency" Type Cargo Ships Constructed in the United States during the Second World War.* 2nd ed. London and New York: Lloyd's of London Press, 1985.

―――. *The Oceans, the Forts, and the Parks: Merchant Shipbuilding for British Accounts in North America during World War II.* Wartime Standard Ships. Vol. 2. Liverpool: Sea Breezes, 1966.

Schofield, William G. *Eastward the Convoys.* Chicago: Rand McNally, 1965.

Strawson, John. *The Italian Campaign.* London: Secker and Warburg, 1987.

Terraine, John. *The U-Boat Wars, 1916–1945.* New York: G. P. Putnam's Sons, 1989.

Truscott, L. K., Jr. *Command Mission: A Personal Story.* New York: E. P. Dutton, 1954.

Valle, James E. "United States Merchant Marine Fatalities." In *To Die Gallantly: The Battle of the Atlantic,* ed. Timothy J. Runyan and Jan M. Copes. Boulder, Colo.: Westview Press, 1994.

van der Vat, Dan. *The Atlantic Campaign: World War II's Great Struggle at Sea.* New York: Harper and Row, 1988.

Wardlow, Chester. *The Transportation Corps: Responsibilities, Organization, and Operations. United States Army in World War II—The Technical Services.* Washington, D.C.: Office of the Chief of Military History, United States Army, 1951.

"War-Risk Bonuses for Seafaring Personnel." *Monthly Labor Review* 58, no. 1 (January 1944): 8–14.

Wilt, Alan F. *The French Riviera Campaign of August 1944.* [Carbondale and Edwardsville]: Southern Illinois University Press, 1981.

Y'Blood, William T. *Hunter-Killer: U.S. Escort Carriers in the Battle of the Atlantic.* Annapolis: Naval Institute Press, 1983.

Index

About the Author

AS A TEENAGER during World War II, Sherod Cooper watched many coastwise convoys steam along the New Jersey coast and occasionally heard the sounds of distant guns. In 1945–46 he served in the Merchant Marine and in 1946–47 the U.S. Army. Later with bachelor's and master's degrees from Temple University and a Ph.D. from the University of Pennsylvania, he taught English for thirty-six years; all but the first four were at the University of Maryland at College Park. His interest in ships and the sea continued through his life, and at the first opportunity he joined Project Liberty Ship, the volunteer organization working to restore the SS *John W. Brown.* Cooper began research on his history of the *Brown* shortly before retiring from the University of Maryland in 1989. He has assigned all royalties earned by this book to Project Liberty Ship.

With his wife, Janet, Cooper alternates between two homes in Maryland: one on the Chesapeake Bay and the other in the Annapolis area. Because their four children and families live close by, the Coopers enjoy frequent lively family gatherings, especially at the house on the Bay in the summer.

The **Naval Institute Press** is the book-publishing arm of the U.S. Naval Institute, a private, nonprofit, membership society for sea service professionals and others who share an interest in naval and maritime affairs. Established in 1873 at the U.S. Naval Academy in Annapolis, Maryland, where its offices remain today, the Naval Institute has members worldwide.

Members of the Naval Institute support the education programs of the society and receive the influential monthly magazine *Proceedings* and discounts on fine nautical prints and on ship and aircraft photos. They also have access to the transcripts of the Institute's Oral History Program and get discounted admission to any of the Institute-sponsored seminars offered around the country.

The Naval Institute also publishes *Naval History* magazine. This colorful bimonthly is filled with entertaining and thought-provoking articles, first-person reminiscences, and dramatic art and photography. Members receive a discount on *Naval History* subscriptions.

The Naval Institute's book-publishing program, begun in 1898 with basic guides to naval practices, has broadened its scope in recent years to include books of more general interest. Now the Naval Institute Press publishes about 100 titles each year, ranging from how-to books on boating and navigation to battle histories, biographies, ship and aircraft guides, and novels. Institute members receive discounts of 20 to 50 percent on the Press's nearly 600 books in print.

Full-time students are eligible for special half-price membership rates. Life memberships are also available.

For a free catalog describing Naval Institute Press books currently available, and for further information about subscribing to *Naval History* magazine or about joining the U.S. Naval Institute, please write to:

Membership Department
U.S. Naval Institute
118 Maryland Avenue
Annapolis, MD 21402-5035

Telephone: (800) 233-8764
Fax: (410) 269-7940
Web address: www.usni.org